MAFIA
LIFE

Also by Federico Varese

The Russian Mafia
Mafias on the Move

MAFIA LIFE

LOVE, DEATH AND MONEY AT THE HEART OF ORGANISED CRIME

FEDERICO VARESE

P

PROFILE BOOKS

First published in Great Britain in 2017 by
PROFILE BOOKS LTD
3 Holford Yard
Bevin Way
London
WC1X 9HD
www.profilebooks.com

1 3 5 7 9 10 8 6 4 2

Typeset in Sabon by MacGuru Ltd

Printed and bound in Great Britain by
Clays, St Ives plc

A CIP catalogue record for this book is available from the British Library.

ISBN 978 1 78125 253 6
Export ISBN 978 1 78125 254 3
eISBN 978 1 78283 055 9

CONTENTS

Life is hard.
And then you die.

INTRODUCTION

On a snow-swept November morning in 2016, I find myself staring at a well-kept grave, inside a sprawling Russian necropolis. The monument is not one of the grandest, yet the full-sized figure of Nikolai Zykov is staring at me solemnly. His image is inscribed on expensive dark marble, and the surrounding space includes a tiny table, a simple white Russian Orthodox cross, and a vase for flowers. Some of his dead associates are not far from him. I last met Zykov in the mid-1990s and, until now, I had not been back to the place where he used to be the local Mafia boss, the city of Perm, in Russia's Ural region. Although I have written a great deal about my time in Russia in the 1990s, I never thought it appropriate to dwell on our encounters. This book will bring Zykov back to life. He belonged to a secret criminal fraternity that has come to play a significant role in Europe's underworld. Members sport impressive tattoos, abide by a secret code of honour and operate in most European countries. In *Mafia Life*, we will encounter equally exotic individuals from Sicily, Hong Kong and Japan, and travel further afield, to Macau, Burma and Dubai, and back to Greece, and across the Atlantic, to uncover the shape of today's badlands. Yet do not for a moment think that a Mafioso is a Mr Big living in a faraway place. He can nest in our midst, in suburban England as much as in Palermo. Let's take just one example.

Recently, in the town of Salford, Greater Manchester, a man was attacked with a machete, and another had a grenade thrown at his house. A nine-year-old boy was shot as he opened the front door of his house: the killer was looking for his father. Thirty children live with the fear of murder in this town, which has a population of

234,000; there are twenty-five organised crime groups here, and the number of shootings in twelve months was nineteen. 'Police don't control the street,' a gang member told the BBC in 2016.

Imagine that you were one of the fans who attended the Manchester United home game against Wigan Athletic on Boxing Day in 2011. If you were, you might remember that Man United demolished Wigan 5–0. Yet something else was going on off the pitch. Professionally dressed 'staff' were directing fans to park near the Old Trafford football stadium. Thousands of people could easily find a spot, for five pounds. A bargain. Large areas of wasteland, car showrooms and empty spaces around office buildings had been turned into parking lots for Man United games throughout the season. The catch was that those attendants worked for local organised crime, using public areas illegally. Occasionally, they engaged in turf wars over who controlled the best spots. On Boxing Day 2011, the police were out in force and arrested thirteen people, aged between fifteen and fifty. The officers were trying to bring to an end a business worth millions every season.

Old Trafford is next to Salford, just over two miles from the centre of Manchester. The Haçienda, the most iconic European nightclub of the 1980s and 1990s, launched acid house and rave music, and produced the records of Joy Division. The doors of the club were managed by one Damien Noonan, a local man from a feared prominent crime family based in Salford. The family was so menacing that, when they got pulled over, the police would let them go, no matter what they had allegedly done. Damien introduced a degree of order at the Haçienda. Gangs were allowed in, but each sat in its own corner, to avoid bloody fights. They got their drinks at cost, so they would not steal them outright and harass the staff along the way. Peter Hook, founding member of Joy Division and co-owner of the Haçienda, recalls that hosting gangsters offered additional benefits: some of the staff took interest-free loans rather than going through banks. And an association with a strong gang carried prestige: 'Our bouncers were so powerful and so bloody violent that anywhere we went we had the cachet of being associated with them,' writes Peter Hook in his book about the Haçienda. Allowing gangsters to manage the doors of a club had some downsides: they controlled the flow of drugs into the place and the doormen were drawn into gang wars, forced to exact revenge for what happened the night before, so as not to lose face. A legitimate business that many of us loved and patronised was complicit in wanton violence.

Some twenty years have passed and most readers will think that the wild days of the Haçienda are over. After all, the club closed its doors in June 1997. Salford Quays is now home to parts of the BBC and ITV, and it has been duly gentrified. And yet, as I was writing this book, the most influential Salford gangster had his life cut short in a carefully planned hit, on 26 July 2015. Paul Massey was shot dead as he climbed out of a silver BMW outside his home in Salford. Shortly after his death, I put this book on hold and travelled to the town, where I met Don Brown, a police officer who started to work these streets in 1983.

> I arrested Massey three times. The first time when he was seventeen. He was a small fellow, not much to look at, but he had the guts to get the job done. He even stabbed a man in front of a BBC crew that was making a film about him. And he served the time for this crime.

Violence is a key ingredient of this trade. Massey and Mafiosi alike must be able to convince a sceptical audience that they have what it takes to pull the trigger. Once they have established such a reputation, people will be more likely to comply with their wishes; it follows that the Mafiosi will need to use *less* violence in their everyday businesses.

These people do not simply buy and sell illegal goods. They organise markets. They control public spaces. Rather than peddling drugs on street corners, they want control over who has permission to sell. Soon, they expand their rackets from a single domain to several elements of the local economy – from drugs to prostitution; from small shops to taxi drivers and hairdressers; from car parks and care homes to construction – until whole sectors are under their rule. They put themselves forward as institutions of governance, ultimately in competition with the legitimate state. Massey's

Paul Massey's elaborate funeral held in Salford, 2015.
The floral tribute describes him as a 'Salford legend'. The
carriage is draped in Manchester United flags.

business interests went beyond pushing drugs. He set up a company
officially named 'Personal Management Security', 'PMS' for short.
Everybody knew that PMS stood for 'Paul Massey Security'. In a
matter of a few years, the company obtained lucrative contracts in
Salford, Manchester and beyond. Clients included Metrolink, Manchester's light-rail network, and the construction company building
the new police station in Manchester (both contracts were rescinded
after a public outcry). 'These security firms are in effect protection
rackets,' says Don Brown. Even Massey, a small-time hoodlum by
all accounts, had a big foot in the legitimate world.

Individuals like Massey, and the people we will come to know
in this book, live in a community. Massey grew up among people
who did not trust the police and the legitimate institutions. Indeed,
the Salford Riots of 1992 were a week-long attack on the police
and the fire services. Those who grass to the authorities have their
name sprayed on the walls in the main shopping area. Four years
ago, in a local pub, a man was shot in front of thirty people. After
the murder, the killer pointed his gun at the witnesses and warned
them not to talk. As in other similar incidents, CCTV footage went

missing. No one was prepared to give evidence. Rather than *omertà*, the Sicilian code of silence, the police call it 'a wall of silence'. But it is the same thing. The former Chief Crown Prosecutor for Greater Manchester concluded in a 2016 BBC interview, 'The impression will be that people are above the law … some individuals will feel that they can get away with murder.' He admitted that 'there is a trust deficit in the police.'

Over time, gangster justice takes over official law and order. Nobody has been arrested for Massey's murder, but a local thirty-three-year-old man was killed by gunmen on a motorbike, a signature crime in the Salford underworld. It is rumoured that the victim was involved in Massey's murder. The informal system of policing Salford even decides the amount of monetary damages that a joyrider has to pay when he hits a passer-by. Members of 'the Salford Firm' – also known as 'the Firm' (two names by which Massey's gang was known) – are alternative authority figures, dispensing their own summary justice to transgressors. The next step is that the gangster himself becomes a community leader. In 2015, the *Guardian* reported rumours that Massey had been asked by police to intervene as mediator following violent incidents in the town, including a grenade and machete attack.* He also acted as a mediator in gangs' conflicts around the UK. In 2010, to cement his role as a community leader, he even ran for mayor of Salford, coming seventh. If the electoral system had been different – say, proportional representation – he would have gained a seat in the local assembly, alongside some of his allies.

These people prey on their communities yet come to be regarded as local authorities, figures to be respected, out of fear, if nothing else. Since they operate in contexts where a set of official institutions exist, gang members and Mafiosi try to influence the process of democracy, by supporting their candidates or even by standing themselves. Some members of the community benefit from the presence of organised crime, but they are a minority. Unfortunately, legitimate authorities often inspire even less confidence than do local gangsters. Indeed, mafias are rudimentary state-like formations

---

* When alive, Massey denied these rumours.

and, if allowed to exist and flourish, they come to replace legitimate institutions.

In some key ways, the mafias discussed in this book – the Sicilian Cosa Nostra, the Italian-American Mafia, the Russian Mafia, the Japanese Yakuza and the Hong Kong Triads – also *differ* from the likes of Massey. While gangs tend to be independent organisations, mafias have made efforts to develop norms of behaviour that are shared *across* Families and they have a lot in common that sets them apart from other types of organised crime. All emerged during turbulent times, when states were not trusted and were unable to properly govern the economy (legal and illegal); they have memorable initiation ceremonies, and tend to have similar hierarchical structures and internal rules, including rules about sex and family life; and they are all active in the same key legal and illegal markets, such as construction, public contracts, drugs and prostitution. A Mafia is in effect a collection of 'gangs' controlling a territory and subscribing to the same rules of behaviour. They might still fight each other, but they belong to the same structure. Above all, they have lasted a long time, much longer than gangs.

Who are the Mafiosi? There is a tendency to describe them as supermen, as demonic sociopaths running a Spectre-type organisation lifted from a Bond movie. This is not the impression I came away with from my limited encounters. I am often asked if I was scared when I met them, and why they would want to talk to me. I think people on the wrong side of the law share with us a most human desire to communicate, to talk about themselves, to justify their actions. Indeed, I could easily see how a different turn of events, a different starting point or personal choice would have led them to live a very different life.

Such people have access to violence but they do not go around killing everybody they meet. My best protection was taking them seriously and not having ulterior motives other than a deep desire to understand, to know how they saw the world, what they thought their life was all about, and whether it was worth it. I put myself in their care for an hour or so, and they rose to the challenge. I acted as a holy fool, an academic version of Pollyanna, and became a tiny observer of a whole world.

Certainly, one has to follow some ground rules when doing such interviews. I never asked about specific details, such as 'who killed whom', as an investigative journalist or police officer would do. For an interview to yield results, one should not show revulsion or moral superiority. In order to reduce the perception of threat, questions should refer to 'people in the same business' rather than to the interviewee in particular. In my case, it proved to be a successful strategy. After a few general remarks, usually the interviewee would refer to a specific case, either his or her own or the case of 'somebody known' to them. I rarely used a tape recorder. In my experience, it makes subjects uncomfortable, resulting in evasive answers. My preferred method is taking notes: it reminds the interviewee of the purpose of the encounter (namely, that of writing a public piece of research) and at the same time reduces the threat of the misuse of the information on the part of the interviewer.

Mafia Life is not based entirely on the interviews I conducted. Far from it. A significant source is judicial evidence, biographical data and conversations recorded by the police in the course of their investigations. I never forget that this material has been collected for purposes that are very different from my own. Yet it would be foolish to disregard such a wealth of information entirely. Buried in court files, one can find priceless insights into the life of the people I write about. Police intercepts, whose subjects are unaware they are being listened to, allow us to become a fly on the wall, gaining access to both the higher echelons and the street level of a crime group, and to discover a great deal about daily life and work. No ethnographer could ever hope to gain such access. I also draw upon investigative reports and published confessions. Mindful of the limitation of every type of data, I have tried to piece together a story that is plausible and consistent with most sources. The reader is the ultimate judge of whether I have succeeded.

With this book, I want to bring to the fore the human side of criminal conspiracies. It describes Mafiosi as people, no smarter than the rest of us, who make mistakes and occasionally get swindled, ending up dead or behind bars. Using the structure of an ordinary life, I narrate the complex challenges faced by Mafiosi as they run their organisations. Just like the rest of us, Mafiosi are born and grow up, perhaps get married, find a job or manage a business, save and invest money, engage in politics, get sick and eventually die. Eight elements form the core chapters of this book: Birth, Work, Management, Money, Love, Self-image, Politics and Death. Each chapter starts with a story, narrated in depth. I then turn to what we can learn from the stories.

In 'Birth', the key character is Nikolai Zykov, the Russian Mafia boss. Very much like Massey in Salford, Zykov was running protection rackets and trying to set himself up as a community leader. He belonged to a secret fraternity that had emerged in the Soviet prison system with an ideology opposed to all things Soviet. The fraternity also had a ritual of admission – a process of rebirth for the future member – very similar to that of other mafias (and absent in the Salford gangs). With the end of the Soviet Union, this fraternity became a major player in the criminal underworld of several countries and aspired, like other mafias, to control markets and territories.

In 'Work', I focus on Antonino Rotolo, the bespectacled boss of the Pagliarelli Mafia Family in Palermo. On the basis of extensive police phone intercepts, I reconstruct how he ran the protection racket in his neighbourhood and how his deputy masterminded the re-entry of Cosa Nostra into large-scale drugs trafficking, thanks to an alliance with the Italian-American Mafia. I also detail the situation that Antonino and other bosses have faced since 2008, including the economic crisis, relentless police pressure, arrests, and the arrival of an immigrant population from across the Mediterranean that is not willing to take the rule of Cosa Nostra as a given. The reputation of the Sicilian Cosa Nostra is not as menacing as it once was.

In 'Management', Merab, the boss of the post-Soviet Mafia clan Kutaisi, takes centre stage. We follow him facing down a challenge from the opposing Tbilisi clan, which has been killing his men across Europe. How should he react? By launching a fully fledged war or by devising a long-term strategy in order to isolate his enemy and only then strike back? Read and find out. In the process, you will learn important management lessons.

Mafias need to do something with the money they accumulate.

In 'Money', I follow the trail of Russian Mafia assets going from Moscow to New York, London and Rome. I identify three key players in this process: the Mafioso, the trusted service providers who work at moving and investing dirty capital, and the bankers who close their eyes to what is going on. We discover that occasionally Mafiosi are cheated by bankers and service providers.

In 'Love', I report an intimate conversation between a Mafioso and his partner. Although she is not allowed to enter the male-only fraternity of Cosa Nostra, he organises a rudimentary admission ritual for her. The power of love leads him to breach key Mafia rules and confide in her. To a great extent, deep affection for one's partner undermines the organisation's integrity and mafias try to keep emotions and familial feelings in check.

In 'Self-image', the main character is 'Broken Tooth' Wan, Macau's boss of gambling, who produced a movie with himself as the subject. Yet the final product was not exactly what he wanted. Film can be a powerful promotional tool. But while mafias would like control over their representation, films produced with their direct involvement do not appeal to sophisticated audiences. The best form of advertising, I conclude, is indirect, as in *The Godfather* movies.

In 'Politics', I follow two Hong Kong Triads who reveal the secrets of the Mafia attack against students on 3 October 2014. It appears that the close proximity of Hong Kong Triads to China is undermining their autonomy and turning them into an arm of a very powerful geopolitical power. More generally, I discuss how a Mafia can become a state and how states often resemble a Mafia.

In 'Death', I describe some of the Mafia's favourite techniques for killing people, and conclude by discussing policies that would weaken, and ultimately kill, mafias themselves. And in 'Post-mortem', I travel back to Perm to visit the grave of Zykov and reflect on the future. At the back of the book I have placed the sources I draw upon, and information on additional reading.

A final word on Massey comes from a person I met in Salford who knew him well: 'When Massey was killed I felt sad. I walked out of my office and just sat on a bench. Why did I feel sad? Yes, he was a criminal, but he was able to keep a lid on things, to keep things under control, and now there will be more violence.' Even the most fearsome Mafiosi start their life as small-time neighbourhood hoodlums, like Massey. While we should not credit these people with superhuman powers, we should also not underestimate them. What fascinates and scares me is the ability of these organisations to produce a kind of social order out of fear and injustice. We can ignore this reality only at our own peril.

A NOTE TO THE READER

The events narrated in this book are factual, and so are the dialogues. For legal reasons and reasons of privacy some names and minor details have been changed. Names written in italics are pseudonyms. When 'Family' is written with a capital letter, it refers to the Mafia basic organisational unit, rather than the natural family. Normally I refer to the Sicilian Mafia with the name used by insiders, Cosa Nostra. The transliteration of some Russian names has been simplified. Sections of this book are based on academic work I published previously. In the endnotes, I make reference to the original sources.

1

BIRTH

Nicolai Zykov in Perm, Russia, 1993

In the very final days of the Soviet Union, I started a voyage of discovery. I was in search of an entity as yet mysterious, the 'Russian Mafia'. Since 1989, I had been travelling regularly to Moscow and St Petersburg, witnessing the sudden collapse of the planned economy. Ordinary people lined the pavements of Gorky Street (promptly renamed Tverskaya) selling contraceptive pills, condoms, bottles of vodka, English-language magazines and children's toys. The more enterprising among them built flimsy wooden constructions known as *kioski*. Russians could now open any sort of shop and engage in any sort of trade. In the meantime, state assets were being auctioned off. The market economy had reached Russia, bringing with it chaos and violence. Russian capitalism was effectively unregulated. Protection rackets were reported everywhere. At the Moscow central market, traders had to pay 100 roubles a day to secure a space. But there was more to Moscow in the early 1990s than contradictory commercial codes and regulations, and burgeoning racketeering. the state to such an extent that all laws seemed Nobody knew any longer what was legal and

Mafia' was said to be behind any criminal activity press that was not entirely random. Words such as 'Mafia' and 'organised crime' were used loosely. For instance, according to Arkadii Vaksberg, Russian journalist and author of *The Soviet Mafia*, 'Mafia' referred to 'the entire soviet power-system, all its ideological, political, economical and administrative manifestations', which was siphoning off the crown jewels of the USSR's military-industrial complex. For others, it referred to a new breed of characters, 'the Oligarchs', originally obscure scientists and students who had amassed fortunes in a matter of months. They were buying the media, influencing the weak-minded president, and had private armies at their disposal – and did not shy away from using them to achieve their aims. It was frustrating for me, as a would-be scholar of the underworld, that most observers called any criminal conspiracy a 'Mafia'. Similarly, countless writers, policy-makers and documents – and this includes the official EU definition of the phenomenon – referred to 'organised crime' simply as a group of more than two individuals who organise themselves to break the law, a notion that covers almost any form of law-breaking.

Few at the time remembered that pre-revolutionary Russia and the Soviet Union had a complex criminal underworld, at whose pinnacle stood a fraternity of bosses, known as *vory-v-zakone*. The expression can be translated as 'men-who-follow-the-code', although it is most often rendered simply as 'thieves-in-law'. Their origins can be traced back to the nineteenth-century 'guilds' of ordinary thieves.* Dissidents who had been confined to the Gulag during the Soviet period met some of these people and described their behaviour.† Maximilien de Santerre, a French-Russian spy born in 1924 and confined to the Gulag for twelve years in 1946, wrote in his memoirs that some criminals in the camp adopted a peculiar dress code and odd mannerisms. They wore 'home-made aluminium crosses around their necks' and were 'often bearded and almost always wore their shirts outside their trousers with one or several waistcoats above'. Tattoos covered their bodies: in particular,

---

* In Russian, *arteli*.

† *Gulag* is a Soviet acronym standing for the 'main administration of the camps'. More generally, it is used to refer to the Soviet system of forced labour camps and prisons.

their chests were adorned with 'a picture of praying angels on each side of the crucifix; underneath are the words "O Lord, save thy slave!" or "I believe in God"', indicating a deep connection to religion. They spoke a language of their own, its grammatical structure being Russian, but with a different vocabulary.*

Varlam Shalamov, who spent a total of fifteen years in the camps (1937–53) and is known in the West as the author of the *Kolyma Tales*, wrote eight essays on the criminal world in the late 1950s, where he described the *vory-v-zakone*. The *vory* had, in his eyes, a consistent attitude of defiance towards Soviet power, as well as their own twisted morality. These law-breakers were organised in groups with their own laws, customs, language, and a rudimentary internal division of labour spread across different districts and even provinces. Caught up in a bitter internecine struggle between the 'honest' *vory* who refused to serve the Motherland during the Second World War and those who agreed to join a special army unit of Gulag convicts, the fraternity was almost completely wiped out in the fifties. Only a few standard-bearers survived.

But these survivors regrouped and expanded their ranks in the 1960s and 1970s and were perfectly placed to take advantage of the chaos of the unregulated market economy of the 1990s, when the *vory* resurfaced in the news as a national fraternity set to have a central place in the new Russia and beyond. During these years a Georgian *vor* became a minister in his country's government and played a crucial role in fostering the ascendency of Eduard Shevardnadze to the presidency in 1992. Eventually, the *vory* also made it into popular culture in the West. The 2007 film *Eastern Promises*, directed by David Cronenberg, tells the story of a cell of *vory* in London. Nikolai, played by Viggo Mortensen, wins the confidence of the old boss and is eventually put up for membership, managing to conceal that he is working for law enforcement. The 2010 novel *Our Kind of Traitor*, by John le Carré, is centred on Dima, 'the world's number one money launderer', who, born in the Russian city of Perm, is a full member of the *vory*'s fraternity, trying to defect to save his family.†

---

* In Russian, *fenya*.
† I was John le Carré's consultant on the Russian mafia.

The *vory* were still unknown in the West in the early 1990s when I decided to travel to the provinces in the hope of getting a clearer answer than I might have found in the whirlwind of Moscow to the question: can the *vory* be the post-Soviet version of the Mafia, or are they just an inconsequential incarnation of old criminal folklore? Since my British university at the time had an exchange programme with Perm, a large city in the Ural region bordering Siberia, that would be my destination. At the time I knew very little of the city. Just before starting my fieldwork, I picked up a copy of *Doctor Zhivago*, the novel by Boris Pasternak published in 1957, whose fictional town of Yuryatin is based on Perm. During the civil war, the real Perm, just like the fictional Yuryatin, was bitterly contested between the Red and the White Armies, with the latter only capitulating in 1919. From 1941, when Stalin moved factories involved in military production to the Ural region, Perm became the central powerhouse for jet plane engines, and the city was closed to foreigners until the last days of perestroika. I arrived when the Soviet Union had just breathed its last. At that time, the best way to reach the city was by train, an updated version of the same carriage described at length by Pasternak. The *Kama* – named after the river that crosses the city – left every afternoon from the Yaroslavsky station in Moscow and arrived some twenty-two hours later.

Outwardly, Perm had not yet disposed of the detritus of the past regime: statues honouring Soviet leaders and heroes, and placards with photos of super-productive workers were all still standing. The hostel where I found a room was on Lenin Street. Superficially, it seemed that life was delayed and that this provincial outpost had yet to catch up with 'the savagery of the capital', as Boris Pasternak put it. I started my sojourn in Perm by interviewing kiosk owners and small entrepreneurs. I learnt a great deal about the complications of doing business in the city, and the erratic inspection regime implemented by tax officials and the corrupt police, while I was getting closer to the people I wanted to meet. Kiosk owners, at the bottom of the pile of the new capitalist class, all paid a protection fee to a gang that controlled the neighbourhood where I concentrated my work. Once, I stayed up most of the night with *Stepan*, a seller I had befriended, to witness the meeting between him and the 'collector' for the local criminal group. Around two in the morning, the emissary sent by the district boss finally showed up. A thick-necked, pockmarked former boxer arrived by car, and invited my new-found friend into the vehicle. I was allowed to follow them. My contact explained who I was and what I was after. I was sitting in the rear seat, my eyes fixed on the backs of their heads, yet I managed to strike up a conversation with this small-time racketeer. He was not a talkative fellow, but he confirmed what I had read in the local press. The name of the person reputed to be the Mafia boss in Perm was Nikolai Stepanovich Zykov, nicknamed Yakutionok.

My break came a few weeks later when I interviewed a local official. Thanks to his good offices (and the efforts of others who shall remain nameless), Zykov agreed to meet me at the Gornyi Khrustal' (Rock Crystal) restaurant in the city's suburbs. I travelled to an industrial district of Perm until I found the place. At the time, the Gornyi Khrustal' was one of the biggest restaurants in the town, housed inside what used to be a Soviet factory making kitchen utensils. It was a Soviet-style diner, a long, dark hall with tables randomly scattered around the room. The place was fuggy, with no windows. Bodyguards searched me before entering, as if I was stepping into a nightclub. I eventually made my way to the end of the smoke-stained hall, where there was a newly built stage. Zykov was holding court, and other customers sitting a few metres away could catch a glimpse of his world. He was sitting at the head of the table, with his back to the external wall. An ethnic Russian, born on 8 June 1953, Zykov was a small, slender, softly spoken man. He was dressed in a white suit, and had almond-shaped, steady eyes. He moved as a man conscious of his power. By the time I met him, he had collected eight convictions for crimes as diverse as rape, drink-driving, and illegal possession of firearms. I noticed small dots tattooed on his knuckles, a traditional way for convicts to indicate the number of sentences they had served. Several cheaply dressed women were bustling around the table. The loud music was spoiling the conversation.

One might expect that I wanted to ask this man about some recent, unexplained events from the city's business wars, or to question him on the rampant corruption of the local administration.

Far from it; and too dangerous. I started by asking Zykov what he thought about the moral chaos that seemed to have engulfed Russia, and what could be done about it. It did not take him long to reply: 'The only moral authorities in Russia today are the Orthodox Church and the *vory-v-zakone*. Both the Church and the *vory* opposed the Soviet regime. When the Communists took over, the *vory* refused to follow the principles of Soviet society: they never wore a uniform and were sworn enemies of the regime. They did not value money or material goods. In the camps, the *vory* only respected religious prisoners,' he continued. More dubiously, he added that the *vory* have always shown respect for women, and in particular their mothers (often the word 'mother' is tattooed on the *vor*'s body). In his eyes, the *vory* were the repository of the moral code that the country had lost.

After much probing, Zykov agreed to describe for me the process – known as 'baptism' or, alternatively, 'coronation' – of becoming a *vor*. Professional criminals who aspire to join the fraternity are closely scrutinised by existing members for several years. They are expected to lead a life governed by a system of strict rules and regulations, and to demonstrate that they have, in the *vory*'s world view, 'deeply held beliefs'. Very much like the Church, they are setting themselves up as the moral authority of a country that has lost its bearing. After a few years of apprenticeship, a senior member sponsors a young criminal for the vaunted title. The ceremony has changed little since the 1920s and normally occurs during a birthday party, although I discovered that Zykov's initiation had taken place while he was in prison. During the event, a serving *vor* speaks first, proposing a novice for membership and extolling his criminal career, recalling his exploits in the criminal world. Senior *vory* come to the conclusion that the prospective member is devoted to the *vory* tradition; that he can become a leader for other criminals; that he can settle disputes in a just and fair way; that he will make effective use of his authority among accomplices; and that he will be able to raise income that will be used to support the communal criminal fund.* The most important point to establish during the

---

* In Russian, *obshchak*.

ceremony is that the future *vor* does not have any connection with law enforcement agencies and has not worked for state institutions. After all this has been established to the satisfaction of everyone present, they take each other by the hand and pronounce an oath of loyalty to the criminal world. Just after the oath, the senior *vor* recites the rules of the organisation. 'Avoid any conflict with fellow *vory* and do not undermine their authority. Respect the rulings of the *vory* tribunals and be active in collecting funds for the fraternity. Never work for the state or join the army, pay taxes or take a job in prison administration. You might have a wife, but the fraternity comes before anything else. Passive homosexuality is strictly forbidden. You can never leave the *vory*!' After the rules have been recited, the member is given a new name. In the case of Zykov, it was 'Yakutionok', a reference to the region of Yakutiya where he had served time in prison. The granting of a new name marks the beginning of a new life, and shares important features with the ritual of renaming practised by the Russian Orthodox Church for its priests and monks (as a Soviet historian noted, it 'amounts to a peculiar taking of monastic vows'). News of the 'coronation' is spread across the criminal world, to friends and foes alike.

Once the ceremony is complete, the new *vor* can finally have the mark of his new status tattooed on his body. The process is brutal, a needle and a razor being used to apply the picture to the skin. Religious images are the most popular. The crucifix is the attribute of an authoritative thief while the number of church cupolas indicates the number of sentences. Serving time for the *vory* is the equivalent of a religious duty. The image of the Madonna and Child, taken from the tradition of Orthodox icon painting, means 'my conscience is clean before my friends' and 'I will never betray'. The Madonna on her own signifies 'prison is my home'. Other images of a legitimate *vor* are the King of Clubs and the King of Spades, skulls and wings (especially those of an eagle, sometimes those of a bat). Stars, skulls and crowns indicate an authoritative *vor*, although religious images will still feature, as will fierce animals.

Over the course of his life, the *vor*'s body acquires a cacophony of images, offering a narrative of his life. The tattooed body of a *vor* is the equivalent of his uniform, complete with regalia, decorations,

Tattoo of a member of a post-Soviet Mafia group operating in Greece. It depicts the head of Christ crowned with thorns, copied from an oil painting by Guido Reni (1575–1642).

The tattoos of an authoritative member of the post-Soviet Mafia serving time in Greece. The eight-point star traditionally indicates that the bearer is a *vor-v-zakone*.

and badges of rank and distinction. All his achievements and fail-ures, his promotions and demotions, his secondments to jail and transfers are accurately recorded on the skin. The tattoo itself is called, in the Russian criminal jargon, 'advert', 'regalia', 'writing' or 'brand', an indication that the practice serves to publicly declare one's allegiance to the criminal world.* No part of the body is off limits: images are inscribed on the eyelids and the penis. A metal spoon is inserted under the lid so that the eye is not penetrated by the needle.

If the *vory* discover an inmate sporting tattoos that he is not entitled to, savage retribution awaits – even death. If, for instance, the impostor has tattooed a ring on his finger, the finger is ampu-tated. In other cases, the tattoo is forcibly removed along with the skin, but the owner's life may be spared. The question put to new arrivals in the prison system by high-ranking prisoners (known as 'criminal authorities') is: 'Do you stand by your tattoos?' If the tattoos do not reflect the criminal's rank, he will be forced to remove them with a knife, sandpaper, a shard of glass or a lump of brick.

The ritual is meant to be the most important event in one's life. 'One feels special. Nobody can touch you after that,' Zykov told me. It soon transpired that he was planning a ceremony for his deputy, who was to be admitted in a few months' time. That event took place in June 1994, to coincide with Zykov's birthday. A key difference between the old *vory* of the Gulag and their new counterparts of post-Soviet Russia is the role of detention. Since the end of Communism, the prison system has played a much smaller role than before in an individual's criminal career. In the Russia of the 1990s, fewer people spent lengthy periods of time behind bars and the opportunities to accumulate riches have skyrocketed. Bosses could become very rich and bribe their way out of prison. The fraternity was quick to adapt: the accumulation of wealth or even working for state institutions were neither prohibited nor dis-couraged any more. Yet prominent *vory* still value the experience one gains inside. The leader of a Georgian Mafia clan lamented in 2012 that some bosses had not served time behind bars. 'How is

---

* In Russian, respectively, *reklama*, *regalka*, *raspiska* and *kleimo*.

it possible? A *vor* should know prison, isolation cells, cold, heat, hunger, tobacco, the latrine. A true *vor* should know all this.' In any case, in Putin's Russia, many mobsters have started to see the inside of prison again.

On 8 June 1994, the sun shone in bright obedience over a resort on the outskirts of Perm, where the birthday party had been organised. Guests from four foreign countries, seventeen regions of Russia and seven towns in the Perm region gathered to pay homage to the city's *vor*, who was turning forty-one. Guests included several fugitives, local politicians, heads of industrial complexes and firms, the director of the central market, a singer, an artist, a football player and four students from the military academy. The initiation ceremony was under way in a private room at the opposite end of the hall, while ordinary mortals were drinking vodka and eating chicken rolls. When the ceremony finished, the criminals walked back into the main hall, upbeat and jolly, one of them holding a precious Orthodox Bible with slivers of papers hanging from the book: the Perm region now had an additional *vor* to grapple with.

This arcane secret society, rather than a vestige of old criminal folklore with no current purchase, mattered in the post-Soviet world, and it continues to matter today. In 2012, the Obama Administration designated the *vory* (under the odd name of Brothers' Circle) as one of the transnational organised crime groups that poses the greatest threat to American security, along with the Neapolitan Camorra, the Japanese Yakuza, the Mexican Los Zetas, and the MS-13 gang. In 2015, the respected Russian news agency PrimeCrime.ru counted 485 bosses of this fraternity around the world. Of these, 118 are behind bars.

From my fieldwork in Perm, it appeared to me that the thieves-in-law had some features in common with traditional mafias: they had a ritual at which a novice was presented by a sponsor; basic rules transmitted to new recruits; an oath; and a new identity conferred on the new member. Associates from other parts of the country attended the event, an indication of the fraternity's national ramifications. In addition, *vory* groups around the country were informed of the latest 'coronation'. The presence of the Bible indicated the religious nature of the event. One key purpose of the ceremony was to *impress*, leaving a mark on the psyche of the recruits, and giving them a sense of purpose and the feeling of having entered into a superior entity, blessed by God. This ritual shared key similarities with the one used by the most established Mafia I knew, which happened to hail from my country of origin: the Sicilian Cosa Nostra.

Nino Calderone joins Cosa Nostra, Catania, Sicily, 1962

In the 1980s, Antonio (Nino) Calderone was one of the most prominent Sicilian bosses to turn state witness for the Italian judiciary. His brother had been the boss of the Catania Mafia Family, and the chairman of the Sicilian Mafia Regional Commission, a body that assembled representatives of all Families from the island. Antonio was himself the deputy head of the Catania Family. When he understood that he was on the losing side of the Mafia war fought in the 1980s, he first escaped to France and then gave himself up. He agreed to tell his story in thousands of pages of court testimony, and in a biographical book, *Men of Dishonor*. He described at length the ritual he went through in 1962.

Antonio was twenty-two when he joined the Catania Family of the Sicilian Mafia. As for Zykov and the Russian *vory*, entry into Cosa Nostra – the name that members use when they refer to the Sicilian Mafia – is not a family right, passed on from one generation to the next. You have to earn it. 'There is observation, a study of the best young men by the eldest. The most senior Mafiosi – friends of the father, relatives of the mother – watch the youngsters, some of whom come to stand out from the others. These are the new bosses, the new men of honour,' explains Calderone in his autobiography. How did he come to join? 'One day my uncle said to me, "You know, Nino, one night this week we are going to go out for a good meal."' Antonio understood that he was about to be 'made'. When the night came, they took him to a village near Mount Etna. Inside a small country cottage, Calderone recognised many people that he had imagined were part of the Family. But there were many others he had not suspected of being in the organisation, a reminder

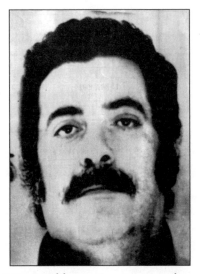

Antonio 'Nino' Calderone (1935–2013), the prominent
Sicilian Mafioso who turned state witness in 1987.

that Cosa Nostra in Sicily is a secret association, and even children brought up in such an environment are not privy to the full list of members.

Together with Antonio, seven other youngsters were about to be initiated. They were looking at one another, nodding excitedly. Then the Catania Province boss – known as the Representative – entered the room and said, 'You boys go over there.' With an official tone, he started to speak: 'My dear young men, do you know why you are here tonight? [...] We're here tonight because we're going to give you a great gift. Tonight we are going to make you.' First, he explained that Cosa Nostra was born when the Sicilian people rose up against the French invaders in 1282 (a totally bogus historical account). The Representative then introduced the audience to the rules of Cosa Nostra. 'First of all, wherever you come across a man of honour who's a fugitive, you must remember that another man of honour's duty is to take care of him, even to hide him in his own house if necessary. But woe to whoever takes another's daughter or wife. If he does, he is a dead man. As soon as you learn that a man of honour has touched another's wife, that man must die.

Second, whatever happens, never go to the *sbrirri* [police], never betray anyone. Whoever does so will be killed. Third, stealing is forbidden.' One boy was startled by the rule against theft, as he was a petty thief. How would he survive if he could not rob? A discussion ensued. It was made clear to him that he could obtain a dispensation, as long as he did not target another made member, or his relatives. The ceremony continued. The boss recited six additional rules: making money from prostitution is not permitted; quarrels with other men of honour must be avoided; silence about Cosa Nostra is to be maintained with outsiders; sober behaviour is to be encouraged; boasting and showing off are not condoned; and one should not introduce oneself directly to another man of honour. Antonio was in awe. 'That evening seemed beautiful and extraordinary. I was entering a new world, a world of exceptional people ready to risk their lives to help comrades, capable of avenging wrongs, more powerful than one could imagine.'

Contrary to what one might expect, recruits were given the option to back out. They all decided to stay. Now there was no turning back. 'If you leave [the Mafia], you will do so with blood because you will be killed.' The ceremony was drawing to a close. The Provincial Representative had a few final words: 'Now, each of you choose a Godfather.' Usually the initiate selects a guardian who has cast a protective eye on him for a while already, and introduced him to Cosa Nostra. He is the man of honour who has assumed the responsibility of presenting the candidate to the Family (just as Zykov arranged his own deputy's induction). In the case of Calderone, it was Uncle Peppino. At this point, Uncle Peppino took a needle and asked Antonio, 'Which hand do you shoot with?' 'With this one,' Calderone replied. Then Uncle Peppino pricked one of Calderone's fingers and squeezed out a droplet of blood, which he dripped onto a sacred image. In this case it was the Madonna of the Annunciation, the patron saint of Cosa Nostra. Uncle Peppino lit a match, put it under a corner of the image, and asked Antonio to take it in his hand and hold it until it burned entirely. 'I cupped my hands – I was quite affected, and was sweating – and watched the little image turn to ashes.' At that point the new recruit recited an oath: 'If I break the Commandments of Cosa Nostra, I will burn like the little image of the Annunciation.' When the oath was over, everyone in turn greeted Antonio. He had become a man of honour. The Representative went on to repeat the ritual with the other young men and, before closing the ceremony, described the Catania Family hierarchy. 'We popped I don't know how many bottles of sparkling wine and ate tons of roast chickens. It was a grand event. I'll never forget that night.' As the *vor* had his party in Perm in 1994, so did Calderone in Catania in 1962.

The rituals of the *vory* and the Sicilian Mafiosi share some profound similarities, despite the cultural distance between the two organisations. In both cases, the ceremony is performed purely by men in front of other men, held in secret and with an audience that is restricted to other members. This key event is not for the eyes of outsiders.

'Upon entering the fraternity, sever all links with society', says one of the rules of the *vory*. The initiate enters a new life. Most remarkably, he is given an entirely new identity, with a new name.* In both cases, the ritual marks a process of rebirth, when all previous ties have to be rescinded, since the Family now comes first. 'He has been made into a man' is the expression that indicates the affiliation of a Cosa Nostra member. Gaspare Mutolo, a Sicilian Mafioso, recalls: 'When I became a member, it was for me a new life, with new rules. For me, only Cosa Nostra existed.' When Sammy 'the Bull' Gravano entered the Gambino Family in New York City in 1975, he was told, 'You are born as of today.' The ritual is an intensely emotional event, so much so that many sweat and tremble. An Italian mobster has this to say about his own ceremony. 'I remember it as if it were yesterday, the holy Monday of 1941, April 7, when the chief of the Family called me *picciotto*. I was intensely moved, when I understood that I had become a member of the Society ... in a clear voice, I swore the oath which I have never forgotten.'

The new member does not simply agree to perform a set of tasks in exchange for a salary or some compensation, as in a modern contract. Nor does he accept enrolment in a professional guild. Being a Mafioso or a *vor* is a permanent transformation, calling into play

---

* In Russian, *klichka*.

one's total physical and social life. And there is no turning back. Judge Giovanni Falcone – a Sicilian prosecutor murdered by Cosa Nostra in 1992 – likened entry into the Mafia to religious experience: 'Becoming part of the Mafia is equivalent to a religious conversion. One cannot retire from the priesthood or the Mafia.' As with those who join a religion, the new member undergoes a near-total change of identity and a redefinition of all previous allegiances: it is, as the Sicilian Mafia calls it, a 'Baptism'. The fire signifies purification, and the holy water is replaced by blood, symbolising the indissoluble bond between the recruit and the organisation. In some instances, the cut made in the upper part of the thumb takes the shape of a cross. It might not be coincidental that the official Cosa Nostra rules read out at the ceremony amount to ten, recalling the Ten Commandments. And of course the role of 'Godfather' is also a key one in baptism and confirmation in the Catholic Church. The *vory*'s ritual, also known as 'Baptism', draws significantly on rituals performed by the Orthodox Church. *Vory* befriended priests at the early stage of Soviet repression in the Gulag prison system and borrowed elements of Church practices and principles. Above all, granting a new name to the *vor* is equivalent to what happens to those who join the priesthood. Early observers noted that, once 'made', a *vor* started to wear a cross around his neck. Most likely the cross itself was bestowed during the ritual. To this day, a Bible is used in every ceremony. When a Russian *vor* was celebrating his birthday in the fashionable Italian skiing resort of Madonna di Campiglio in 1997, the only object of value that he put in the hotel's safe was a precious Orthodox Bible. A black cloth with verses in Old Russian engraved in gold and scrolls containing Russian Orthodox prayers were later found in his rooms. Only his untimely arrest by the Italian police prevented him from performing an initiation ritual for a new member.

One can trace the raw elements of Mafia ceremonies all the way back to the covenant between Abraham and God in the Old Testament (Genesis 15:5–12 and 17). Abram forms an alliance with God that transforms him, starting with the change of his name. His flesh and that of all his offspring will bear an indelible mark of the pact. Mafia rituals take us back to the most ancient act of binding. In Western cultures, taking an oath involves entering into the realm of religious forces. Indeed, every oath comes with a curse: you will suffer unbearable pain if you do not fulfil your promise. As with other solemn rituals, the Mafia's oath contains three elements that cannot be separated: a promise, the invocation of superior and menacing forces, and a punishment for those who commit perjury. To put it differently, it contains what we normally call magic, religion and the law. Religious imagery is used in Mafia ceremonies to acknowledge an irrevocable change of status, to impress the watchers, and to confer moral authority on the organisation. And nor are such rituals, or indeed the concept of 'Mafia' itself, unique to Western culture, as we'll see in the following section.

Sakai joins the Yakuza, Southern Japan, 1978

Today the Yakuza is the largest Mafia in the world. Most authors agree that the word 'Yakuza' refers to the worst hand in a Japanese card game: the cards *ya-ku-sa* ('eight-nine-three'), when added together, give the worst possible total. Alternatively, it might be a contraction of the old Japanese phrase '*yaku ni tatazaru*', meaning 'good for nothing'. The National Police Agency estimated that there were some 78,600 affiliates in 2010. The organisation enjoys a quasi-legitimate status and can operate in the open to a great extent, facilitating growth to a size that is unimaginable in any context where the government puts up a decent fight against organised crime. The three big syndicates are the Sumiyoshi-kai, the Inagawa-kai and the Yamaguchi-gumi, the largest and most famous of all. Each of these syndicates receives pledges of allegiance from hundreds of independent gangs around the country. Within each gang, senior members build their own group of loyal enforcers and helpers. The entire architecture of the Yakuza is a complex set of fragile alliances, sealed by elaborate ceremonies. The glue is a common set of rules and a shared ritual. Each gang pays a monthly due to the headquarters. According to a recent estimate, the Yamaguchi-gumi receives some $50 million every month in fees.

In return they bestow the seal of Yakuza authenticity upon the fee-paying gang.

In the late 1970s, an American ethnographer, David Stark, acquired unprecedented access to a Yakuza gang. In his unpublished doctoral dissertation we find a description of a man called Sakai and the ritual he underwent.* To this day, the ritual is identical. Sakai was just twenty when he was jailed for murder. Six foot tall, with an inch-long cut above his eye, he had broad shoulders and large hands and feet. 'His nickname was "jumbo size", a reference to his big penis. His large physique, the scar above his eye, and his stern facial expressions gave him an appearance of toughness,' writes Stark. In jail, he met Oda, a member of a gang affiliated with the Yakuza, who was serving one year for assault, battery and extortion. Oda suggested to Sakai that he should visit the gang headquarters when released. After prison, Sakai could not find a job. Jailed at a young age, he had no qualifications, and the time spent behind bars had weakened his body, making him unable to do proper work. Because of his criminal record, ordinary people did not want to have much to do with him. Short of options, he decided to visit Oda's Yakuza gang.

Oda's gang was affiliated to the Yamaguchi-gumi. Oda had grown to like Sakai but he did not yet have the standing necessary to take him under his wing. So he introduced Sakai to Murata, the underboss of the gang. Murata was about to be promoted to the national structure of the Yakuza. He agreed to take Sakai as his apprentice, although reluctantly because he did not like the fact that Sakai had served time for a violent crime. Unruly behaviour was seen as a potential indicator of trouble ahead.

After six months of apprenticeship and close scrutiny, Sakai was deemed ready to join. An auspicious day was chosen, and all members of the gang attended, with Murata acting as the guarantor. Rice, whole fish and piles of salt were placed in the alcove of the Shinto shrine, in front of which the boss† and the novice‡ sat facing

---

* This paragragh and the next are based on Stark's work.
† In Japanese, *oyabun*.
‡ In Japanese, *kobun*.

each other. The guarantor arranged the fish ceremonially and filled the drinking cups with sake, adding fish scales and salt. He then turned solemnly to the novice and warned him of his future duties:

> Having drunk from the boss's cup and he from yours, you now owe loyalty to the Family* and devotion to your boss. Even should your wife and children starve, even at the cost of your life, your duty is now to the Family and the boss.† The boss is your only parent; follow him through fire and flood.

The most important rules transmitted at the ceremony are: never reveal the secrets of the organisation; never violate the wife or children of other members; have no personal involvement with narcotics; do not withhold money from the gang; do not fail in obedience to the superiors; and do not appeal to the police or the law. The lightest punishment for breaking one of these rules is the removal of a finger. Temporary expulsion is next in severity, followed by irreversible expulsion. Death or lynching is the heaviest sentence. After the ceremony ended, Sakai was given a gold-plated badge displaying the gang emblem and the number six inscribed on the back. A lavish party followed.

As with the rituals of the *vory* and the Sicilian Mafia, the Yakuza's entry process consists of four key elements: scrutiny, presence of a guarantor, recitation of the rules, and oath taking. Admission carries responsibility for the new member, as it gives him access to the collective reputation of the Mafia, a reputation that can be improved or harmed by the behaviour of its members. The rookie has, in all instances, a sponsor, who is ultimately responsible for his past and future behaviour. Responsibility is entrusted in a person, rather than a formal structure, such as a committee.

The Yakuza rules are remarkably similar to those of the *vory* and the Sicilian Mafia, despite their different contexts. Rules of all mafias cluster in three areas: norms of mutual help and obedience;

---

* In Japanese, *ikka*.

† An alternative rendering is: 'from now on you have no other occupation until the day you die.'

norms regarding sexual behaviour; and rules prohibiting consorting with the authorities. For instance, where the *vory* say, 'be honest
and helpful to one another', the Japanese agree, with the injunction 'don't betray your gang or your fellow gang members. Don't
fight with fellow members or disrupt the harmony of the gang.'
Women attached to fellow Mafiosi are off limits not because they
are respected, but because wives and girlfriends are the property of
the criminal, so coveting somebody's woman amounts to stealing.
If left unchallenged, the 'theft' irremediably undermines the reputation of the man. How can you be a Mafioso if you cannot even
protect your own property? The norms related to obedience and
to women help to minimise internal conflict. Mafia groups cannot
survive if members constantly fight among each other, pursue each
other's wives, and do not accept basic discipline. In addition, these
organisations are under threat from state agents, who are always
trying to recruit Mafiosi as informants or trying to induce them
to defect altogether. Not surprisingly, the third cluster of norms
prohibits consorting with authorities, informing on the Family and
becoming a witness for the state.

In the Yakuza, the recruit swears an oath of allegiance and a new
identity is acquired through a fictive kinship between himself and the
boss. The process of rebirth implies that the neophyte has acquired
a new father (he is 'your only parent'). The central moment is the
formal exchange of sake cups. The gods witness the ceremony, as
it is performed in front of a shrine devoted to Shinto, Japan's indigenous religion. Aside from the emotional impact of the ritual, the
process has a functional aspect: it helps establish who is a *bona fide*
member. 'The Mafia is the organisation of people who have taken
an oath,' as Antonio Calderone put it. The ritual clearly marks the
boundary of those who are members of the organisation. At the
ceremony, the newborn obtains an official 'birth certificate'. Yet the
context in which each Mafia exists is different and this accounts for
some variation in rules and rituals, and the extent to which they can
reveal openly their membership. Although disclosing membership
would help to reduce confusion over who is a certified Mafioso, the
revelation might lead to trouble with the authorities. In Italy, Cosa
Nostra has been a fraternity pursued by the authorities since its

birth in the nineteenth century, albeit with varying intensity. Today, according to the Italian criminal code, it is illegal to belong to the Sicilian Mafia. Thus it is not surprising that Cosa Nostra has strict rules about who can reveal membership status; indeed, Mafiosi in Sicily deny the very existence of the organisation. In Japan, however, the Yakuza is almost legal. Lists of members, including rank and professional history, not only exist but are made public: in fact it is easy to find DVDs of major Yakuza ceremonies, such as succession ceremonies for the bosses of major syndicates. I have watched one such video of a succession ceremony for the Yamaguchi-gumi, a long and excruciatingly tedious procession of flags being raised and lowered in a large hall, with all attendees dressed in traditional costumes. Most fascinating are the bored faces of gang bosses forced to endure such an ordeal.

Mafiosi are expected to keep their membership and most of their activities shielded from the public eye, and some mafias have also developed covert signs of recognition, but it is the level of police pressure that determines the degree of secrecy. Business would run more smoothly if Mafiosi could easily recognise each other through obvious signs of belonging, such as a certificate, badge or name card. Secrecy is a cost for an organisation that undertakes a varied set of economic activities. Since membership of the Yakuza is not illegal, it has developed the most elaborate and visible way to identify mobsters, including the use of tattoos.

Once Sakai had formally joined, he could, like a newly crowned *vor*, get himself a traditional handmade tattoo, a practice that had been legalised by the occupying US administration in 1948. Most Yakuza members have tattoos. They receive them in their late teens and early twenties when they join or still hold a low rank. When asked, they say that such images give them a manly appearance, and increase their sex appeal. But senior members and bosses stress that they are proof that a man can endure pain. The cost is very high and normally the boss of the group gives an enlisted man a leave of absence and foots the bill. In 1978, at the time of Sakai's initiation, a back tattoo, stretching from the collar of the neck down the entire back to the buttocks, came to US$4,000 and took 100 hours to produce, according to David Stark. Today it costs up to US$20,000.

Every image is unique and the tattoist is an artist. If the recipient sits for four hours every day, it takes about a month to complete a full back figure. Most members begin with a shoulder tattoo, which covers half the upper chest, a shoulder blade and the corresponding biceps. They later have one on the other shoulder. Eventually, for complete coverage of the upper body, a back image is added, reports Stark. When this is done, they get a stomach tattoo. As for the *vory*, eyebrow tattoos and penis tattoos are considered the ultimate test of pain endurance and coverage, and confer great prestige.

Yakuza tattoos are carved by hand.* Most of the members are unaware of the origins or details of the legendary figures depicted: all they want is an eye-catching image. Many of the tattoos are selected from sample drawings that the tattooist has copied from famous woodblock prints by the nineteenth-century artist Utagawa Kuniyoshi. These include a fabled drunken Buddhist monk; an early Yakuza fiercely fighting a dragon; a demon, who terrifies and eats children; a chrysanthemum in full bloom representing the beauty of youth; and an ascending (or descending) dragon. Bathing and sweating will make the tattoo shine.

After formally joining the gang, Sakai was given additional responsibilities and was well liked.† He was obedient and loyal, yet he never bonded with his fellow initiates, nor developed independent sources of income. Ultimately, he could not accept the rigid life of the Yakuza. He was insecure, tense and nervous. He had also become obsessed with sex, and spent most of his time in the local hostess club. After a while, Sakai started to disappear without alerting Oda, who always needed to know where his men were. Oda had often scolded Sakai over his absences. After ten months of service, Oda had had enough.

On what was to become his final night as a member, Sakai was nowhere to be found and Oda reported him to Murata, who concluded that he should be expelled from the gang.‡ Murata took the case and his recommendation to the boss, who agreed. In the

---

* The process is called *tebori*, 'to inscribe by hands'.
† This paragraph and the next are based on Stark's work.
‡ In Japanese, the expulsion process is called *Hamon*.

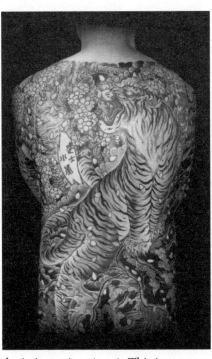

A Yakuza tattoo, depicting a tiger (*tora*). This image, representing courage
and strength, is meant to protect against demons, diseases and bad luck. As
one of the four sacred, elemental animals, the tiger is said to control the wind.

highly ritualised world of the Yakuza, when a member is expelled,
an expulsion postcard is written up and circulated among allied
gangs as well as rival Yakuza groups throughout the country via the
ordinary mail. The text of an expulsion card reads as follows:

> We welcome the prosperity that your group has attained. The
> person on the right (___ generation, ___ group, ___ rank, ___
> member, ___ age, and ___ city of residence) has lost his good
> conscience and is not good for our group. We expelled him on
> ___(date). He has absolutely no relation to our group.

Anthropologist David Stark notes that this procedure underscores the general openness of the Japanese Mafia. The internal
structure of gangs becomes public knowledge through these

missives (reinstatement cards are also sent out, in the case that discharge is not permanent). The office walls of Sakai's (former) gang were covered with expulsion and reinstatement notices from other Yakuza groups, a display that makes the system of internal control readily visible to the members. Most significantly, the cards also serve as a method of checking the status of those claiming to be affiliated with other gangs.

The quasi-legal status of the Yakuza and the lack of an effective anti-Mafia policy in Japan explain why misfits, like Sakai, can be simply let go, rather than being executed for their errors, as would happen in Cosa Nostra. (Such process has a parallel among the *vory*: for serious errors a *vor* can be stripped of his title permanently or for a fixed period.) The organisation is so sure of itself that it does not fear what a disgruntled former member might say. And it does not worry that the authorities could use Sakai as a part of an investigation. Tellingly, the Yakuza is the only Mafia not to have an explicit rule against informing the authorities, the closest relevant norm being, 'don't betray your gang or your fellow gang members.' This is because such investigations are few and far between.*

Sakai had to return his badge and name card. He could stay in the gang's territory but could not use his past membership to make money nor could he join another gang, or behave like a Yakuza. If he breached these stipulations, he could be punished. In Sakai's gang, a person who had been kicked out continued to extort money within the territory of the group. Once he was found out, he escaped to Hokkaido, in the north of the country. Soon after, the gang found him. Punishment was death. No one escapes the bullet (*tama*) of the Yakuza, as the motto goes. With this in mind, Sakai accepted his fate and disappeared. Unlike the *vor* in Perm, he was unable to embrace his new identity: the process of rebirth into a new Family is not easy. He was never seen or mentioned again.

---

* This description applies above all to the pre-1992 period. After the introduction of the 1992 law against 'violent groups' (*burakumin*) there have been more prosecutions, but still the Yakuza has not been outlawed.

George Cheung enters the Triads, Fulham, London, 1992

Rituals are highly flexible. They can be performed in settings that are far from the Mafia's birthplace and cater for recruits that understand little of what is going on, as in the case of Wai Cheung, who joined the Hong Kong Triads in London. Even Mafiosi can be clueless.

Wai Hen Cheung – known as George Cheung – was born in Leicester in 1964 to Chinese parents who worked in a restaurant.* When he appeared in court in late 1992 people saw a small fellow, short-sighted and with acne. He did not at all look the part of the 'sadistic assassin' that had been presented in the press. Yet there was something special about this defendant: he was the first self-confessed member of a Triad gang who had broken his oath of allegiance and given evidence in a British court. The Hong Kong Triads, also called societies, although shrouded in mystery and with allegedly ancient origins, emerged in the early twentieth century. By the 1950s, the Triads had thousands of members in Hong Kong, clustered in fourteen main gangs, which are still active today. Some estimates suggest that there were 160,000 members at the beginning of the twenty-first century, which is most certainly an exaggeration. The two main Triads – based in Macau, Hong Kong and Taiwan, with branches in London and North America – are the Water Room Triad† and the 14K.

George had come into contact with the Triads because a few years earlier he and his flatmate had been beaten up by some thugs. His uncle suggested that they seek the protection of the Water Room Triad. The first of many Wo Triads, the Water Room was founded by a group of workers in a soft-drinks factory in the north-western part of the Kowloon Peninsula in the 1930s. It is known for controlling the red-minibus routes, as well as several underground gambling dens, brothels and some drug trafficking in Hong Kong. On the back of migration to the UK, it became the most significant player in London's Chinese community. Based in Queensway,

---

* The narrative below is based on Tony Thompson's *Gangland Britain* and newspaper articles cited in the references at the end of the book.
† Also known as Wo On Lok and as Shui Fong.

it often clashed with the 14K in the 1990s. For instance, the 14K purchased a restaurant in the heart of the Water Room territory, opening a brothel above it. Such 'invasion' could not be left unpunished and a low-intensity war started between the two gangs, until the brothers back in Hong Kong ordered them to come to a peaceful settlement. Since 1997, mainland Chinese gangs involved in human smuggling have come to the fore and now challenge the traditional Hong Kong-based Triads.

Through his uncle, George and his flatmate met a man known as Flying Man in the basement of a restaurant in Gerrard Street. He reassured them that the problem could be solved if they joined the gang and accepted his authority. George said in court: 'I understood this meant we would have to be loyal to him and do what he asked. In return he said he would look after us.' In due course, George was to undergo the Triad ritual in London. Unusually, the period of scrutiny was rather brief, suggesting that the gang had a serious shortage of men and that the bosses were ready to take risks with untried recruits.

After three weeks, George went to the Princess Garden Restaurant in Greyhound Road, Fulham, in West London. Nine other people were there for the ceremony. They were all told to strip and were then taken to the basement. In the middle of the room there was a table covered in red paper. George saw a knife, wine and a piece of paper in the shape of a man. 'A makeshift altar made of more red paper had been taped to a bare wall and beneath it were nine or ten sets of pieces of paper laid out in triangles. The air was heavy with the scent of burning incense,' writes Tony Thompson, a reporter who was at the trial. The altar was decorated to represent the mythical Triad capital of Muk Yeung.

The Incense Master – who was the restaurant manager – recounted the history of the Triads and reminded the recruits that their decision to join was entirely voluntary. They could all leave now, but they decided to stay. 'We were told to kneel on the pieces of paper on the floor and hold joss sticks between our fingers,' said George. Speaking in ancient Chinese, the restaurant owner listed the thirty-six oaths of allegiance. George did not understand what was being said but mumbled along. He later realised that they meant he should 'never betray a brother, never steal from a brother and never commit adultery with a brother's wife'. Although he did not quite comprehend, he also swore to 'obey the Incense Master, never inform to the police, keep secrets nor create discord'. The gang is seen as a Family and everyone in it is a 'brother'. 'If we broke these oaths we were told that we would be punished severely. We could be crippled or we could be killed.'

The Master then asked George, 'If one of your brothers is in trouble and the police are seeking him and willing to pay for information, do you take the money or do you stick by your brothers?' He answered, 'My brothers!' He was then struck with the back of the flat blade of a knife. Next, George's middle finger on his left hand was pricked with a pin. The blood was then collected in a glass while the teacher continued to recite words that George did not understand. 'I was then told to place my bleeding finger in my mouth and he asked me how it tasted. I said it was sweet.' In an alternative version of the modern ritual, the recruit drinks a mixture of his own blood and that of other initiates (although concerns over HIV infection have apparently led to a change in the ritual). In the traditional ceremony, the head of a chicken is chopped off and recruits drink its blood.

The paper cut-out in the shape of a man represented an informer. The Incense Master declared that punishment for brothers who betray the gang is death. 'He asked us what we would do and everyone said "death". He said "louder", and we all shouted "death". He took the knife and hacked the piece of paper to pieces.'* Then George was taught secret hand signals to communicate his membership to other Triads.

George had now become a '49' – a fighting member of the Triads. 'According to Triads mythology, he had died in his former life and been reborn as a gang member,' concludes Thompson. At the ceremony, the recruit enters not only into the particular society concerned, in this case the Water Room Triad, but the Triad fraternity as a whole. This feature is in stark contrast to gangs such as that of Massey in Salford. Indeed, brothers can transfer from one

---

* In alternative versions, an egg with a human face drawn on it is smashed, to show what would happen to those who betray the society.

society to another without having to undergo another ceremony. However, the member wishing to switch normally pays financial compensation to his Big Brother. In addition, this universal membership also permits an ordinary affiliate from one society to accept promotion in another. Nevertheless, one is not allowed to be part of more than one Triad at a time. 'Once a Triad, always a Triad' goes the saying. Although membership is lifelong and cannot be revoked, a brother may be expelled from his particular society. In 1957, for example, a document dealing with the expulsion of an official from the Water Room Triad, copies of which had been circulated to other gangs, was seized by the Hong Kong police.

Equality is a common feature of Mafia rituals. The ceremony stresses the importance of brotherhood among the recruits and explicitly eradicates any sign of a member's previous social position. A willingness to embrace a new self is the prime requirement to join, rather than family background or social rank. Since one is born naked, George and the others were made to remove their jewellery and were stripped of their clothes before the start of the ceremony. The mixing of novices' blood in the traditional ritual creates a brotherhood bond that forms the central part of the initiation: 'We are now brothers regardless of our blood families.' This is especially attractive for those who are barred from upward mobility due to a lack of family power and prestige. Indeed, all mafias offer a peculiar ladder for social advancement. This is most evident in the case of the Yakuza: while roughly 0.5 per cent of the population is considered ethnically Korean, and 2.5 per cent belong to the outcast group known as *burakumin* (descendants of individuals associated with occupations considered impure or tainted by death), a majority of members of the Yamaguchi-gumi are either Korean (10 per cent) or *burakumin* (70 per cent). Speaking in 2006, a former member of Japan's Intelligence Agency estimated that the *burakumin* make up about 60 per cent of the entire Yakuza. In the Soviet period, estimates suggest that at least 30 per cent of the *vory-v-zakone* were born in the Republic of Georgia, and another 30 per cent in the Asian Soviet Republics.

While some mafias in multi-ethnic societies tend to attract minorities, it is rare to find rules that explicitly forbid somebody to join *because* of their skin colour or ethnic background. 'I think mob guys are the most unracist people in the world. They are just greedy,' says Sammy 'the Bull' Gravano, the underboss of the Gambino Family in the late 1980s and early 1990s. In Sicily, anybody can join Cosa Nostra, at least in principle, and Neapolitans have been admitted. The entry requirements of the Italian-American Mafia are stricter. Since the 1970s, to be eligible, your father has to be Italian, while before that, one had to be Italian on both sides. For the Yakuza and the *vory*, there are no rules preventing anybody from joining, although, as we've seen, they tend to attract ethnic minorities and outcast groups. While in principle mafias are motivated to 'hire' on the basis of merit, in practice, bosses are sensitive to issues of trust: if they admit individuals whose family background is unknown and who come from distant lands, it is much harder to recognise an undercover agent, as in the infamous case of Joseph D. Pistone, aka Donnie Brasco, the FBI agent who penetrated the Bonanno Family in New York City in the 1970s. Criminal organisations tend to recruit locally, including among relatives of existing Mafiosi, in order to increase control. If a member feels disgruntled and is tempted to defect, the organisation will be able to punish his most immediate relatives, who are in effect hostages. Indeed, Sicilian Mafioso-turned-state-witness Tommaso Buscetta had a dozen of his relatives – including two sons and a brother – murdered.

Other Families want a say over how many people each clan recruits and usually there are rules regarding numbers. For instance, the Italian-American Mafia 'closed the books' for many years, meaning that no Family could expand its ranks. When 'the books' were opened again, the available spots were limited. This is what a Mafia captain told Donnie Brasco: 'The books are gonna open up for membership at the end of the year. I can propose five guys, which I got already … But next time the books open up, maybe next year, you're gonna be the first guy that I propose.' However, at times of bitter internecine wars, Mafia Families have a strong incentive to replenish their ranks as quickly as possible, without much regard for old traditions and proper vetting, as was the case during the Mafia Wars in Sicily in the 1960s or with the recruitment of Sicilian-born killers into the American Mafia in the 1980s, the so-called 'zips'. Indeed, during another US Mafia war – the Castellammarese war of the early 1930s – the need to expand recruitment led to a change in basic rules, allowing Italians of Neapolitan descent to be admitted into the ranks of the Families.

Back in London, meanwhile, George is now a 'made member'. First, he is sent to a gun club in Chingford, Essex, to learn how to handle weapons. Soon he is ready to carry out the orders of his new bosses. On one occasion, George and two others burst into a Chinese restaurant in North London armed with iron bars in order to teach the owner a lesson over his outstanding debt with the Water Room Triad. He also attacked the owner of a video shop in Cardiff, and travelled to Glasgow to give a man a 'good beating', all on instructions from his superiors. His clean record would also come in handy – he was asked to sign a lease for a Bayswater flat that was later turned into a brothel.

His most consequential task was to shoot a brother who had been sent by the Hong Kong headquarters to rein in the London branch. Naturally, the London bosses were not pleased at the idea of relinquishing power and tasked George with murdering him. Cheung cornered the target in Chinatown but on two separate occasions he found that he did not have the guts to kill. 'I was scared. I started to feel dizzy. I looked around and looked away from him.' On the third attempt, George 'got changed and prepared the gun. I decided not to be scared any more and made the decision to shoot. I decided to end it. I walked up close to [him], checked to see if anyone was watching, and I pulled the trigger twice. I saw three marks on his trousers. I did not see any blood. I thought he wasn't hurt.' In reality, the badly wounded man survived, but was crippled for the rest of his life.

George was arrested shortly after. Initially, he stuck by his oath of silence and loyalty, denying that he and others were involved in the attempted murder. But after a while he began to lift the veil of secrecy on the Water Room Triad. He detailed a catalogue of other offences he had committed but, as soon as his gang leaders found out, a plan to silence him was put into operation. Two of his bosses visited him in prison and, using false names, reminded him of his vow and threatened to kill him.

The trial ended with an unexpected twist. The five men whom George had accused of organising the murder with him were acquitted, although two were found guilty of attempting to intimidate George while he was in prison. The court believed the defence's argument that Cheung was protecting his real Triad bosses and simultaneously attempting to get a reduced sentence for helping the police. George's story is a counterpoint to Sakai's – both men were initiated almost by accident, but made very different fists of it.

Perm–Oxford, 1998

After I returned to Oxford from my field trip to Perm in the 1990s, I had a better idea of what mafias were and where the *vory* stood among them. Mafias are not just a shifting collection of individuals committing crimes on a varying scale. They all have a secret initiation ritual and a distinctive set of rules, which are shared among competing Families. Massey's gang, by comparison, does not have a formal ritual, and while rival US street gangs such as the Bloods or the Crips have their own rituals, neither group would dream of using the same ceremony and sharing information with their enemies over who is initiated. And while some rules are specific – the Sicilian Mafia forbids members from engaging in pimping and outright theft, for example – most are found in different mafias.

When I had just completed my dissertation on the Russian Mafia at Oxford, I received a phone call from a police officer I had interviewed in Perm. I felt a shiver down my back. He told me that Zykov had been murdered. It happened shortly after his forty-fifth birthday, in June 1998, as he walked out of a nightclub. The officer had something else to tell me. When the police searched the body, they found several photos in his pocket. One was a picture of a meal we had shared in his favourite hang-out. We were all raising our glasses, making a toast, most probably to friendship, or to Russia. Who can remember? In an unlikely setting, a passing bond was forged.

2

WORK

450 Via Michelangelo, Palermo, 2003–2008:
Antonino Rotolo and the neighbourhood tax

In 2005, two middle-aged men are talking in thick Sicilian accents, huddled inside a garden shed. The space is tiny and unadorned. If they stretch out their legs, they could touch each other. Two chairs stand next to a picnic table covered with old newspapers, pressed against a window looking out onto a neatly kept lawn. None of the tools of the gardening trade are hanging on the wall. The only concession to modern comfort is a small radio tuned into the local news. One of the men picks up what looks like a Wi-Fi box.

Francesco Bonura: What's this thing?

Antonino Rotolo: I tell you, with this, nothing comes in nor goes out, no communication, nobody can bug us.

Francesco Bonura: Really? Amazing.

Antonino Rotolo: Yes, really.

Francesco Bonura: What do I need to do to have something like this?

Antonino Rotolo: Well, you have it made. If you want, I could ask.

Francesco Bonura: If it's not too much bother …

Antonino Rotolo: For it to work, the space must be small.

Francesco Bonura: Like a garden shed [*laughing*].

Antonino Rotolo is over sixty and bespectacled, and he has recently suffered a stroke. Devoted to his faithful wife and a proud father, he cannot quite afford to retire yet. He is the Godfather of the Pagliarelli Mafia Family in Palermo. Among the seventy-eight Families operating within the Province of Palermo, the Pagliarelli Family, headed by Antonino, is one of the most influential and complex to manage. Located within its territory are both the university and the City Hospital, and many prestigious shops. This is a diverse urban environment. Antonino needs to mediate among the hundred or so members of the Family, to oversee protection racketeering, to fend off challenges from rivals, and to keep an eye on the money he has invested in construction projects, shopping malls and drug deals. He is serving a life sentence under house arrest and is barred by a court order from leaving his detached house within a gated community at number 450, Michelangelo Street, Palermo. (When I visited the house in April 2016, I realised that this was the same compound where police had arrested top boss Totò Riina in 1993.) Antonino is allowed limited contact with the outside world. If he cannot communicate, he loses his power. He must, however, be constantly vigilant if he is to avoid additional prison time. This is a central challenge he faces in what are most likely the final years of his life. And he is not letting his guard down, now or ever. He needs to make sure that nobody is listening in; hundreds of Mafiosi are behind bars because of bugs strategically placed by the police in cars, garages, sitting rooms and even in the toilets of reputed Sicilian mobsters. 'How is it possible that when we talk about something, cops know about it next day?!?' lamented a boss a few years earlier. Since the 1990s, the Italian state has kept up the pressure against the organisation: from 1992 to 2006, 557 fugitives were apprehended in Sicily alone. In 2011, some 6,300 individuals were in prison in Italy for Mafia-type crimes (the figure for 2002 was 5,295 people).

In order to outsmart the authorities and his many enemies, Antonino adopts some ground rules. First and foremost, never use the telephone to arrange a meeting or to discuss matters of importance. Second, every guest must be introduced and accompanied by somebody Antonino trusts. Since the police keep an eye on anybody who comes and goes, every visitor must have a plausible reason to meet

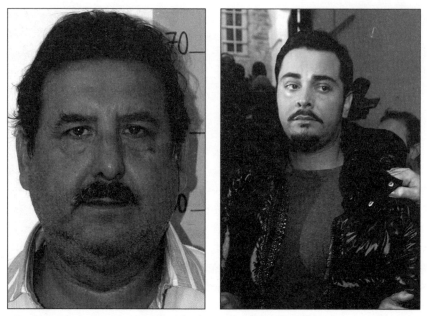

(Left) Antonino 'Nino' Rotolo, the boss of the Pagliarelli Family in Palermo. *(Right)* Giovanni 'Gianni' Nicchi, second in command of the Pagliarelli Mafia Family in Palermo. Says Rotolo of Nicchi: 'For me he is like my own son.'

the boss. He is obsessed with his conversations being listened into, reprimanding an interlocutor who has his mobile phone switched on while talking to him: 'You need to keep it turned off and remove the sim card. It is a listening device!' His concern with secrecy is one reason we find him hiding in the shed at the bottom of the garden: it is a small space, easy to check for listening devices, and if his enemies raid the house to kill him, the shed allows an easier escape route. And to ensure that the shed is not bugged, he asks an engineer to build the device that we heard him explaining to Francesco.

Despite Antonino's best efforts, the police have placed a secret camera that bypasses his new gadget. This is a cat-and-mouse race and the Italian state is a step ahead. Totally unsuspecting, he talks freely about many topics: the complications of running an extortion racket; the links with the US Mob; recollections of the 'second Mafia war' of 1981–2; the challenges of setting up a new drugs importation system. With a visitor, he even comments on the death of John Paul II. While he agrees that the Polish-born Pope has been 'a great man of the twentieth century', the head of the Catholic Church has managed to offend 'all Sicilian men' when he openly condemned the Mafia during a trip to Sicily in 1993. Antonino has not forgotten that affront.

Antonino runs the Family with the help of a regular visitor to the garden shed, Gianni Nicchi, his right-hand man. Born in 1981, Gianni has moved up the ranks on his own merits, rather than through influential blood connections (his father is serving a sentence for Mafia-related crimes, but is a minor player), and he has earned the trust of Antonino. Always impeccably dressed, with a preference for cashmere sweaters and Moncler jackets, the dark-skinned Nicchi combines entrepreneurial spirit with ruthless violence. For Antonino, Gianni is like a son. This boy is the future of the Family, not his own children, who do not want to follow his path into crime. In a conversation with the head of another Mafia Family, he says:

> Gianni is my godson. So I tell you, for me he is like my own son, he is right. You must know that when you talk to him you are talking to me.

Gianni deals with the day-to-day problems of the Family on the ground, while keeping an eye on the financial investments and the common fund used to support members in prison. He interacts effortlessly with the well-groomed and suave local politicians, all of them much better educated than he is. He is also Antonino's ambassador to other Families. Despite his young age (he is not even thirty), he is allowed to attend key Mafia meetings and speak even when older and more experienced Mafiosi from his Family are present. To cap it all, Gianni is entrusted with the highly delicate job of delivering the missives that Antonino writes to the most influential Sicilian Mafia boss, Bernardo Provenzano, who is in hiding. While a fugitive, Provenzano consults with important players such as Antonino on the future of the organisation. Things are not going well: internal discord is coupled with relentless police pressure, and the plan to re-enter the lucrative drugs trade is not favoured by all bosses. In addition, new players in Palermo are making it harder to control the territory. To some extent, even the core activity of the Sicilian Mafia, extracting protection money from local businesses, is not as easy as it used to be.

Antonino and Gianni's day job is, first and foremost, to try to impose a tax on the economic activities that take place within their neighbourhood. Large and small firms alike – undertakers, construction companies, street vendors, contractors, shopkeepers, local speculators and newly arrived foreign business people – in principle should pay. Dressed up as a donation to help the poor folks behind bars, the protection payment establishes a principle of authority. Gianni calls it 'the neighbourhood tax'. In 2005, Francesco Bonura, the man who admires Antonino's electronic device in the garden shed and a Mafia boss in his own right (he is underboss of the Uditore Family), makes the point that every penny counts:

> I am going to ask for 500 euros every month from the [car dealership]. I'll also ask 500 from [another shop]. So all in all it is 1,000 euros a month, and that is enough to feed two people.

This is a reference to inmates who will receive 500 euros each. Francesco Bonura recalls a conversation he had with his mentor, many years before:

> I told [my Godfather]: 'It might make sense to leave small fishes alone. If we have a large prawn, a lobster, then it makes sense [to extort them], but if we have just a few small mackerels, we can let them go.' He replied: 'No! I cast the fishing rod and pick up all kinds of fish ... I catch them all.'

In Palermo, Mafiosi expect business people to pay. In the past, violence was seldom needed to convince them. Normally, the shop owner was approached with the request of a loan or asked for a donation to support the prison population. At other times the request was framed as an 'act of friendship', or simply the need to 'settle the issue'.* Those asking often claimed that they could

---

* In Italian, *mettersi a posto*.

The ledger was found in January 2005 in the house of Giuseppe di Fiore. The first entry in the table refers to a construction company that has won the contract to build a car park in front of the town's cemetery: 2,500 euros. The following two entries refer to car parks built respectively in Mattarella Street (named after a victim of the Mafia) and Saint Isodoro Street. A firm building an extension at the School of Accountancy in Bagheria pays 10,000 euros, in two instalments, one in December and one at Easter. 'Santa Flavia Brokerage' refers to the fee paid for the construction of an apartment block. 'Zagarella' is a hotel: 10,000 euros. The business of burying people does not escape Mafia taxation: the undertaker IFOR is taxed for a total of 14,000 euros over a period of five months in 2004. Other entries refer to a fruit and vegetable vendor (2,500 euros), a timber yard (5,000 euros), a builder (5,000 euros), and the construction of sports facilities (10,000 euros). As for arithmetic: 134,000 + 27,000 = 161,000 rather than 159,000.

obtain a discount on the official 'tax'. The collector presented himself under the guise of a friend helping the business person to avoid further complications. In some cases, the victim felt a sense of misplaced gratitude towards the people who approached him. Fear of retaliation turned into tacit acceptance of a twisted morality where everybody paid a Mafia Family. Often, the entrepreneurs volunteered to pay before being asked.

Even today people pay the neighbourhood tax. Around the time that the police are listening to the conversations in Antonino's shed, they pick up a small-time mobster from a Family allied to Antonino, in the town of Bagheria. In a hidden partition of a bedside table, they find several items: cash, yellow Post-it notes, small pieces of paper, cheques and promissory notes worth 900,000 euros, as well as a notebook. This last item contains several pages with the headings 'Revenues' and 'Expenditures' related to the year 2003–4. Occasionally, the headings are a + or − sign. It is a Mafia ledger.

Revenues

Parking Lot Cemetery	2,500
[As above] Mattarella Street	2,500
S. Isidoro Street	2,500
S. Flavia Brokerage	2,000
Accountancy Schools December	5,000
Accountancy Schools Easter	5,000
Bellacera Pool	12,000
Rubbish Collection	2,000
Siciliano Firm	5,000
ASPRA December 2003	10,000
[as above] Easter 2004	10,000
Zagarella 5	5,000
Zagarella	5,000
IFOR January 2004	5,000
[as above] February	2,500
March	2,500
April	2,500
May	1,500

Amusingly, it appears that on page two the accountant gets his arithmetic wrong. When questioned by police, the vast majority of the business owners listed denied having paid any protection money. The consequences were severe: they were charged for aiding and abetting Cosa Nostra. Only one readily admitted to having contributed once to 'needy people currently behind bars'. Eight more confirmed paying at the trial.

Unlike those in a state system, each Mafia tax is individualised, and often Mafiosi ask for additional payments in kind. Typically, construction companies are forced to subcontract to firms also connected to the Mafia and to hire friends of the Family. For instance, in 2005 the owner of a retail chain with shops across Sicily contacts Antonino, who orders the business person to pay a lump sum of 10,000 euros every six months. It will be up to Antonino to distribute the fee to other bosses. Antonino asks, in addition to the money, that twenty-two people suggested by him be hired in shops across the city. Jobs are a valuable commodity and help build social support for the Mafia, so in this way Antonino is able to gain additional benefits for himself, without sharing them with the other Families. (Antonino also suggests that the businessman joins an anti-racket grass-roots association to better disguise his connection to Cosa Nostra.)

In a context where the fight against organised crime is relatively effective, a Mafia Family tends to control a rather limited territory. Yet Families cannot be too small. Once a Family is able to have credible control of a shop or a portion of a street, it normally expands its reach over a larger area, usually a neatly defined neighbourhood. In the province of Palermo in 2013, the size of each Family ranged from fifty to a little over 300 people. Antonino's Pagliarelli Family was reputed to be ninety-four strong in 2013. Since the 1990s, a series of important studies have shown that the Sicilian Cosa Nostra, the Italian-American Mafia, the Hong Kong Triads, the Russian Mafia and the Japanese Yakuza are essentially forms of governance specialising in the supply of protection. Extensive evidence suggests that Mafia protection is mostly genuine, limiting extortion and theft by other gangsters and police officers, helping with collecting informal loans and with the settling of a variety of social disputes. Mafias can, of course, side with those who operate in the underworld, helping thieves, prostitutes, loan sharks and drug dealers at the expense of law-abiding citizens. A rather sophisticated form of market protection undertaken by mafias is the enforcement of cartel agreements. Producers have an incentive to enter into cartel agreements but also to undercut fellow conspirators. The Mafia is able to enforce the cartel agreement among producers, thereby deterring conspirators from cheating on the deal. In general, the fee paid to the Mafia is reasonable.

Although it might benefit some entrepreneurs, if the price of extortion is not too high, Mafia rule has devastating collective consequences on economic development. In a world controlled largely by the Mafia, legitimate businesses do not want to 'attract attention', and opportunities are forgone in order to avoid complications and genuine danger. Mafia interference acts as a deterrent against expansion, every attempt at which involves time-consuming negotiations and a cut in profit margins. Those who expand their business know that it is thanks to Mafia support rather than the quality of their services or goods. Mafia Families can ask for additional favours, such as the use of areas where fugitives can hide and arms can be stored. The entrepreneur is not simply liable for protection money but is forced to become complicit in the much more serious crimes of aiding and abetting. Although most firms are not taken over directly by the Mafia, key decisions are not in the hands of the legitimate owners. Not surprisingly, firms in Sicily are smaller and have less capital than those in other parts of Italy, and they perform less well. Obviously, the Mafia foments illegality and crime by supporting unlawful activities.

Yet in the new century things are changing dramatically in Sicily, a place where the Mafia used to have the most secure control. Pressed for money – and especially so after the 2008 financial crisis – some mobsters disobey Mafia rules and have a tendency to overcharge. Increased police pressure on the organisation weakens it, leading to fly-by-night gangsters passing off as real Mafiosi. Finally, the arrival of immigrants – whether law-abiding or law-breaking – is challenging the Mafia grip on key neighbourhoods and markets. Mafia-watcher and scholar Antonio La Spina writes that 'the organisation does not seem capable of recovery. Especially in the area of Palermo, the organisation is in crisis because of the arrest of all prominent bosses and the huge seizures of the proceeds of crime.'

In the late 1980s, two brothers connected to a Mafia Family got into the habit of shaking down firms in a different territory. When top boss Totò Riina found out, he ordered their execution, with the approval of their Godfather. Shortly afterwards they were duly punished: one was strangled with a rope and another found with twelve bullets in his body. More recently, the Families seem unable to stop cases of fly-by-night extortionists unconnected to the Mafia. For instance, in 2015 two petty criminals had been harassing shops in the Santa Rosalia neighbourhood, using typical Mafia warnings, such as putting glue in the shops' locks. When the local Mafioso was informed, he pretended that these people were police officers, so that he was not shamed into admitting that he did not know about their activities, and could not stop them. Since so many mobsters are either in prison or under house arrest, like Antonino Rotolo, control of the territory is difficult.

Increasingly, Mafiosi seem short of money and bend old-time regulations. For instance, it is widely accepted that a protection payment is not automatically renegotiated if somebody from the Family is arrested or dies, because the deal is made in the name of the Family rather than the individual Mafioso. However, mobsters seem to now wilfully forget this directive. In one case, Antonino has to intervene to protect the owner of a trucking company operating across two provinces. One of the Families has a change in leadership, and the new boss wants to renegotiate the deal upwards. Ultimately, Antonino manages to shield the man from the additional charge. A great deal of Antonino's time is spent ensuring that other Families do not harass those who pay protection money to his Family.

Another attempt at rule bending takes place at the time of Italy's adoption of the euro in January 2002. Shortly before that date, a builder in Palermo agrees to pay 250 million lire for permission to proceed with a construction project. In the meantime, Italy joins the new currency and the request jumps to 250 thousand euros. This trick amounts to almost doubling the tax, as pointed out by one mobster who intervenes in favour of the business person: 'This is a play on words, 250 million, 250 thousand euro …' Since at the time of the currency changeover a euro was worth 1.936 lire, 250 million lire are the equivalent of 125 thousand euros.

The situation gets worse after the 2008 financial crisis. The jailed boss of the Porta Nuova Family, Giovanni di Giacomo, is serving a sentence in the northern city of Parma when he is overheard saying to his visiting brother in 2014, 'All we have left are four restaurants, four pubs, which are always empty ... Restaurants, hotels, they all close down, they change management all the time, there is nothing left ... there is no more work, no more building sites ... We might as well give up [collecting extortion],' he concludes dejectedly. Indeed, the economic situation in Sicily is worse than in the rest of Italy. Between 2008 and 2012, the island's GDP has lost 11 percentage points, with 86,000 jobs disappearing in the same period.

Profit margins are low, extortion payments are becoming unbearable, and more cases are reported to the authorities. In 1985, only 189 cases of extortion had been investigated by the authorities.* The number jumped to 593 in 1996 and to 811 in 2007. In 2013, 736 cases were investigated. Since we know that protection racketeering has been pervasive on the island for a long time, we can take this upward trend as an indication of more effective policing and the higher willingness of individuals to defy the Mafia. Grass-roots associations – such as Addiopizzo and Libera in Sicily – support entrepreneurs that refuse to pay protection money and promote shopping only in outlets that do not condone extortion. The situation is so dire that some Families have decided to collect protection money only twice a year, at Christmas and Easter, rather than monthly. 'Nobody wants to pay the *mesata* [extortion fee] any more,' says a Mafioso in 2014.

Some Families have even adopted an 'austerity budget'. In 2014, the Porta Nuova Family was not able to collect more than 7,000 euros in extortion, not enough to pay salaries, legal expenses, and to support those in jail. The Family thus decided to cut spending. This included money that was owed to a car dealer for a BMW X5 bought by a prominent member of the clan, Tommaso Lo Presti, for which the Family had originally promised to pay. Under the new austerity regime, however, they were not prepared to keep honouring the monthly payments. 'There are still 20,000 euros outstanding,' said a member of the clan. The car dealer was not impressed by the

---

* This data refers both to people who voluntarily reported extortion attempts to the authorities, and cases that have been uncovered by police.

Mafia powers of intimidation and nor was he prepared to renegotiate the debt, so much so that Lo Presti was forced to return the car, a serious blow to his reputation.

Even the authority of a ruthless boss like Antonino has been challenged recently. In 2005 it emerged that a firm had obtained a contract to supply meals to the University of Palermo and the City Hospital. Antonino demanded that the firm pay him 3 per cent of the total value of the contract as part of the neighbourhood tax, yet he had no role in securing the deal and neither he nor Gianni Nicchi knew the value of the contract. There is no evidence that they did eventually manage to extort anything from the firm. In another instance, in 2007, an entrepreneur operating in the neighbourhood was intent on applying to the court to settle a dispute with a competitor. Such a move would undermine the authority of Antonino and the Family. The boss involves the man's American relatives, who call him, asking him to reconsider. 'Do not involve cops or lawyers,' he is told. The businessman is ultimately convinced and submits to the authority of the Mafia instead. Yet the power of Antonino's intimidation does not seem to have been enough.

Most worryingly of all for the Sicilian Mafia is the arrival in Palermo of foreigners who challenge Cosa Nostra territorial sovereignty, do not respect age-old rules and are occasionally tough enough to take on local mobsters. Several Chinese shopkeepers sell food and knick-knacks in Calatafimi Avenue, in the middle of Antonino's territory. They are the victims of constant small-scale harassment. For the Mafia enforcers, it is hard to tell whether they genuinely do not understand or are merely pretending not to. In any case, they are defying the iron law of western Sicily: everybody pays a tax to the Mafia. Gianni is getting restless. When he shows up, asking them to contribute to the common fund for 'the poor fellows in prison', they politely send him away. Gianni, Antonino's second in command, cannot accept that the Chinese are avoiding paying their 'fair' share. He announces to Antonino that he has had enough:

> Thursday we'll smash up all the Chinese in Palermo. So far we have cut up their shop awnings and they simply repaired them and reopened the shop. This time, we're burning them down.

Antonino suggests caution. Brazen acts of violence would attract police scrutiny and land them in prison. Rather than arson, he favours putting glue in the shops' locks. But this message might just be a little too subtle to achieve the ultimate aim of having the Chinese pay up. These shopkeepers plant seeds of dissent that threaten the local equilibrium. Globalisation and the influx of new people create problems for the Mafia.

Indeed, Chinese nationals have continued to challenge Cosa Nostra. A network of criminals from China had been sending fake euros to Palermo until the ring was dismantled in 2014. The gang was based in Naples and received the notes from Shanghai. When Italian investigators got wind of the scheme, they were able to seize a delivery of more than half a million euros destined for Palermo. A couple originating from Ghana who were running a stall in the Ballarò street market of Palermo (a traditional Mafia stronghold) would travel to Naples, stuff the money into suitcases and travel back to Palermo. Two local business people introduced the fakes into the local economy, while Cosa Nostra remained completely unaware.

Giovanni di Giacomo is the boss in charge of the Ballarò street market, in the Porta Nuova neighbourhood. Giovanni is serving a life sentence in the northern city of Parma. His brother Giuseppe visits him regularly until his murder in 2015. During a conversation in 2013, Giuseppe mentions the worrying fact that a gang of Romanians have been robbing flats in the neighbourhood, scaring elderly people. 'Are these dickheads (*crasti*) still robbing people in their homes?' asks the jailed boss. His brother replies that yes, they are, 'they are from Romania, but we do not know who they are', an admission of impotence. The boss suggests caution: 'Be careful, because Romanians can be tough (*cornuti*) if they want.'

When I was in Palermo in April 2016, I spent time in the Ballarò street market. A casual stroll in the neighbourhood suggested that immigrants were feeling very much at home in what is possibly the most multicultural part of Palermo. Immigrants originating from Bangladesh run stalls selling cheap plastic gadgets, such as iPhone covers, souvenirs, snacks and bottles of water. People shouting on the phone rarely speak in Italian. After I had just left the main artery of the neighbourhood in the early afternoon, a disconcerting crime took place. Three Gambians were walking in the market area when they were insulted by two men. The Gambians reacted to the insults and shouted back. Within minutes, some ten people started a fight. A local thug involved in extortion and theft, Emanuele Rubino, retrieved a handgun from a nearby building and shot a young Gambian migrant, Yusapha Susso, through the head. Yusapha, born in Gambia in 1995, had come to Italy from Libya. He worked as a bricklayer, a miner, a cook and a carpenter, and in Italy got a qualification in hotel management. He was a keen singer, from a family of nomadic singers that travel through West Africa playing the *kora,* a twenty-one-string harp. The attempted murder of Yusapha sparked demonstrations in Ballarò. Bangladeshi stallholders led the response. With the support of the local business association, Addiopizzo, these poor sellers, often without residency papers, marched, started to report instances of harassment, and organised their own community-based security. Yusapha is now recovering from his wounds in Milan. Although badly shaken, he plans to return to Palermo. Rubino was arrested.

I had been in the Ballarò street market because it had emerged that a powerful gang of Nigerians was entrenched there. Indeed, local informants told me that the gang controls drug distribution and a profitable prostitution ring. Small dealers have now to pay a fee to the Nigerians. As for prostitution, a 'madam' manages several young Nigerian women, most likely victims of human trafficking. The Nigerian gangsters have been able to create their own code of silence, their own *omertà*. Rather than a group of disorganised thugs, they belong to two different criminal fraternities originating in Nigeria, the Black Axe and the Eiye. They have rituals, a rudimentary internal structure and strict norms of behaviour. They are fighting over this patch of streets in central Palermo, while Cosa Nostra bosses are languishing in jail or forced to sit in a garden shed, like Antonino.

There is no evidence that Cosa Nostra has entered the most lucrative new market, the smuggling of migrants across the Mediterranean to Sicily. Mafiosi do not have the connections in Libya or the expertise to oversee thousands of trips from a war-torn territory.

It is impossible for Mafiosi to demand protection money from smugglers based across the Mediterranean Sea. As most migrants are intercepted at sea, there is no way for the Mafia to charge a 'landing' fee. Even if they did, the smugglers could easily change the landing site to an area the Mafia cannot reach.

Technological changes also affect mafias. As more transactions take place in the virtual world of the internet, the harder it becomes for the Mafia to practise extortion. If the corner shop disappears, the Mafia will lose one of its victims. The likes of Antonino and Gianni have no way of reaching as far as Amazon and Netflix.

There is only one way in which the organisation can regain its importance: it must get back into the drugs trade, where it played such a prominent role in the 1980s. The forward-looking young bosses, such as Giovanni Nicchi, understand that.

Gianni Nicchi and Nicola Mandalà scheme to make the Sicilian Mafia re-enter the drugs trade

The drugs business beats all others for easy money, as Antonino Rotolo is well aware. When he joined the Mafia in the 1970s, he was at the forefront of heroin trafficking. In the 1970s, Sicily was a key node of the international drugs trade. Morphine was bought in the Far East and sold to Sicilians by Turkish traffickers. It was then refined on the island. Between 1980 and 1982, prosecutors uncovered four refineries in the Palermo area, each producing fifty kilos of heroin a week. The heroin was then sold to Italian-American Mafiosi in New York who distributed it across the entire eastern side of the United States and Canada. In 1983, Antonino bought two tons of basic morphine from a Turkish trafficker for US$55 million. Another associate of Antonino was a Swiss-Turkish trafficker. When arrested in 1984, he was quick to reveal Antonino's role.

Yet the massive profits the Palermo Families made in the trade led to bitter disputes and eventually to a full-blown 'war', which was fought out in the streets of Sicily, New Jersey and New York in the early 1980s. Some bosses complained that other Mafiosi were not sharing in the profits made through heroin trafficking. In particular, the powerful Corleone Family felt that it was treated as a second-class citizen of the Mafia Republic, and taken advantage of. Antonino sided with the Corleone Family and took an active part in the fight. 'I have done things,' he said, when talking in the garden shed of that period. Friends betrayed friends and relatives informed on relatives. Antonino's side was responsible for some of the most gruesome murders in the history of the Sicilian Mafia. They lured unsuspecting victims to a filthy three-room flat – dubbed 'the flat of death' – where rivals were strangled and dissolved in acid, their remains thrown into the sea. Antonino's allies ambushed and killed Stefano Bontade, a leading figure in the opposing camp. That murder was a turning point. Antonino's side – led by the ruthless Totò Riina, head of the Corleone Mafia Family – was now on course for a thorough victory. Yet success in this 'war' came at a price. The final tally came to more than 500 dead, and many arrested. The carnage was so extensive that the American Mafiosi – who had relatives among the losing camp in Palermo – begged the warring factions to stop. The winners agreed to spare the lives of some of the losers if the latter moved to the US and never set foot in Sicily again. The decision was underwritten by the Mafia Commission, the collective authority representing the seventy-eight Families operating in the Province of Palermo (there are more than a hundred Mafia Families in Sicily). Some members of the Inzerillo Family, who are related to the New York City Gambino Family, had their lives spared and became known as *gli scappati*, 'those who escaped'. Yet the unforgiving leader of the winning faction demanded that some prominent Inzerillos be killed in the US. Pietro Inzerillo, who had escaped to Philadelphia and was managing a restaurant, was betrayed by his own brother. Killers from Palermo put a bullet in his head on 15 January 1982 in the car park of the Hilton Hotel in Mount Laurel, New Jersey. The killers cut off his genitalia and stuffed his mouth with a wad of cash. The message was clear: this is what happens to Mafiosi who are too greedy to share profits.

The war brought such attention to the Sicilian Mafia that several investigations were started, crippling the organisation. Bosses were

Defendants at the Palermo Maxi Trial, 1986.

arrested and tried en masse. A landmark trial against Cosa Nostra was held in Palermo between 1986 and 1987 with 474 defendants, 360 of whom where ultimately convicted, with nineteen life sentences. Investigators such as Giovanni Falcone in Italy and Rudy Giuliani in New York brought an end to the transatlantic traffic in heroin. The most influential boss of the Sicilian Mafia and the winner of the war, Totò Riina, reacted violently to the arrests of the late 1980s and started a terrorist campaign against Italy, in the hope of forcing Italian democracy to grant concessions to the Mafia, halt the trials, and relax prison conditions for mobsters. This strategy broadly failed and Riina was arrested in 1993. In addition, the Italian parliament passed laws making it easier to confiscate assets of people suspected of Mafia crimes, made the prison regime harsher, and created incentives for members to turn state witness and for victims of racketeering to come forward. While Sicilian Mafiosi were busy killing each other and launching a devastating attack on the Italian state, the Calabrian-based Mafia, the 'Ndrangheta, forged links with Latin American traffickers and became a prominent importer of cocaine to Italy.

Over time, however, the role of the Sicilians was bound to be diminished. In the 1980s, they had been crucial to the importation of heroin to the United States. The drugs were arriving at the docks of New York City, which were controlled by Sicilian allies in the Italian-American Mafia. At the time, this was the main route for the importation of heroin to the eastern United States. A decade later the situation had changed dramatically: now there were multiple points of entry in the US for drugs, including Mexico and Canada. Other ethnic groups had better contacts with source countries than the Sicilians: Latin American gangs and East Asian Triads could talk directly to producers and organise more effective transport into the US. Cosa Nostra's role thus became much reduced due to globalisation.

Of course, there is big money to be made importing and selling drugs on the streets of Europe. In 2012, it costs just over US$2,000 to buy a kilo of cocaine in Colombia or Venezuela, pure at 85 per cent, and by the time it reaches Europe it goes for US$55,000. It is better than construction, extortion, and even heroin. Gianni Nicchi knows this and he does not want to miss out. In fact, he has taken some baby steps already. For instance, in 2005 he informs his God-father, Antonino, that an international dealer is about to buy a large quantity of cocaine in Uruguay and is capable of supplying them with 'five to ten kilos a month'. Gianni also has contacts in Milan, where he buys several kilos of cocaine, coordinating four people, and in Naples too. Yet he is keen to exploit Mafia contacts in the US in order to expand his involvement in narcotics. The New York Families have direct connections in Latin America and can open up remarkable opportunities for the folks in Sicily.

Gianni and the new generation of Mafia bosses want to forge an alliance across Families to re-enter the narcotics industry. Rather than embarking on individual and uncoordinated ventures, the entire Cosa Nostra should set aside old rivalries and pool capital to buy large quantities of drugs. 'If we make a deal, we can touch God's feet,' he says. In this plan, he has a key ally, Nicola Mandalà, a balding, rather chubby, up-and-coming boss in charge of five Families to the east of Palermo, himself the son of a prominent Mafioso. Nicola lives the high life, travelling first class and staying at luxury hotels. In Italy, he drives expensive cars, gambles at the Saint Vincent casino and racks up 15,000 euros a month in credit card bills. To keep up his lifestyle and to pay the people who work for him, he needs 600,000 euros a month. This is why he needs to make more money. He starts by raising the protection racket fee, and dreams up schemes to build a giant shopping centre in the village of Villabate. But he knows that the solution is in narcotics.

In 2003, Gianni and Nicola start their diplomatic offensive with the three top bosses of the Sicilian Mafia. The influential Salvatore Lo Piccolo is easy to convince: he is a one-time ally of the Gambino Family in New York with drugs contacts in Latin America. He also hopes that closer ties with the Americans will pave the way for the Inzerillo to come back to Sicily and challenge the authority of Antonino. Nicola's mentor, top boss Bernardo Provenzano, wants to heal old wounds with the American fugitives. He is also a man of vision, and knows that the future of the organisation is in drugs. The hardest one to convince is Antonino himself. He worries that his enemy Lo Piccolo and his relatives the Inzerillo will gain in authority as a consequence of the deal, and demand revenge for Antonino's role in the wars of the 1980s, when he was fighting against the Inzerillo. Gianni reassures Antonino that the Inzerillo would still be barred from moving back to Sicily and would not be able to exercise revenge against those who had taken part in the war. After much thinking and some misgivings, Antonino gives the nod: he knows that if he refuses, others will do it behind his back and this might be even more dangerous for him. Once the support of the three bosses is secured, the other Godfathers fall into line. A whirlwind of meetings takes place. More and more Families approve the plan. Eventually, an exploratory trip to New York City set for November 2003 is officially approved and funded by the entire Cosa Nostra. Gianni and Nicola are tasked with going.

The two young men are ecstatic. Nicola's girlfriend and Gianni's fiancée have been invited in order to quell suspicions by law enforcement. They open bank accounts and obtain new credit cards on which to charge all expenses. They start by buying the appropriate attire in the best shops of Palermo: *la bella figura* is the first ingredient of any successful business plan. Their contact in New York is

Frank Calì (b. 1965), the son of a Palermo shopkeeper with a clean criminal record who moved to New York City in the 1960s, where he ran a video store on 18th Street, in Brooklyn. Frank grew up between Brooklyn and Cherry Hill, catching the attention of a capo in the Gambino Family and the self-styled King of 18th Street.* With this support, Frank reportedly joined the Family in the late 1990s. Soon he impressed fellow Mafiosi. He is serious yet amiable, and keeps his word. Within a few years, he is close to the boss and is capable of forging links with mobsters in Canada and drug traffickers in Latin America. When he marries Rosaria Inzerillo, an heiress of the famed Inzerillo transatlantic dynasty, he has finally joined Mafia royalty.

Gianni and Nicola arrive in New York City on 26 November 2003. Frank is there to pick them up. The weather is a far cry from Palermo's, and they speak no English. But they are about to have the best time of their lives. They visit the city's landmarks, go shopping and eat out. In a case of life imitating art, they are seen patronising trendy bars in the East Village, some modelled on the speakeasies of the 1930s.

Longing for a degree of normality, the girls take many photos to remember the trip. But snapshots can also be used as evidence. The women are told to destroy the pictures after they have shown them to relatives and friends back home. But one fails to do so. She treasured her memories so much that she hid the photos at a friend's house, which was later raided by police. In one photo, we see Frank Calì, Nicola and Gianni having dinner with their partners in an empty restaurant. One cannot fail to notice that Frank is not accompanied by his wife, Rosaria, who was probably working in the family's restaurant in Brooklyn, where you can savour stuffed baked sardines and bowls of pasta bake.† Indeed, Frank spends a lot of time in a red detached house in Long Island with a front garden and a porch, the address of the woman in the photo. (When the FBI eventually come to arrest Frank, they find him there rather than at the family home.)

---

* Jackie D'Amico.

† In Italian, *sardine beccafico* and *anellini al forno*.

In another photo, the two couples from Palermo are immortalised shopping in downtown New York City.

It later transpires that Gianni Nicchi and Nicola Mandalà have overspent. Nicola's credit card bill alone is 40,000 euros. Nicola's fiancée, *Amalia*, is complaining that the Nicchis went way above the allocated budget. Nicola is quick to reassure her: 'Don't worry. It is not our money', meaning that the tab will be picked up by the Sicilian Mafia. What matters is that the business talks went well. Gianni will later inform Antonino: 'We were introduced to Frank Calì. Frank Calì is a friend of ours, he is everything over there.'

Calì puts the Sicilians in contact with a trafficker based in Miami, who in turn has direct connections to Venezuela (the main transit country for cocaine worldwide and the largest 'country of origin' of shipments to Europe). The trafficker travels to New York to meet Gianni and Nicola. They agree on a regular supply of cocaine, and a favourable price. Everybody is happy. Large consignments of drugs start to arrive in Sicily less than a month later. On 9 December 2003 Nicola says: 'Next week 500 kilos of cocaine are on their way. I'll take ten.' Cosa Nostra is paying 5,000 euros for each kilo of cocaine arriving directly from Venezuela through the deal negotiated in New York City. Each Family can buy some and sell it on. For this, they can enlist local dealers and pushers, even some of those newly arrived immigrants.

Thanks to the work of the new generation of Mafia bosses represented by Gianni and Nicola, the transatlantic connection has been rekindled. They have put Cosa Nostra back on the map of big-time global crime. Nicola now travels regularly to the US. He is spotted a few times in Miami. He even plans to buy a farm in Venezuela. And the money is flowing in.

Yet dealing in cocaine can also have an effect on the personal lives of Mafiosi. Nicola Mandalà lives with his fiancée, *Amalia*, in a luxurious flat stretching over three floors in Via Meli, Palermo. Just as Nicola is not an old-fashioned don, *Amalia* is not the typical Mafia wife. She is inquisitive, critical yet totally loyal and beautiful, with long, blonde hair, green eyes and the sweetest of smiles. Nicola, who knows that he is far from the most handsome guy on the block, has never loved anybody as he does *Amalia*. There is no indication that he has ever looked at another woman since they got together, unlike many of his friends, who regularly cheat on their partners. She is his rock. He confides in her, in breach of those old-fashioned Cosa Nostra rules forbidding bosses from talking to their spouses about business. They are a modern couple. Yet frictions emerge after large consignments of drugs start to arrive in Sicily once the New York deal is forged. Cocaine is the cool drug, taken by the jet-setters, the rich and the powerful. She knows that it is hard to resist. *Amalia* makes Nicola promise never to get into the habit. 'It is just business, we sell it but never use it, promise me!' she says. Yet one evening, as they are about to go out for dinner, she senses that Nicola is different, sweating profusely, over-alert, nervously excited, his eyes scarily hollow. Unceremoniously, the police pick up the conversation.

> *Amalia*: Come here.
> Nicola: Do I have to come?
> *Amalia*: Yes.
> Nicola: Are you upstairs?
> *Amalia*: Yes.
> Nicola: Are you going to make the usual speech?
> *Amalia*: Yes.
> Nicola: Come on, stop it …
> *Amalia*: Come here.

Nicola, the cold-blooded killer and Mafia boss, knows that he cannot keep a secret from *Amalia*. She can see through him in a second.

> Nicola: OK, I'll tell you right away.
> *Amalia*: What?
> Nicola: I snorted, half an hour ago.
> *Amalia*: And why did you do it?
> Nicola: Because … because I did it. Because I had to pick up a
>   cargo and I had to … to taste it. And it is …
> *Amalia*: And it is what?
> Nicola: Amazing …

At this point in the conversation, she is disappointed.

> *Amalia*: But we made a promise to each other ...
> Nicola: Well, what could I do ... I was there, there was only me and I had to test it. It was just a little amount ...
> *Amalia*: And you need to snort, right?
> Nicola: Well, just a little. My love, I have never done this before ...
> *Amalia*: We made a promise to each other ...
> Nicola: Well, but at least I am telling you, I am not hiding it.
> *Amalia*: And this is meant to mean what? Does it mean that it is OK?
> Nicola: I am just telling you ...
> *Amalia*: But what are you telling me for? You are telling me that it happened, a snort and that is all. And now what do we do? We need to go out for dinner, with other people. What are you going to do? Not eat?

Nicola sheepishly concedes that he has breached their promise not to be sucked into the world of cocaine. It is just business, he used to tell her, but now it has become personal, they are quarrelling like never before. Nicola is now torn between guilt and an enduring desire to get more.

> Nicola: OK, let's go to dinner ... But I must tell you, it was awesome, unbelievable, I felt like ... big.

Cocaine does that to you. It affects a neurotransmitter called dopamine, which normally delivers its limited dose of pleasure from a neuron to other, larger cells. After the pleasure has been delivered, it goes back to the neuron and does not stay in the brain. Cocaine blocks the flow of dopamine back to its rightful place. The cells are lit up, one after another, like a swarm. The effect is powerful: one feels confident; everything becomes easier. But quickly the brain adapts to the higher level of dopamine in the cells. The natural amount is not enough, and you experience depression, fatigue. Mood levels become low and mood swings prevalent. The brain craves more, and more. *Amalia* might not know the precise medical effects, but she knows enough. She is furious and hurt. She shouts.

> *Amalia*: You are a jerk. A promise is a promise. One does not
>   break a promise. And you say you have to do this again.
> Nicola: Well, what can I do?
> *Amalia*: What do you mean, 'What can I do'?!

Nicola tries to convince her that he snorts small amounts, just for work. But then his craving for the white powder creeps back. He tells *Amalia*:

> Nicola: I tell you, it is amazing ... Fuck, I feel ... beautiful, I
>   feel special, and the effect lasts all the time, not just every
>   ten or twenty minutes ...
> *Amalia*: Oh my God!
> Nicola: It is ... awesome.
> *Amalia*: Is it very strong?
> Nicola: It is amazing, the end of the world.

From this conversation about broken promises and forbidden pleasures, further details of the newly established transatlantic business begin to emerge, thanks to *Amalia*'s relentless questioning that mixes the personal with the professional. Kilos of cocaine are now reaching Sicily from Latin America. Once the cocaine is on land, it is easy to hide it in the numerous establishments that pay protection money to the local Families, and businessmen cannot say no when asked. One such hiding place is a car repair shop opposite the City Hospital, in the Pagliarelli neighbourhood, where Gianni and Antonino Rotolo work. The Sicilian Mafia then sells the drug to local dealers. They do not care if it destroys kids from the neighbourhood, or even themselves. 'We do not keep it, we just sell it,' Nicola tells *Amalia*. 'Well ...' Nicola concedes, 'after we sell it, we can keep some, provided we pay the guy.'

Amalia is worried that the habit is costing her fiancé and his crew a huge amount of money. Nicola, as usual unable to hide anything from her, is quick to admit: 'Well, it is costing us something.'

Cocaine is also clouding their judgement, she fears. She is puzzled as to why Nicola buys his doses *after* selling the cocaine on to the trafficker. Here Nicola enters into lecturing mode. It is the boss talking, but his woman is not easily swayed.

> Nicola: No … my orders are to sell it as we get it, so [the buyer] can see that nobody has messed with it. Then you can say, 'I need some for personal use', and one just pays, do you understand?
>
> Amalia: But do you pay him more than the wholesale price?

Nicola is impressed. 'She is so smart,' he thinks. He also detects a change of mood in *Amalia*. Might it be possible that she too is coming under the spell of the white stuff? It is hard to say conclusively, but a few days later the subject comes up again. She is definitely interested.

Nicola continues telling her how wonderful he feels every time he tries it. 'It is amazing. I snorted at 9 a.m. today and I still feel high, after nine and a half hours. It is the most amazing thing I have ever tried, you cannot understand.' *Amalia* replies, 'Is it really possible?'

> Nicola: Yes, now try it and I will show you.
>
> Amalia: Ah … ah … ah … no …

Amalia then appears to give in and asks him to keep a few grams for her ('keep it for me then').* Nicola assures her that he has got stuff of the highest quality, 81 per cent pure; and there is plenty of it coming in. Consider that by the time it reaches the streets of Europe or the US its purity can be down to 60 per cent. The first consignment of cocaine to the Sicilian Mafia amounts to a whopping 500 kilos. Nicola keeps only two kilos for his group, the rest being bought (and quickly resold) by other Families. *Amalia*, ever the businesswoman, asks why he keeps only two kilos. He reassures

---

* It is conceivable that *Amalia* suggests to Nicola to keep it for her in an effort to make him stop consuming.

her that he will get more the following week. She is getting ready to travel to Venezuela, closer to the source country, where they have bought a farm. Things could not be going better. She is happy to share this side of Nicola's life as well. And there is more. She is pregnant.

Cocaine, however, has a destabilising effect on the Palermo Families. Frank Calì's Family in New York, the Gambino, are closely related to the Inzerillo, the 'fugitives' from the war three decades before. On the back of the drugs partnership, the Inzerillos are now back to Sicily and, as feared by Antonino, reclaiming their lost ground. A Sicilian mobster describes their renewed importance:

> The Inzerillos have started to walk again ... they have ways of bringing in large quantities of drugs.

Antonino Rotolo is sure that the Inzerillos are trying to kill him. This is why he is taking so many precautions in his shed. He plans to strike first. Among his targets are Salvatore Lo Piccolo, his old-time rival and a supporter of the Inzerillo, and Lo Piccolo's son. Francesco Bonura, in charge of the Uditore Family and a regular visitor to Antonino's garden 'office', is ready to go to war siding with Rotolo. Antonino's plan would set in motion a new war, bringing to an end the profitable new transatlantic alliance, attracting police attention and, most likely, landing everybody in jail. It would also split Families. Would Gianni be willing to jeopardise the deal he brokered in New York and side with Antonino, or would he betray his Godfather and facilitate his death? Such are the dilemmas of those who live in the Mafia. In any event, Cosa Nostra seems incapable of burying old rivalries and agreeing on a common long-term strategy. Passion and revenge rather than cool business planning tend to characterise the Mafiosi mind.

While Antonino plots his revenge, and Gianni and Nicola deal in cocaine, special units of the Italian police and the FBI are ready to strike. After having listened extensively to the bosses' plans they choose to act precisely because they want to avoid a new bloodbath on the streets of Palermo. On 20 June 2006, they nab Antonino

Rotolo, Nicola Mandalà and Francesco Bonura. *Amalia*, also on the wanted list, is caught while she is about to board a plane for Venezuela, where she was hoping to go and live in the villa she had bought with Nicola, and raise their child there. In total, fifty-two people are arrested in Palermo. Top fugitive boss Bernardo Provenzano had been caught two months earlier. Less than a year later, Lo Piccolo too is arrested with his son. Frank Calì is arrested by the FBI in Long Island. The only boss who manages to escape is Gianni Nicchi, who goes into hiding, living mainly in Calabria under an assumed name with his partner and daughter. He is apprehended in 2009. By 2012, harsh final sentences are meted out by the higher courts of Italy against the top bosses of the Sicilian Mafia: Nicola Mandalà gets life, Lo Piccolo thirty years, Francesco Bonura twenty-three years, Gianni Nicchi twenty years, and Antonino Rotolo sixteen years and eight months. *Amalia* is acquitted. Frank Calì is behind bars for just one year (he was never convicted for drugs trafficking). Unconfirmed reports suggest that he has become the boss of the Family.

Today, the Pagliarelli Family is still active but much diminished in its ambitions. A committee of three youngsters has been appointed to replace Antonino and Gianni. They have not given up on drug trafficking but they do not have the ability to set up complex transatlantic deals. They buy the cocaine from a Neapolitan trafficker and distribute it in Palermo. Police pressure also continues. In June 2015, the Palermo carabinieri arrest thirty-nine members of the Family and find 250 kilos of cocaine in their possession. This new investigation originated partly from a business person who had obtained a contract at the hospital and had been asked for a payment of 500,000 euros, although the Family had had no role in securing the contract. He called the authorities.

3

MANAGEMENT

Greece–Milan–Bari, 2010–2012: A battle between two post-Soviet mafias, and a boss tries to save his organisation

Kvicha has a job to do. He has just arrived in Italy from Greece and, after a short stopover in Naples, is now holed up in a flat located in a nondescript dormitory town near Milan-Linate airport. When he arrives, it is early in the morning and he goes straight to bed. In his mid-thirties, he is fit and lean, medium height, with a slightly receding hairline. He does not drink or take drugs, but he has a temper, and people say he is hard to manage. He rests for most of the day and, at 8 p.m. on 4 January 2012, he is back on the road, driving south for an all-night trip. By the early hours of the following morning, his mobile phone connects to a tower in a little town on the outskirts of Bari, a city best known internationally as the home of the Basilica of St Nicholas, an important pilgrimage destination for Orthodox Christians. But Kvicha is here for a different reason. He is part of a crew of four, all working for one of the most powerful clans of the post-Soviet Mafia, originating in the tiny Republic of Georgia – the Tbilisi clan, named after the country's capital. The clan has branches in most Western countries, a common fund worth billions of dollars, and safe houses throughout Europe.

Kvicha's clan has been battling a rival outfit – the Kutaisi clan – in the streets of Europe for the past five years over profitable business opportunities, most recently the Sochi Winter Olympics. From 2007, bosses and soldiers of both groups have been killed in Belgium, Russia, France, Spain and Greece. Despite their bitter rivalry, the two clans belong to the post-Soviet Mafia, composed of hundreds of groups scattered around three continents. They all subscribe to the same arcane rituals, rules of behaviour, and their own version of the code of silence. They form a global criminal network that has been alarming Western officials since the collapse of the Soviet Union.

Kvicha's mission is to kill a member of the rival clan based in the southern Italian port city of Bari. This particular feud starts with a woman: Maka, a young, blonde business person with nerves of steel. In 2010 she moved from Georgia to Bari to better herself, where she found a job in a company shipping parcels from Italy to Georgia. The owner of the business is paying hefty sums of money to the Kutaisi clan in order to ensure the safe passage of his merchandise through Greece. The pay is meagre and the owner spends most of his time in Georgia, leaving Maka to do all the work. She quickly realises that her fellow countrymen have greater needs than simply shipping goods home: the Georgian community in Bari amounts to almost 2,000 people, most of them with legitimate jobs. They need office services, translation, and advice on how to navigate – and possibly deceive – Italian bureaucracy. It occurs to her that, if she started her own business, she could make some decent money. Buy a house, raise a family. This is her way out.

Maka's plan to establish a competitive shipping company could have momentous consequences. If the company obtains the necessary permits, it would undermine the monopoly of the only existing firm. Maka is not one to let an opportunity pass her by. In early 2011, she makes her move. She travels secretly to Athens, to meet the boss of the Tbilisi clan, the one Kvicha works for. Greece has become a stronghold of the Georgian clans for a combination of reasons. At the beginning of the twentieth century, Turkey massacred its Greek population, which escaped to Georgia, Russia, Armenia and Greece (such tragedy is recognised by some countries as a genocide). From 1988, the Soviet-based people of Greek origin, the so-called Pontic Greeks, left the USSR, settling across Greece and now numbering some 400,000 people. After 2003, police repression in Georgia forced criminals to escape, joining the vast community of people in Greece born in the Soviet Union. The Georgian Mafia runs protection rackets in Athens and Thessaloniki targeting local businesses, especially nightclubs, as I discovered when I travelled to Thessaloniki in October 2016. There are no fewer than 100 post-Soviet gangs active in Greece today.

Maka knows that she needs protection from a Mafioso if she is to break away from her current job and set up a competing shipping company. The equilibrium will be broken. Traffic will have to be re-routed. She needs the reassurance that somebody will back her up. After four days in Greece, she emerges victorious. When she returns to Bari, she officially opens *GlobalDelivery*, offering 'photocopying services, documents preparation and any other office-related support systems, and worldwide shipping'. *GlobalDelivery* is located directly opposite Maka's previous firm, where Bari's Station Square widens out a little. From her brand-new desk, you can see the interior of her former shop.

It does not take long for Maka's business to take off. She is educated, smart, speaks perfect Italian, and knows how to handle the paperwork and the people. Tensions, however, loom large in the background. Maka's former employer rushes back to Italy from Georgia and accuses her of having embezzled funds, although hard evidence of this never emerges. He also mobilises his own protector: Rezo, a balding old-timer with the Kutaisi clan, with a permanent disparaging grin plastered on his face and tattoos almost entirely covering his chest. Rezo carries a gun and threatens Maka with it: 'This will spill your blood one day, bitch.' A source in the police told me that Rezo and Maka had briefly lived together in Austria. If this is true, this matter is personal for Rezo.

Rezo's job is to harass Maka and her new boyfriend, who, like Maka, is connected to the Tbilisi clan. He creates scenes in her office, throwing papers and slamming doors, scaring the customers away. Once, he even hits one of Maka's assistants with a gun. Things are starting to get out of control and the boss of Maka's clan in Greece calls Rezo with a simple message: 'Do not touch her.' But the harassment continues. In July 2011, Maka's protector in Greece decides to send three people to straighten things out with Rezo, at a meeting that takes place a few metres from the two offices. Rezo attends alone. Kvicha is there. The conversation gets heated as Rezo is not in the mood to compromise. He continues to refer to Maka as 'the bitch who stole our money'. Although he has no right to open his mouth, Kvicha steps into the conversation:

> Kvicha: It is a good thing that another shop is open. This is the way things should be.

Competition is the essence of commerce, seems to be his theory. Rezo cannot believe that Kvicha dares to speak up.

> Rezo: What, are you in love with her? And who the fuck are you? You cannot talk to me. I am a bigger fish than you.

Any hope of defusing the conflict is gone.

> Kvicha: I will make you find out who I am.
> Rezo: I don't talk to kids.

Rezo cuts the conversation short and throws the can of Red Bull he is holding in his hands at Kvicha, who immediately pounces on him. His pals separate the two men. Rezo is furious; he cannot allow a youngster to have the final word. He quickly goes back to the office, grabs a kitchen knife, and is back on the square in less than a minute. He shouts, 'son of a bitch' – an extremely serious insult for any Mafioso.

In a matter of seconds, Rezo stabs Kvicha in the lower back. The wound is deep and Kvicha almost collapses. An elderly woman, witnessing the scene from her window, shouts in horror, while the police are on their way, albeit slowly. Kvicha is whisked away to a safe house, in a village in the outskirts of Bari, almost bleeding to death. Six months later, on 5 January 2012, he is back in the same flat, after an overnight car trip from Milan.

In the early hours of the 5th, Maka meets the team. She hands over two pistols that she's been holding for a while – and has been planning to use should nobody act against Rezo. But now the time has come to pass the small arsenal to the professionals. Kvicha is in charge, acting on the orders of the Tbilisi clan boss. Rezo must die.

The stakes are high for Kvicha: entry into the elite of the post-Soviet Mafia. If the mission succeeds, if he manages to take revenge on Rezo, Kvicha will be put forward for the greatest honour, the title of Man-Who-Follows-The-Code.* He would become a leader of men, a boss. The ceremony amounts to a spiritual rebirth, although the title also has practical consequences, opening up possibilities of recruiting subordinates, claiming control over emerging businesses, and having a say in how to spend the common funds. In Mafia terms, it is the equivalent of an academic obtaining a professorship, or a business person becoming a CEO of a large corporation. Above all, a *vor* is a judge who is called upon to apply the law of the criminal world in a fair and dispassionate way (*zakon* means 'law'). It is the opportunity of a lifetime, a dream come true.

The following day the crew is ready for action. The team has been waiting for Rezo since early morning but the target has not yet shown up. Maka is sitting at her desk, monitoring the square. At 11.31 a.m. Rezo arrives with a *vor* named Avto. They pop into the office for cigarettes, and are out again, smoking in the small square. They barely pay attention to the tramp sitting some fifty metres away, holding a half-empty bottle of beer.

A fraction of a second elapses and shots are fired. The execution is faultless. Guided by the spotter pretending to be a tramp and by Maka from her office, with the fourth man waiting in the car, Kvicha and his comrade fire one full round of bullets apiece. Rezo is taken by surprise, although he manages to pull out his gun and fire a random shot, while his friend Avto is just a metre or so away. The killers do not stand around to observe the aftermath of their action: they run for the car. They drive madly through the city. They hear sirens in the distance, but nobody stops them. They are back in the flat on the outskirts of Bari, but only for a quarter of an hour. They grab their bags and disappear in different directions. Kvicha is on his way to Naples and Spain, hoping to reach Greece

---

* In Russian, *vor-v-zakone*; in Georgian, *kanonieri qurdebi*. See chapter 1.

eventually, while the others go directly back to Athens on the ferry to Patras.

As Rezo is gunned down, Avto is just a few steps behind him, but the killers fail to notice him. As soon as he hears the shots, Avto runs for his life, down a passage that leads to a parallel street, away from the railway station. Soon, he is talking on the phone, terrified.

By 2.40 p.m., Rezo is declared dead. The news spreads fast. Rezo's sons in Georgia are immediately informed and vow not to shave their beards until the murder of their father has been avenged. A few days after the murder, even the Orthodox priest of Bari enquires into the fate of Avto, who by this time is a fugitive from Italian justice. The interlocutor reassures him that Avto has managed to escape, and is heading for Turkey.

The day after the murder, three Kutaisi guys arrive from Milan. They have 7,000 euros to pay for the repatriation of Rezo's body to Georgia and for the funeral. Rezo's Mercedes is also sent back to his family. More money has been put aside for Rezo's family, who desperately needs it: Rezo was supporting nine people behind bars, including his two children, the youngest already boasting the title of Man-Who-Follows-The-Code.

Over the next few days, the news of Rezo's murder, and its consequences, start to sink in. The Kutaisi clan members are beginning to show their frustration and fear: 'They slaughtered him like a pig, they violated the rules of the fraternity of the *vory*, but nobody gives a damn,' says one, while others point out that 'they had assured us that stabbing Kvicha would not lead to this! That could have been settled in a meeting!' The decision to kill is a breach of the *vory* Code of Conduct. Instead of spilling blood, a formal meeting – a Gathering – should have been called to discuss the situation. Only mere gangsters would simply kill each other. In any case, the rank and file have been shaken.

The problem now rests on the shoulders of the boss of Rezo's clan, *vor* Merab, the head of the Kutaisi clan. Just over fifty, tall and lanky, slightly stooped, he has cropped black hair, any dash of white ruthlessly disguised by a good dose of dye. He does not dress elegantly, and has serious liver problems. When he is not in prison, Merab travels through Europe: Italy, France, Spain, the Czech

Republic, Hungary, Greece, Lithuania, Russia, as well as Turkey and Israel. He is driven in a black Mercedes S5000 with Czech plates. He uses perfectly produced Russian passports in the name of other people. He is also conscious of security: after buying a computer, he sends it to a trusted hand in Moscow to encrypt it. Unless the police intercept the computer before the password is set, it is nearly impossible to plant malware which would allow them to spy on him.

Merab lives in five-star hotels and in safe houses. In Rome he is particularly fond of the Parco dei Principi, a luxury hotel next to the Villa Borghese Park, the design of which is inspired by the elaborate style of villas fashionable among late seventeenth-century Roman nobility, with impressive panelling in the hall and gilded stuccowork. He has visited the Parco dei Principi with a string of girlfriends. The most recent is *Anna*, a pale brunette who is not yet thirty, seemingly unfazed by consorting with some of the most prominent organised criminals in the world. When officers monitor her at an airport as part of an undercover operation, they can hardly take their eyes off her. Their quarry has a suitcase full of designer clothes and lingerie, an encrypted new PC, twenty-two telephone cards issued by a British provider, and a large amount of undeclared cash.

The clan over which Merab rules is named after an ancient city on the banks of the River Rion, in the north-western part of Georgia. Kutaisi is where Jason and the Argonauts finished their mythical journey to retrieve the Golden Fleece, but in recent times Kutaisi has gained a reputation for being the birthplace of many prominent *vory*. According to a local lawyer, 'every street had its own *vor-v-zakone*', until the pro-Western government swept to power in the aftermath of the 2003 Rose Revolution, and started a ruthless campaign to drive the criminals out. Many left for Russia, Germany, Spain and Greece. Although rooted in Greece and Georgia, the Kutaisi clan is a transnational group subscribing to the spirit of the *vory*.

All groups belonging to the post-Soviet Mafia are led by powerful *vory*.* While Merab is in charge of the Kutaisi clan, the 75-year-

---

* Such groups include the Solntsevskaya, Dolgoprudnesnkaya and Izmailovskaya in Moscow and the Tambovskaya in Saint Petersburg.

old Grandpa Khasan is the boss of the rival Tbilisi clan. Grandpa Khasan is based in Moscow and travels regularly to Athens. Although the two men are bitter enemies, they both belong to the fraternity of the *vory* and have met at parties and dinners, and have crossed paths in prison.

Merab is ruthless enough to do the job, but does not have a penchant for violence as such: when it comes to spilling blood he economises. In one instance, he dispatches six henchmen to Turkey to avenge a wrong. He urges them to use a proper 'technique': 'First hit him and knock him out. Take him by car to a secluded place. Then cut off his nose or ear. Nose or ear!' But Merab also implores them to double-check if the victim is willing to apologise for his misdemeanour, so they can all save themselves time and aggravation.

Behind the façade of a merciless and successful global criminal, Merab is a troubled man, occasionally displaying the telltale signs of insecurity. Bosses – like the canonical Great Men of the past – are invariably described as monumentally self-assured and driven to fulfil their destiny. We never read about a dull moment or a false start in their lives. But just like the rest of us, Merab has bad days at the office and complains about the stress of the job. After all, he is an acting leader. When in 2009 the old boss of the Kutaisi clan, Tariel Oniani, was arrested in Moscow, Merab took over as acting boss. The old boss, who is serving a ten-year sentence in Russia, still commands considerable influence within the clan and keeps calling to give advice and warn him against a particular course of action. 'Do this, don't do that' is the tone of most conversations between the two men in 2012 and Merab can't resist making the occasional dig at him when speaking to others. But Merab's grip on the clan is slipping. The murder of Rezo in Bari is just one in a series of episodes. On 15 January 2010, hitmen setting out from Barcelona try to break into a luxury apartment on Rue Andrioli, Nice, a prime Côte d'Azur location less than 100 metres from the promenade. The combatants fire thirty-three bullets; while escaping, they discard a Hershel machine gun, used by the French army in combat situations. The target – the Kutaisi's representative in France – survives, and a second attempt on his life takes place in Nice on 15 February, but again fails. By March, however, while walking along a street in

Marseille, the Kutaisi man is gunned down, with three bullets to the chest and head. The police find a burned-out car nearby, along with a machine gun, automatic pistol, and empty 9mm shells used at the scene. Another Kutaisi *vor* has to be buried. Similar episodes occur in Israel, Turkey and Greece.

Internal morale is low. Merab knows that three prominent associates are thinking of defecting to the Tbilisi clan. Others start to make a show of challenging his authority. A young *vor* accuses him of 'swearing too much' and 'taking decisions without ever consulting anybody'. Merab is not even sure any more whether Avto, the man who was with Rezo on the day of his murder, is to be trusted. Maybe Avto led the killers to Rezo and made sure that he would not get hurt? Betrayal is all too real in the lives of Mafiosi. In a phone call from his Russian prison cell, Oniani's own frank assessment, with more than a hint of understatement, is that 'the situation within the clan is not ideal'.

What can Merab do to thwart the haemorrhaging of members to the other side and to infuse strength and confidence in the ranks? One way would be to start an all-out war with rivals, dispatching death squads all over Europe. This option, of course, is always on the table and is occasionally pursued by Mafia clans. Indeed, this was the path chosen by Totò Riina and his allies in Sicily – including Antonino Rotolo – for over twenty years, and which led to the crippling of Cosa Nostra. Such a strategy would not be wise in the long run. The use of violence has to be coupled with the adoption of legitimate means. One has to invoke accepted rules, twist them enough to suit one's own aim, convince everybody else that the project is legitimate, and find a way to coexist with internal rivals. Mafias are most effective when they operate like states in the modern international system, where a mix of might and right, guns and UN-style noble principles go hand in hand.

Merab's strategy is vintage Mafia. First, he plans to promote some of his loyalists to the role of *vor*, so that he can face the competition with broader support. The newly made *vory*, once called to attend collective meetings, would support his plans and, if necessary, be ready to fight in the streets of Europe on his behalf. For his plot to succeed, he has to organise legitimate induction ceremonies.

These Gatherings can be called by any member of the fraternity, and function as courts of law, meetings and induction events: under discussion are matters of common interest, reviews of recent events, reports on how the common funds have been used, explanations and apologies, future plans, or judgements on fellow *vory* who have besmirched their title. Any *vor* can attend, even if he belongs to a different clan. 'The most important part of our way of life is that one becomes a *vor* at such a Gathering,* and not in a forest,' muses Merab in a conversation with an associate in 2012. Bestowing the title of *vor* on somebody is a collective decision, taken in accordance with strict procedures and on the basis of close adherence to the norms of the fraternity, rather than as a favour granted by one person to a loyal friend.

In the spring of 2012, Merab starts planning a major meeting to be held within the year. Usually the Gatherings of *vory* are made to coincide with somebody's birthday, so that, if the police raid the place, participants can offer a plausible excuse. Such was the case with the meeting organised by Zykov in Perm in 1994. Nowadays, coordinating the event is very expensive. A *vor* interviewed in 2014 claimed that it could cost up to $1.5 million in Russia: 'Lots of money is necessary to bribe everyone under the sun ... to ensure that the event takes place quietly. Otherwise people get arrested. The police are very greedy.' Merab's first choice of location is Italy, where many of his allies already live or can easily reach. Also, life in Italy is less stressful than in other places. Russia is making the life of *vory* increasingly difficult. A boss, who is planning to buy a house in Italy, has this to say about the place: 'In Russia they do not let you live in peace. Here we have freedom ... would it ever happen in Moscow that so many *vory* all go out together without being arrested?'

But whereabouts in Italy? Merab picks Calabria, the region where a powerful Italian Mafia known as the 'Ndrangheta is rooted. Like other traditional mafias, the 'Ndrangheta is a confederation of Families, most of which (eighty-six) operate in the province of Reggio Calabria in the south of the region. Entry into the 'Ndrangheta is marked by a ritual that shares several features with that of the Sicilian

---

* In Russian, *skhodka*.

Mafia. Internationally, the Ndrangheta traffics cocaine that reaches Europe from South America. Indeed, the Gambino Family (whose deputy boss is reportedly Frank Calì) appears in several investigations into transnational drugs trafficking between Calabria, Latin America and New York City. After the failed attempt to collaborate with Cosa Nostra (narrated in chapter 2), it has now understood that the future lies with the Calabresi. Locally, the Ndrangheta maintains a firm grip on the territory: it forces local entrepreneurs to pay protection money, corrupts officials, and penetrates politics. Anti-Mafia activists and honest officials have been threatened, wounded and killed, while bosses have stood successfully in local elections. From 1991 to 2007, the Italian government ordered the dissolution of thirty-eight city councils due to the Ndrangheta's ability to subvert local elections.* A few weeks after Merab's decision to hold his meeting there, the City Administration of Reggio Calabria, the most important metropolitan area, was disbanded. The Ndrangheta is now considered the most powerful crime syndicate in Italy, with a revenue stream of around US$72 billion. This is the first time that hard evidence of the cosy relationship between the post-Soviet Mafia and the Ndrangheta has been brought to light.

'We can ask our friends in Calabria to have the meeting in their territory,' suggests Merab in the spring of 2012.

'There should be no problem,' replies his associate. 'There will be some 100 people. Forty *vory*, plus those to be inducted, the drivers and the bodyguards ...' Merab replies: 'We can hold it in the same place where we went for the wedding; the owner is a friend of theirs' (that is, a friend of the Ndrangheta bosses).

---

* The Ndrangheta is infamous for a massacre it carried out in Germany in 2007, when a crew travelled to Duisburg, in north-western Germany. The killers made their way to an Italian restaurant, Da Bruno, where six people were celebrating the eighteenth birthday of a Calabrese man. As the six friends walked out of the restaurant and got into their cars, the killers started shooting: no fewer than seventy shots were fired. All six people were hit, and each of them received a final shot in the head. These executions in the heart of Europe brought the ruthless nature and international reach of the organisation to the TV screens of most Europeans.

'Ndrangheta weddings are used by Families to forge alliances and cement partnerships. It is highly significant that Merab was invited to such an event. What is behind the warm relationship between these two mafias? Current investigations tell us that the post-Soviet Mafia is trying to take over the distribution of cocaine in Eastern Europe. Until 2012 groups from Serbia and Montenegro had privileged access to cocaine arriving from Colombia into the port of Gioia Tauro, in Calabria, which is controlled by the 'Ndrangheta. The Serbians then distributed the drug across Italy, Eastern Europe and several other Mediterranean countries. The *vory*, however, have a well-oiled European network of distributors and want a piece of the pie. They are trying to convince the Calabrians to dump their old partners and forge a new alliance with them. Their plan is to work alongside the 'Ndrangheta, buying vessels from impoverished Greek shipowners in order to transport drugs between Italy and Greece, while using their cash to bribe port officials. With the prospect of continuing economic hardship in Greece, the country could one day become the main destination of cocaine from Latin America (in June 2015 alone 3,500 kilos were seized in Athens).

'Good,' says one of Merab's associates, 'I'll tell everybody that we are celebrating a birthday in Calabria, so they bring gifts!'

Merab: 'Yes, but even if we get raided, nothing will happen, this is not Moscow.' (In Moscow, *vory* could be arrested if caught holding a meeting.)

'Calabria is the best choice,' concludes Merab. 'We need somewhere out of the way because we are a very loud bunch!'

In August 2012, Merab travels with his bodyguard to Calabria in order to inspect the location. He is the guest of the four Italian Mafia Families based in the city of Reggio Calabria, who work together, sharing risks and profits. The climax of the trip is the evening meal. Their hosts take the two Mafiosi on a scenic highway which runs along the southern tip of Italy until the town of Scylla, a twenty-minute ride from Reggio Calabria. Scylla is famous for its views over the strait of Sicily and for its seafood cuisine. It also makes an appearance in Homer's *Odyssey*.

The beauty of the place is stunning and the meal is exceptional.

We do not know the menu they were offered but the local speciality is the swordfish *alla Ghiotta*, marinated in olive oil, salt, lemon and oregano and then roasted, and a soft-textured, spicy salami typical of Calabria (*'nduja*). As for dessert, the traditional Bagnara nougat, made with almonds and orange blossom honey, is a hit. Merab is speechless. Naturally, he is not allowed to pay: 'I wanted to settle the bill but the waiter would not even let me see it.'

But after a few days have gone by, the Calabresi send back a message suggesting that their region might not be a good place to hold the summit after all. 'The police are always on the lookout, so it is better if you find a different location,' they tell him. Is it an excuse? Has the rival Tbilisi clan been informed and intervened to thwart the plan? Or is there true concern about police interference? Merab cannot be sure, but he reluctantly accepts their pronouncement and gives up on the idea of holding the meeting in Calabria. Trans-Mafia collaborations are not easy.

With the south of Italy now out of the question, Merab turns his mind to Rome as a possible site. After consulting with his most trusted aides, he makes up his mind and starts to invite as many bosses as he can to the Italian capital, still planning to initiate a new batch of *vory*. His objective is still to increase the ranks of his Kutaisi clan and then strike at the Tbilisi clan. The date for the meeting is now 12 September 2012. Merab works the phone. He extends invitations and orders a travel agency to hire a venue, sign contracts, book hotels and rent Mercedes cars. Instructions are precise. 'Sixty guests, no need to hire waiters, just leave the food on tables and we'll serve ourselves.' Clearly they are afraid of potential undercover officers. The travel agent makes sure that everything goes according to plan. A seventeenth-century castle in the Roman countryside, on the Bosco di Bracciano estate, is the chosen venue. The price tag is significant.

One should not underestimate the work that goes into organising such an event. For it to be a success, as many *vory* as possible must attend. But it is not just about numbers. Some bosses have more political clout than others, so Merab does his best to ensure that the most influential ones come. He is very keen on the attendance of two bosses in particular, living in Riga and Berlin. A delicate diplomatic mission is arranged: Merab sends trusted associates to both cities, as a medieval king would send his ambassadors to a foreign country. This is the conversation Merab has with one of his envoys in Riga, who is about to meet the local *vor*:

> Merab: Where are you?
> Associate: We are out already. Soon Slava will join us and we will talk.
> Merab: Where are you meeting?
> Associate: Just near the hotel.
> Merab: Do not create tension, make things smoother, for the benefit of our brotherhood.
> Associate: Yes, yes …
> Merab: The most important thing is not to blow things up.

One can sense a touch of anxiety in the tone of his voice.

'Sure, don't worry,' Merab's emissary in Riga reassures him, in a rather patronising tone.

There are more setbacks around the corner. Prominent members of the Tbilisi clan make it clear that they will not attend if new *vory* are to be crowned. In addition, two bosses from Merab's organisation now have doubts about putting forward new names for the coveted title of Man-Who-Follows-The-Code. An important member of the clan, *vor* Jemo, had a son killed by the Tbilisi. He wears the Russian Mafia trademark leather jacket and expensive shoes with an air of juvenile defiance. His attitude of permanent anger stems from resentment against Merab. He had hoped to become boss, and he now does what he can to undermine Merab's plan, discouraging others to attend. At one point, Merab bursts forth: 'If you don't want to come, don't! We shall go ahead with our meeting without you!'

The bickering and strategising are taking their toll on Merab. In a moment of self-reflection, he admits to a friend: 'I have lost weight over this meeting. At 1.90 m tall, I now weigh 69 kg … This is going to kill me.'

He now takes pills for his blood pressure, which climbs as high as 220/90, suggesting hypertension.

On the other hand, things are progressing. The logistics have been sorted out, and a sufficient number of people have promised to attend. Merab is forced to postpone the event by a few days because some have not managed to obtain a visa, while another has fallen ill. But everything is ready for the grand party, now scheduled for 18 September 2012. To avoid suspicion, attendees have started to converge in Rome since the beginning of the month. This event will be a major coup for Merab, demonstrating his prestige to the world of the post-Soviet Mafia.

Merab has to ensure that no blood is spilled before or after the formal event. One of the distinguished guests is caught by police in Rome carrying a seventeen-centimetre-long jack-knife. Apparently, he has every intention of using it, as he openly discusses plans to kill a man against whom he bears a grudge: 'We should stab him like a bitch before the meeting starts!' he says to one of his buddies on 6 September.

If violence breaks out, the entire meeting would be called off and Merab's efforts would have been in vain. He has to stop his own men from doing something rash. In this instance, the police lend an unwitting hand by arresting the man. This is a stroke of good luck.

But few things ever go according to plan in the life of Mafiosi.

On 7 September Merab is staying at a hotel hidden inside a lush designer garden, in the exclusive Parioli neighbourhood of Rome. As is customary, he orders breakfast in bed. It is already past noon, the hour when most guests stream to lunch. When he opens the door to welcome the waiter, he sees a familiar face, a middle-aged woman of Russian origin, well built and with dyed blonde hair. She has been helpful in the past. Putting the tray down on the grand table in the adjacent drawing room, she looks worried. Merab starts to chat to her, but she quickly puts both hands on her mouth and signals to him that they should go out onto the balcony to talk. Three French windows lead to the terrace, which overlooks the main entrance of the hotel. The restless hubbub of the lobby is audible below: taxi drivers coming and going, the clinks of plates from the dining room, the footfall of employees, the brittle voice of a young Italian beauty sitting at a red-lacquered, faux Louis XV reception desk. At least, this is what I noticed when I stayed in the same hotel room in the autumn of 2015. As I walked on the landing, I found myself picturing the scene: there were several plants on the balcony, including a small palm tree, but it must still have been possible to see the Kutaisi boss, overlooking guests and staff entering and leaving the posh establishment, talking to the maid.

'The police have been asking about you, and are listening to all your conversations, the room is bugged.'

Merab is stunned and furious, but manages to disguise his rage. Fuming, he grabs his coat and takes his car out for a spin, doing some seventy miles in order to check if he is being followed. The next day, he distributes ten new telephone cards to his associates. He also suggests to the Mafiosi already in Rome that they take a short trip around Italy, in order to baffle the police. Another ominous sign of police attention is that a close friend, Aleksandr Timoshenko-Bor, has been searched thoroughly upon landing in Rome. Gradually, even close allies start to hint that he should consider cancelling the event altogether and reconvening in a different country.

Eventually, Merab comes to the same conclusion. The deciding factor is a meeting with a rather mysterious figure from Tbilisi, somebody who does not belong to the criminal world. A trusted confidant calls Merab and urges him to 'pay close attention to what the man who is meeting you has to say, he is a very *serious* person'. (I interpret this to be a code word for somebody who works for the secret service, but I have no way to confirm this intuition.) Dutifully, Merab goes to pick him up at the airport. They have a long tête-à-tête.

The mystery man informs Merab that Italian and Georgian police know all his plans and that they will arrest him. He elaborates further: 'As Georgia is going through a closely contested election, the raid will be used to score points politically. My advice is call the meeting off or you and your guests will end up behind bars.'

An international arrest operation against Georgian *vory* in Rome would indeed be an ideal opportunity for the ruling pro-Western government led by Mikheil Saakashvili. Since coming to power in 2008, the Georgian government has carried out an extremely harsh (and arguably effective) campaign against the *vory*, in the hope of freeing Georgia from the grip of pervasive organised crime. However, in pursuing the *vory*, the government has violated human rights, ruthlessly crushed prison riots, and conditions in jail are appalling, especially in the wards where the *vory* are housed. Indeed, this is the country with the highest prison population per capita in Europe. The opposition, led by billionaire Bidzina Ivanishvili, is making rapid gains and is set to win many seats. With the October 2012 elections approaching, September is the month when things get very hot politically. Anti-government forces get hold of a compromising video showing horrendous abuse. In one clip, a male prisoner is brutally raped with a broom. In another clip, a man being humiliated (and possibly raped) is forced to shout that he is a *vor*. The images are from ward n.7 of Tbilisi prison where the *vory* are held. The video shocks the nation. In an attempt to control the ensuing damage, the government is trying to show that organised crime is a serious menace. But elements within Georgia are rooting for the opposition and spoil the operation by informing Merab in advance.*

Whatever the reasons, the warning received by Merab in September 2012 is indeed quite extraordinary. It clearly undermines highly secretive, Europe-wide police murder investigations. The boss does not doubt for a moment the truthfulness of the message and agrees to cancel the meeting. The organisation goes into damage limitation mode: all guests are told to leave the country as soon as it is safe to do so. Merab will stay behind until everybody has left, a gentlemanly touch that underscores his style. He is not a man to run away, leaving others in trouble. On the evening of 18 September, the day when the Gathering is to be held, the castle in the Roman countryside stands ready to welcome its distinguished guests. Nobody shows up. That night, Merab is drenched in a sorrowful mood:

---

* The opposition wins the 2012 elections. Merab and Oniani are heard on the phone devising schemes to rig the vote. Pro-government television stations broadcast images meant to prove that some opposition politicians met members of organised crime – the politicians in question strongly denied any wrongdoing. Yet one may assume that there were rigging attempts by both sides and it may be that these opposing efforts effectively cancelled each other out.

'How much money we have thrown away, how much effort, how much energy wasted.'

The boss is forced into a strategic rethink. If he gives up on holding the event in Italy, his role as the key organiser will be diminished, and he will not appear as central as he had hoped. On the other hand, he could agree to share the limelight, and hold the ritual of admission into the fraternity in a city where another *vor* is based. Merab also understands that he needs to galvanise the clan into backing his leadership. In order to do so, it is best to reach out to prominent *vory* outside his own clan, as well as to insiders who do not feel fully integrated. One of them is the influential Jemo, who has been lukewarm about the Rome event. Jemo often travels to Dubai and is close to a local *vor*. Behind the scenes, the old boss Oniani also favours the United Arab Emirates as the new venue. At first Merab worries that it might be difficult to obtain visas, but by the end of September he agrees to convene the meeting in the Middle Eastern city. The new date is set for 10 December 2012. Meanwhile, in another positive development for Merab, a Gathering organised in Greece by the opposing Tbilisi clan has been raided by police.

I visited Dubai in August 2015. This is a concept city, the brain-child of a visionary sheikh who decided some forty years ago to build the most luxurious metropolis in the world, using labourers forced to live in crammed accommodation and unsanitary conditions in a neighbourhood far away from their homes. Everything here is grand, fake, expensive, wasteful and hidden. Dubai is a set of high-security, privatised spaces, with the highest ecological footprint in the world. Life takes place in shopping malls, conference centres and luxury apartments rather than in streets and squares. Behind closed doors, anything goes. Although officially illegal, prostitution is arguably the largest business in Dubai. When I visited in August 2015, I befriended a Russian sex worker who explained to me how the system works. In upscale bars and expensive hotels, women pay up to 10,000 dirhams (£1,750) a week to hotel security to be allowed to loiter around in the bars. The industry here is highly tribal: tourists from Japan seek out Japanese sex workers, Arab men prefer Arab women, and so on. Russians are no different.

By the beginning of December 2012, several bosses have already landed in Dubai. 'How many are coming?' asks an associate of the Kutaisi boss.

'Thirty-six are confirmed, but two have dropped out. There are more than thirty of us,' Merab gleefully replies.

'Are you also counting those who will be made *vory*?'

Merab replies: 'Yes, of course. Givia is coming, and he is worth ten people! Four people will be flying directly from Italy.'

Ever the gentleman, Merab books the guests into a complex of five-star villas within a short walk of the Mall of the Emirates, the largest shopping area in the world, with 700 stores and an indoor ski resort. He reserves two villas, each accommodating eight people. When I visited the place, the manager of the resort told me that two single beds could be added for a modest fee. Each villa has three large bedrooms, a large sitting room with dining space, an enormous flat-screen interactive LCD television, a modern kitchen, en-suite bathroom, a separate laundry room ('should you get in the mood for washing,' suggests the brochure I was given) and a private garage, allowing discreet access. Private dining facilities are available in the landscaped garden, among the cascades of bougainvillea in the flower beds.

Merab is understandably anxious, yet he is also pleased with himself. In the early afternoon of 10 December, all convene in one of the villas. They sit around the large dining table, and draw the curtains. Surprisingly, I discover that bosses who cannot secure a visa join the meeting via Skype, some of them from their prison cell – mafias are quick to adapt to cheap and secure technology. The officer in charge, an authoritative *vor* in his sixties, places a Bible on the table. The meeting can now begin, starting with the traditional formula:

> Long live the *Vory*, prosperity and peace to our common Home, we salute those who are in prison and those who have died following the traditions of the Fraternity.

The introduction ends with a ritualised invitation to all those who are eligible to attend if they so wish: 'All *vory* who work together to preserve the Fraternity are welcome to attend this meeting.'

The first item on the agenda is money. Since significant sums are paid into a common fund, estimated by police to be in excess of

$100 million, the person in charge of it has to account for how the money has been spent. A long-running dispute with the Tbilisi clan over the assets of a boss arrested in Dubai in 2005 is mentioned, although there is no progress to report. But the Kutaisi clan has not given up, and as one of Merab's associates reminds everybody, stealing from the common fund is punishable by death. It's a clear reference to Grandpa Khasan, the boss of the Tbilisi clan, perhaps even a death sentence in disguise.

The second item on the agenda is 'un-crowning', meaning expulsion from the fraternity. For those in jail, this measure could easily lead to death. By now, a couple of *vory* from Merab's clan have been stripped of their titles at ceremonies where the accused is not present and cannot defend himself. It is agreed that this practice does not conform to *vory* traditions and should not be allowed. Merab reminds everybody that 'brothers can come without fear to the meeting and admit to having committed some errors. Their fate will be decided at the meeting by all.' Everybody agrees and toasts his wisdom and knowledge.

The third item on the agenda is the induction of new men. As I had discovered in Perm in the mid-1990s, each new recruit is introduced by a sponsoring boss. The future *vor* needs to have lived according to the 'Code of Conduct'* and be honourable. This is what a sponsor has to say about his protégé:

> He is respected and clean both within the criminal world and beyond it. There is nothing that puts his honour in any doubt. He is correct in the way he lives, the way he treats people, and the way he behaves. He is capable of resolving problems in the criminal world, so everyone can work without constant conflict. Finally, he despises 'dogs' [the police], like all of us!

The rules are then recited. Eventually, all attendees join hands and bestow the coveted title on the person, who is then allowed to stay in the room for the rest of the ceremony. In the Dubai meeting, this procedure is repeated sixteen times. Some of those inducted,

---

* In Russian, *ponyatiya*.

however, are unable to be there, so they are called on the phone and hear viva voce the part of the event that refers to them. When the meeting is over, the new *vory* start sharing the news with their friends. As with any promotion in the workplace, the event generates a buzz. There are commiserations for those who fail to make it ('next time you will be in!'). Enzo, a newly made *vor*, recounts how he breaks the news to his comrades in Greece: 'Back in Greece, everybody is very happy, they say: Hurrah to the *vory*! They wanted to know how things went, and I told them everything ...'

By any measure, the meeting is a success for Merab. Everything has gone according to plan. By sharing the limelight with other prominent *vory* he came across as even-handed and chiefly interested in the prosperity of the fraternity. Bosses who were not his close allies have attended, and they have conferred credibility on the decisions taken. Most of the people he wanted to promote are promoted, although he had to compromise on a few names, so the final count includes individuals from Belorussia and Chechnya, and Russian cities like Rostov, Tolyatti and St Petersburg. Out of sixteen, seven new *vory* are aligned with Merab's clan (one of them is particularly close to *vor* Jemo). The Kutaisi clan has replenished its ranks. In the end, the aggravation and high blood pressure have been worth it.

The next step is to announce the decisions taken at the ceremony to the rest of the world. In Soviet times, letters were written using a secret code (quickly deciphered by the police) and sent to other prisons. The tradition is followed today, when an announcement* is released and signed by all who attended. The text is fine-tuned over several phone conversations. Eventually, two handwritten A4 pages with the following announcement are produced:

Peace to our Home and the good people that live in it.
    For the good of the Fraternity, We, the undersigned *Vory-V-Zakone*, inform you that on 10.12.12 a Gathering took place. During the Gathering, we considered the issue of passing judgement on people who are absent from the event. The *Vory* who

---

* In Russian, *progon*.

attended and those who were connected [by Skype] all together agreed that we should not change our Laws. The destiny of a *Vor* can only be decided at a Gathering at which he is present. All of us who know our Way of Life understand what we are talking about. Those who want to know more, we the *Vory* will give you more details when we meet. Bear in mind that the *Vory* solve their problems on their own. We do not need any intermediary or any lawyer. Nobody should dare to interfere in our affairs except ourselves.

To avoid any misunderstanding, do not take into consideration telephone calls where in one way or another someone tries to besmirch the Name of *Vory* regardless of whoever makes that phone call. This also applies to SMS messages.

With all our soul, we inform you that the following Brothers have joined our Family.

Sixteen first names, followed by nicknames, are then listed. For instance, we find 'Tolian Toliattinsky'. His nickname is a reference to Tolyatti, a Russian city 500 miles south of Moscow where he most certainly operated or had served time. (Tolyatti was a breeding ground for Russian criminality, witnessing an estimated 110 contract killings between 1998 and 2004. In the local cemetery, a special section is devoted to Mafiosi graves, complete with grimly humorous footnotes engraved in marble, such as 'Don't worry, Dima, we got the guy who did you'.)

The document is signed using the formula 'With the blessing of the daring bosses … ' The names of thirty-two *vory* follow. Merab's name is fifth from the top. Tariel Oniani, who is connected by Skype from his prison cell, is the eighth name from the top. The official document needs to be circulated as widely as possible. After some discussion, it is agreed to leak the text to PrimeCrime.ru, a respected webpage that has been keeping tabs on *vory* matters since 2006. The man behind PrimeCrime.ru is the elusive Alexander, who has put his passion for all things *vory* to good use by creating the most exhaustive site on Russian organised crime. Eurasian mobsters check it regularly and often add their comments to news items published there.

In a matter of a few days, the Dubai Declaration is online under the title 'Vory announcement of the coronation of sixteen people, 10.12.2012'.

Despite Merab's efforts, the boss of the Tbilisi clan, the 75-year-old Grandpa Khasan, declares the Dubai meeting invalid, and vows to kill all those who were inducted on 10 December. Merab is outraged, reminding everybody that it is Grandpa Khasan who has been creating new *vory* via Skype, without following procedures (some thirty people in 2012 alone, people say). After a round of phone calls, Merab senses that his sworn enemy is isolated. This is why he takes the bold decision to travel to Moscow later that month to plead for the legitimacy of his actions with the other clans of the post-Soviet Mafia. The trip is carefully planned. His brother arrives in the Russian capital a few weeks in advance, with a bag full of cash. He is to gauge the political mood, call old friends, and offer plenty of bribes to all those who might embarrass – and arrest – Merab during his trip. He finds many doors open in the Russian capital. When the boss of the Kutaisi arrives, he has meetings scheduled with the royalty of Russian organised crime, including a former ally of Grandpa Khasan. He reaches out to the so-called 'Slavic' faction of the *vory*. During those meetings, it becomes clear that there has been a switch in the balance of underworld power. Grandpa Khasan is now regarded as a *vor* who does not abide by the Code of Conduct of the fraternity; a man who does not strive to create peace and uphold the rules, who spreads discord, organises meetings that lack legitimacy, and kills with impunity.

When he is in Moscow, Grandpa Khasan eats every day at a restaurant near Moscow State University. I visited the place one evening in November 2016. A security person stood outside a poorly lit and badly signposted entrance that had a minuscule metal porch. That night a white Rolls-Royce was parked outside, with the driver also on guard. The restaurant's theme is that of a nineteenth-century coach house, yet to Western eyes it simply looks like an alpine-style, noisy tavern. After I entered and was warmly welcomed, I left my coat and sat down to sample the excellent Azerbaijani wine, salmon shashliks, and cake. During the summer, patrons usually dine in the

The signatures appended
to the Dubai Declaration
announcing the coronation
of sixteen *vory-v-zakone*,
10 December 2012.

courtyard in a spacious pavilion, and each table in the main hall is
separated by wooden partitions covered in greenery. The staff are
from Southern Russia and the former Soviet Republics. The rowdy
party led by the Rolls-Royce owner was at the far end of the room,
and I did not consider it polite to bother them. They were speaking
a variety of Caucasian languages. I tried to imagine where Grandpa
Khasan would normally have sat. I had been told that he favoured
a private room at the back, where he sampled dolmas and lamb
kebabs in complete privacy. A large stocky man who seemed happy
only when sitting down, he projected a sense of assured authority:
this was what I was told by those who had met him in Thessaloniki and Athens. His four-car motorcade and bodyguards would be
visible outside. After dinner, I found refuge next door, at a shisha
lounge bar that I imagined people from Grandpa Khasan's detail
would also have patronised.

Facing the restaurant is a tall, tastefully restored residential
building. At around lunchtime on 6 January 2013 a man entered

this building with a large bag, wearing a winter coat and hat. None of his features were visible on CCTV cameras. He walked up to the fifth floor and opened a window in the stairwell. I traced his steps and walked up myself. Nobody stopped me. The man carried a bag containing a silencer and a Val, a sniper rifle with a range of up to 400 metres, normally used by elite units of the Russian army. He slowly assembled the gun, while an accomplice checked that nobody walked up behind him. As Grandpa Khasan left the restaurant after lunch, a single shot hit the old boss in the neck. The sniper fired a second round to make sure the target was dead, but missed and hit a waitress instead. In any case, the first bullet did the job: he died a few hours later in hospital. Grandpa Khasan, often described as the boss of bosses of the post-Soviet Mafia, head of the Tbilisi clan, sworn enemy of the Kutaisi clan, the man behind the murder of Rezo in Bari, friend of politicians and celebrities, finally met his end. The sniper calmly placed the gun and the silencer in his bag and left the building from a side exit. To this day, he remains at large.

The death of Grandpa Khasan sent shockwaves throughout the Russian criminal community and was reported by news agencies all over the world. Police and pundits expected a new war to start soon between the Tbilisi and the Kutaisi clans, as most observers blamed the murder on the Kutaisi clan. Naturally, the *vory* turned to the website PrimeCrime.ru to confirm the news and check reactions from fellow criminals. One, whose telephone is monitored by the police, shouted to a friend: 'PrimeCrime.ru!! Look there!!'

In a call intercepted shortly after Grandpa Khasan's death, a *vor* from Merab's clan appears to confess to a friend that the man who acted as a lookout had just called him. 'Half an hour ago I got a call from that person in Moscow and he told me he saw how they took the shot! I told him, "What? Are you there and are you calling me on the phone? And he answered, "Yes".' This suggests that the murder might have originated within the Kutaisi clan. Grandpa Khasan is dead. Ultimately *vor* Merab is the winner.

The most important message of Merab's story is that legitimacy matters, and that violence has to be used judiciously by the bosses. Mafias are organisations governed by myriad rules and a code of conduct. Such a code can be twisted, up to a point, but its total

People lay flowers at the grave of crime boss Grandpa Khasan in Moscow's Khovanskoye Cemetery. Grandpa Khasan died in hospital after being wounded by a sniper in the centre of Moscow.

disregard does not pay in the long run. Merab proved to be a more skilled statesman than Grandpa Khasan. Although under pressure from his enemies, who had been killing his soldiers for years, and from his friends, who were ready to defect to the opposition or stage a coup, Merab held the line. While supporting minor acts of retaliation, he opted for a long-term strategy. He decided to replenish the ranks of his clan by conducting legitimate induction ceremonies. When he understood that Italy was too dangerous a place to hold the meeting, he was willing to share the limelight with the *vory* based in Dubai. He was able to 'make' enough of his own to strengthen the Kutaisi clan, while accepting others' requests for new *vory*. He followed proper procedures and could legitimately claim a moral superiority over Grandpa Khasan, his arch-rival, whose unruly reaction proved to be his death sentence.

Mafias have not only rules and norms of legitimacy, but also organisational structures that have been created to deal with challenges that the groups face. The *vory*'s Gathering is part of a company chart. Quite remarkably, all mafias covered in this book have virtually identical structures. We now turn to them.

Salvatore Lo Piccolo is arrested with the Constitution of the Sicilian Mafia, Giardinello, Palermo Province, November 2007

Four men are sitting inside a garage next to a cottage in Giardinello, a small town some forty kilometres south-east of Palermo. It is Sicilian Mafia heartland. The men are reviewing the accounts of the local Family: who pays and how much. On hearing some commotion outside, they retreat into the house and barricade themselves inside. They have eight guns, two each, and for a moment it seems that they are prepared to use them. But after a few minutes, they accept that they are surrounded by police and signal that they are ready to give themselves up. One of the Mafiosi shouts, 'I love you, Dad.' Dad is Salvatore Lo Piccolo, the arch-rival of Antonino Rotolo and one of the three most powerful men of the Sicilian Mafia. He is sporting a black leather jacket, a white T-shirt and designer glasses. He is of medium height and has white hair, with a carefully trimmed beard and moustache. On his wrist he wears an expensive Rolex Daytona.

Salvatore Lo Piccolo has with him his portable archive, his most treasured documents. One of these consists of two typed A4 pages, written in capital letters. It is no less than the Constitution of the Sicilian Mafia, setting out rituals and rules, duties and responsibilities, electoral procedures and sanctions. It shows us how the 'Family' is the basic cell of this organisation. The document spells out how each Family is structured.

HOW EACH FAMILY IS COMPOSED

HEAD OF THE FAMILY

DEPUTY HEAD

ADVISOR

CAPO DECINA[*]

SOLDIERS

Top positions are allocated as follows:

---

[*] Head of a ten-man unit.

THE HEAD OF THE FAMILY IS ELECTED BY ALL MEMBERS
OF THE FAMILY. THE SAME FOR THE ADVISOR.

THE DEPUTY HEAD IS CHOSEN BY THE HEAD OF THE
FAMILY. THE SAME FOR THE CAPO *DECINA*.

THE FUNCTIONS OF EACH MEMBER

THE HEAD OF THE FAMILY HAS THE FINAL WORD.

THE DEPUTY HEAD ACTS WHEN THE HEAD IS ABSENT.

THE ADVISOR STRIVES TO KEEP EVERYBODY UNITED IN THE
FAMILY — AND GIVES ADVICE FOR THE GOOD OF THE FAMILY.

THE SOLDIERS ARE DIRECTED BY THE *CAPO DECINA*
AND SERVE THE NEEDS OF THE FAMILY.

Indeed, the structure of the Italian-American Mafia is identical to that of the Sicilian Mafia, although some titles differ. For instance, the *capo famiglia* (Family boss) is called Father in the US. According to Jo Bonanno, the head of the New York City Bonanno Family, the 'election' is not truly democratic but is intended rather to 'establish consensus'. The ballot is not secret and normally the decision is unanimous. This practice mirrors what happens in the legitimate world of business. An entrepreneur who has been on many companies' boards told me that voting there reminds him of the way in which mafias 'elect' bosses. In the corporate world decisions are taken in advance of board meetings, and voting simply ratifies them. Bonanno adds that it would be unthinkable for a boss to obtain a simple majority and rule over a divided house. When a relatively free election was held in a Palermo Family in 1979 in order to reconfirm the existing boss Stefano Bontade, he was duly elected, but not unanimously. While he forgave the dissenting minority, he was gravely weakened by the process. Two years later, he was murdered. Unlike in the corporate world, those who lose a Mafia vote do not get a second chance.

The deputy and the *capo decina* are chosen by the boss, both in the Sicilian Mafia and in the Italian-American Mafia. The deputy represents the Father but has no power of his own. If a boss is sent

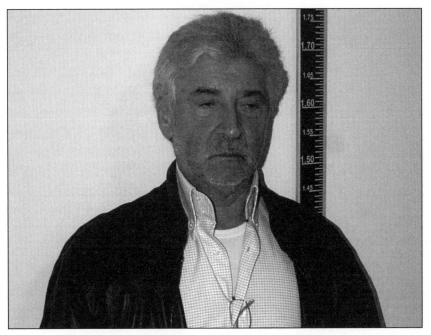

Italian police arrest Sicilian mafia boss Salvatore Lo
Piccolo in Palermo, Italy, on 5 November 2007.

to jail, the deputy does not automatically take over. It is up to the
Father to delegate as much authority as he thinks best. In the US
and Sicily, the boss chooses group leaders who carry out the orders
and assigns tasks to the ordinary members called soldiers or 'sons'.

Mafia groups in Sicily, the US and Russia all have a boss pre-
siding over a loose organisation composed of internal subgroups:
the *Decina* (Sicily) and the *Brigada* (Russia). While the boss is a
powerful figure, he rules as long as the leaders of subgroups lend
him their support. Merab's story is instructive: during his tenure, he
tries to accommodate the different personalities, such as *vor* Jemo.
While all Mafia Families seem to have an advisor, the role is more
codified in Italian mafias, although it carries no real power. Outside
the formal hierarchy stand associates and prospective members,
groomed for later induction. The Hong Kong Triads and the Japanese Yakuza have a remarkably similar structure, which I spell out in
Appendix 2.

A key challenge for Mafia organisations is to manage violence. Soldiers are good at using violence, so they have a tendency to resort to it in order to settle any disagreement. The instance of Merab's guest who had been caught with a seventeen-centimetre knife, ready to kill another participant at the *vory* Gathering in Rome, is a case in point. A crucial Mafia rule is that members cannot use violence against fellow members, or, indeed, against non-members, without permission from the boss. Above all, permission must be obtained to kill police officers, prosecutors, judges, and prominent people more generally. Mafia members must also inform bosses if they want to go into business with a member of another Family, and they are forbidden from entering into certain business ventures, such as prostitution in Sicily. Often they are asked to take the blame for crimes they have not committed. In Japan the practice is so common that there is even a name for it, *migawari*. When released, the fall guy is celebrated in an elaborate prison release ceremony. Obedience is rewarded by promotion and money to the soldier and his family. The top management of a Mafia group should help its soldiers actively – find them jobs, lend them money, offer legal aid, pay fines and bribe officials on their behalf. In short, a soldier's duties, and the rights he enjoys, go well beyond what employees of a firm would expect.

The exercise of the boss's authority must be viewed by members as legitimate and can be judged against the rules recited at the ritual. If you break them, you should expect punishment. As pointed out by Henry Hill in *Wiseguy*, 'You got out of line, you got whacked. Everybody knew the rules.' But in any organisation, superiors can be nasty and jealous. Only saints act fairly all the time. In the case of mafias, bosses have already broken the law. Why should we expect them not to break the rules of the organisation? Sammy 'the Bull' Gravano, underboss of the Gambino Family in the 1980s, candidly admitted that 'there's a hundred rules. We broke ninety-nine of them.' Indeed, while he was a soldier, he killed a businessman without permission. A former member of the Sicilian Mafia noted: 'if one was disliked, [the boss] could simply dispose of him without informing anybody.' Mafia executives have committed other 'crimes'. For instance, Frank Scalise, the underboss of the Gambino Family in the early 1950s, sold membership of Cosa Nostra for $50,000 per head, with the apparent approval of the boss, who had gambling debts. Numerous instances of senior *vory* sponsoring novices to join the fraternity for money have been reported since the 1990s. Similar instances occurred in the Yakuza as well. A boss in Iwate Prefecture forced a subordinate to go to prison in his place but failed to provide adequate support and remuneration when the subordinate was released. The solution to this organisational dilemma is to create organs above the single boss, some sort of Employment Tribunal of Made Guys: this is the role of the Commission in the Italian-American Mafia and in the Sicilian Cosa Nostra, and the Gathering in the post-Soviet Mafia. Equivalent institutions exist in the Hong Kong Triads (the 'headquarter system') and the Japanese Yakuza (*kanto*).

Commissions

Who punishes a boss who breaks the rules? Soldiers could gang together and assassinate him, but such an action would generate an endless spiral of retaliation and vengeance. Mafias have tried to overcome this conundrum by creating a forum above each Family and devising a rudimentary 'due process'. This is what Merab is trying to accomplish with the Gathering in Dubai, and what the Commission in the Sicilian and American mafias is meant to achieve. The document found in the possession of Lo Piccolo describes the Sicilian Commission as follows:

THE COMMISSION IS FORMED BY ALL CAPI MANDAMENTO.* THE COMMISSION ELECTS THE HEAD OF THE COMMISSION AND HIS DEPUTY, AND A SECRETARY. THE LATTER FIXES THE TIME OF THE MEETINGS.

THE ROLE OF THE COMMISSION.
IT HAS BEEN CREATED TO ENSURE THAT THERE IS EQUILIBRIUM WITHIN THE FAMILIES AND WITHIN COSA NOSTRA. AND TO DISCUSS AND DECIDE OVER THE MOST DELICATE MATTERS.

---

* Bosses each representing three families.

In Sicily each member of the Palermo Provincial Commission, created in 1957, represents three geographically connected Families.* In New York, where five Families – Bonanno, Lucchese, Genovese, Gambino and Colombo – operate, the five bosses each have a seat on the Commission. This body has a supervisory role and is competent to make decisions about all issues that affect the organisation as a whole. It also manages major economic ventures, such as entering into drugs trafficking, which cannot be reduced to the business of a single Family, and even gives collective orders regarding which political party the Mafia should support in elections. For instance, in 1987 it ordered members to switch their allegiances from the Christian Democratic Party to the Socialist Party. The Commission approves the murders of prominent people, such as judges, prosecutors, police officers, businessmen and politicians. As these actions will unleash the full force of the state against the entire organisation, each Family must be happy to take the heat, and bosses cannot resort to recriminations against each other for such decisions. Indeed, the head of the Cosa Nostra Commission from 1978 to 1986, Michele Greco, was found guilty for all the murders approved during his tenure. In the Mafia Commission Trial (1985–6), the heads of the New York City five Families were all indicted by US Attorney Rudolph Giuliani for extortion, racketeering and murder, regardless of the fact that they had not committed the crimes directly.

Mafias understand that the Commission allows them to better coordinate the Families' activities: it is a flexible collective system of governance. Yet it is very hard to maintain this institutional structure. This is because of police pressure, as well as the tendency of some factions to take over and settle internal disputes violently. Due to the relentless police pressure on the Sicilian Mafia, and the disregard of the rules by Totò Riina in the 1980s, the Commission has not met in years. It is in many ways a figment of a bygone past.

---

* A layer up from the Palermo Commission stands the Regional Commission, set up towards the end of the 1970s. At its head is a *rappresentante* or *segretario*, 'the first among equals', in the words of former member Antonio Calderone.

The Commission in Sicily was created in 1957 at the suggestion of American Mafiosi and operated until the 'war' of 1963. It started to function again in the mid to late 1970s. By the early 1980s, Cosa Nostra Families were at war with each other again and the Commission, now seen as a mere power instrument of the Corleone Family led by Totò Riina, lost any residual authority. In 2008 there was an attempt to revive the Commission, which would, at that point, have greatly benefitted the organisation, given its attempt to re-enter the drugs trade and to identify new leaders. This failed badly, however, and all those involved were arrested, in a sweep known as the 'Perseus Operation'. According to these calculations, then, the Commission was fully functional for some ten years only.

The New York City Mafia Commission has not fared much better than the Sicilian one. Created in 1931 by Lucky Luciano, it has not held a meeting since 1985, according to the testimony, given in 2011, of the former boss of the Bonanno Family, Joseph Massino. (Massino was in charge of the Bonanno between 1991 and 2004 and is the first boss to turn state's evidence.) After Paul Castellano, the boss of the Gambino Family, was killed, there were no more Commission meetings. Police pressure is surely part of the reason: in 1985 Castellano was on trial with fellow bosses in the so-called Commission Case. The resulting convictions and life sentences convinced future bosses that such meetings were dangerous. According to Mafia expert Thomas Reppetto, 'Today it is too dangerous to meet. The *de facto* destruction of the Commission is one of the reasons that the New York Mafia is a shadow of its old self.' While formal meetings do not take place any more, informal encounters between single bosses to discuss matters of common interest still occur. It is indisputable, however, that the heyday of the Commission has gone.

Several things are remarkable about mafias. First, all have a similar structure. Power resides in the Family, which is the site of the military might of the organisation. Families are organised hierarchically but are part of something greater than themselves, and they subscribe to shared rules and norms of behaviour. They recognise, too, that it is better to minimise conflict within the group. So they have devised a coordinating body monitoring adherence to the rules. This entity also serves to agree on some key decisions.

When it works, the Commission keeps conflict in check, and allows the voice of all Families to be heard. It is a democratic body meant to prevent the emergence of a 'dictatorship' that would inevitably lead to Mafia infighting and ultimately all-out war. Yet the story of Merab's efforts to convene a single meeting testifies to the difficulties of coordinating across Families. It took some nine months for the Gathering to take place. Police pressure adds to these difficulties, making the organisational life of Mafia groups a mighty headache.

Epilogue: Maka talks, Merab is arrested, Bari, 2014–2016

Back in Bari, Maka has been arrested. She quickly crumbles under police pressure and starts to cooperate, her contribution to the investigation proving to be immense. Prosecutors also sympathise with her for another reason: by the time of her arrest, she is pregnant. Officials are happy to take the view that she has been caught up in a game bigger than expected, and are willing to offer a reward for her cooperation. After a few months in prison, she is granted house arrest.

When I saw a prosecutor in Rome in the summer of 2014, she was furious: Maka had breached her house arrest orders and fled Bari. There is now an international warrant for her arrest. It seems that she has moved to Greece, where her boyfriend – and father of her child – is also hiding. While it is possible that she has simply decided to defy Italian justice and join her boyfriend, an alternative explanation is that she did not feel safe in Bari. With the triumph of Merab, she was at risk of being severely punished for her betrayal. But Merab himself was now a fox hunted by the hounds. The Europe-wide investigation had continued to follow Merab around the world, despite the Rome setback in 2012. In June 2013, Merab was hiding in a large bunker villa, in the Hungarian town of Dunakeszi, on the outskirts of Budapest. If you are ever in the Hungarian capital, just take a bus to Dunakeszi. It's a pleasant small town, with a paved square where children play ball games and run over the splash fountain pads to avoid getting wet, often failing in the process. The café is friendly and the customers do not question an unfamiliar face. When I was there in July 2016, I was told by a local who sat next to me under the summer sun: 'This is the best place to live if you want to run away.' And yet police finally caught up with him: he was arrested on 18 June 2013 and shortly afterwards transferred to Bari prison to serve a four-year and eight-month sentence for aggravated theft, extortion, money laundering and use of false documents. Given the close proximity to the boss of the rival clan, it's no wonder that Maka did not feel comfortable. After serving his sentence in 2016, Merab is a free man again and he has never been charged for the murder of Grandpa Khasan. The Russian government has revoked his passport and nationality. In January 2017, Maka and Kvicha were found guilty of the murder of Rezo, and both were sentenced to twenty-four years in jail.

And what of Kvicha's induction? After a few months on the run in Europe, he surfaced in Portugal, where he was arrested for possessing a fake passport. The local police realised that he was wanted for murder, and he was due to be extradited back to Italy. Yet his boss, Grandpa Khasan, kept his word and arranged an induction in prison. Through Skype, Kvicha obtained the title of *vor-v-zakone* while in Portugal. This is what he had killed for on that early morning of 5 January 2012. In the warped world of the Mafia, this is the bargain he had strived for.

4

MONEY

Moscow–Italy, 1996

Dima is a former KGB agent turned businessman turned money launderer. Born just after the end of the Second World War, he's been around for a while and he knows how the world of the mafia works. During his time in the Russian security service, he had the opportunity to travel to the West and gained some insight into the workings of the capitalist banking system. And – just in case he ever needs it – his military training has also made him combat-ready. As the new era of market freedom and democracy commences after the collapse of the Soviet system, this peculiar combination of muscular heavyweight and bespectacled financial expert is ready to go global, offer his services to innumerable clients and strike some deals on the side for himself. In the 1990s, he lives in France, Austria and Italy. In France, he is known to the authorities as a counterfeiter, a scammer and a cheat. In Austria, where he owns a villa, he has been charged for polygamy and fraud. In Italy, his criminal record includes illegal possession of firearms, threat with the use of a gun, assault and the use of forged documents. Ordered to leave the country, he does not comply: in fact, he is in the process of applying for citizenship on the strength of a fake marriage. Over the years, he has used no less than four aliases, probably more. In Rome, he sets up an import-export company and lives in luxury in an exclusive neighbourhood with his family. Official papers state that his company deals in the import and export of frozen meat and other food products, along with oil, alcohol, timber and coal. The company also conducts 'market research', or so the official documents claim. What they do not say is that he also deals in fissile materials, particularly so-called 'red mercury', which he tries to sell to South East Asian countries. Red mercury is a hoax: supposedly used to build (or substantially increase the power of) nuclear bombs, there is no evidence that such a substance exists, although a major in the Taiwanese Army falls for *Dima*'s scam. On top of all this, *Dima* has commercial accounts in Vienna, Geneva and New York City. He wires large sums to accounts in Rome, and quickly moves them onwards to beneficiaries in Istanbul and Spain, before sending them back to Austria in the guise of legitimate transactions. He also imports forged US dollars from Russia, by depositing significant amounts in cash (some $700,000 in nine months), usually in $100 denominations. The money arrives in parcels of $30,000 to $50,000 at a time. Nobody seems to notice. Simultaneously, he registers several commercial vehicles at the same address. *Dima* is nothing if not an enterprising provider of financial services.

The service providers

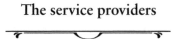

Dima's access is considerable. In Moscow, he is close to a senior manager at a branch of European Bank; *Dima* calls this amiable and obliging man 'our banker'. The bank manager is keen to help, although he does not come cheap: he is offered an under-the-table 4 per cent fee for his services (though there is no evidence that he accepts the offer). The manager's help is extensive. He is instrumental in the opening of several bank accounts at a European branch of his bank for *Dima*'s friends and family, and gives him detailed advice on how to avoid anti-money-laundering legislation. *Dima* tells his brother: '[he] told me to split the amount into several smaller transfers, over a period of time, and not to go above US$12,000. Above that sum, controls might kick in.' As well as a business partnership, a friendship of a sort has grown among the two men. *Dima* is often a guest at the banker's villa. The last time he is seen there is at the end of August 1996. In a call to his brother, *Dima* praises the beauty and comfort of the house.

Dima is a service provider, and one of his clients is the mightiest Russian organised crime group to emerge from the wreckage of the Soviet Union, the Solntsevskaya Fraternity.* Based in the run-down, working-class district of Solntsevo (or 'Sunnyside') in the western and southwestern part of Moscow, the Solntsevskaya becomes a significant player in the Russian underworld only with the spread of market freedom. By the mid-1990s, the organisation has grown in strength. An FBI report in 1995 describes it as the most powerful Eurasian organised crime group in the world in terms of wealth, influence and financial control. In a 2014 *Fortune* magazine investigation of the biggest organised crime groups in the world, the Solntsevskaya tops the list, with US$8.5 billion in revenues. It is bigger than the Camorra, the Ndrangheta, and the Mexican Sinaloa Cartel. Estimates of the size of the brotherhood (possibly exaggerated) range from 5,000 to 9,000 members. The group subscribes to the principles of the *vory* and comprises no fewer than ten semi-autonomous brigades,† which operate under the umbrella name of Solntsevskaya. It controls about a hundred small and medium-sized enterprises. The organisation is governed by a council of twelve individuals, who meet regularly in different parts of the world, often disguising their meetings as festive occasions. The money generated is pooled: 'All the criminal activities of the Solntsevskaya feed into a common fund‡ that is administered by several banks', a former member has told the FBI. 'The organisation's council oversees the investment decisions', he adds. All of this means that the Solntsevskaya need sophisticated financial arrangements: and people outside the organisation to help them with it.

Dima works closely with *Andrei*, a financial wizard with a mild stutter who works with the Solntsevskaya back in Moscow. Born in

---

* In Russian, *solntsevskaya bratva*.
† In Russian, *brigady*.
‡ In Russian, *obshchak*.

1950, *Andrei* hails from the remote island of Sakhalin, in the North Pacific Ocean, the last outpost of the Russian-Soviet empire. This is Siberia's Siberia: in winter temperatures are minus 40 degrees Celsius. You have to have been extremely bright or well connected, or both, to make the leap from a forsaken military outpost to the capital. After high school, *Andrei* wins a place at the prestigious Moscow University to study mathematics. When the Soviet Union collapses, he leaves his job in a state-owned bank and tries his luck in the private sector. Soon, he starts working for the Russian Mafia. And he seems to be doing well: a boss admits in an April 1996 conversation that 'out of all of us, *Andrei* is the only one who has the brain to conduct any type of financial operation.'

Dima oversees the laundering of criminal capital in Europe. In several instances, the funds belong to various Mafia groups, not just the Solntsevskaya. 'Money belonging to people from Magadan [in the Russian Far East] to Moscow', according to *Dima*. He invests the money coming from Russia in a vast array of import-export ventures. The deals range from purchasing sparkling wine to buying frozen meat, wood, furniture, wheat, steel, pharmaceutical products, computers, food products (including fish), Armani suits, works of art, gold, helicopters and antennae. The Russians even plan to buy a fishery in Tuscany – a scheme that fails. They also negotiate the establishment of a casino in Korea, another failed venture, and the purchase of goods in Venezuela. The group controls a small arms shop in Moscow and arranges for several shipments of firearms to be sold there. The Russians seem to import anything.

When a member of the Solnstevskaya ruling council moves to a European capital, *Dima* helps him buy a villa which costs more than half a million US dollars. The money flows into the bank account of *Dima*'s client in small amounts, travelling via New York, Vienna and Rome. One partner institution is a private bank based in London. *Dima* collaborates with Solntsevskaya on several projects. For instance, he helps transfer vast sums from Russia via Austria, using his own bank account in Vienna. Once the money arrives, *Dima* cashes it and transports it by car to the final destination. He also collaborates on the importation of oil products from Chechnya.

The banks

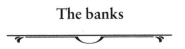

The first lesson we can learn from *Dima* and *Andrei*'s activities is that banks are a crucial means by which to move black capital. In the 1990s, the complex international anti-money-laundering legislation seemed easy to bypass. Indeed, such legislation had only recently been introduced, money laundering having become a federal crime in the US in 1986, a move instigated by Ronald Reagan's 'War on Drugs' and at first applied only to profits from narcotics. For the first time, banks were obliged to support federal efforts to combat crime. Since such a 'war' had to be global, the US pushed for the creation of the 1988 'United Nations Convention against Illicit Traffic in Narcotic Drugs and Psychotropic Substances', which was signed by some 150 countries. By the mid-1990s, states realised that it was illogical to outlaw drugs money on its own, so a host of other crimes, such as illegal gambling, robbery, tax evasion, bribery and kidnapping were added to the list of predicate offences. Principles such as 'know your customer' and the 'reporting of suspicious transactions' were born. Yet some countries were smart enough to carve holes in their legislation. For instance, Switzerland did not include tax evasion in a different jurisdiction as a reason to refuse deposits, while Dubai required bank officials to have actual knowledge that money was the product of criminality. If the client did not volunteer that information, they were not obliged to ask or report it. A well-placed bank official – 'our banker' – can do marvels for a Mafioso. He is instrumental in opening accounts, negotiating loans and bypassing inspections on large money transfers.

The importance of banks for money laundering has not changed. A report by the British government, published in October 2015, found that the vast majority of dirty money is moved through financial institutions rather than, for instance, through digital currencies, such as the famed bitcoin. Banks top the table of risks, with a Total Vulnerability Score of 34, while digital currencies come last in this list, with a score of 5. Stephen Platt, in his 2015 book *Criminal Capital*, writes that 'well over half of [drugs money] is laundered through standard banking products.' Indeed, over the years several banks have failed spectacularly to prevent their channels being used for illicit purposes – often to their own significant cost. Between 2005 and 2007, the North Carolina branch of Wachovia was entangled in a particularly shocking scandal. The problem arose because Wachovia was providing corresponding banking services to twenty-two Mexican currency exchange businesses, the so-called *casa de cambio* (CDCs). Wachovia offered wire transfer services to the CDCs, which in turn transferred money from their Mexican customers to recipients around the world. The system worked as follows. A trafficker was paid in dollars by buyers in the US. He took the money back to Mexico, changed it into the local currency and had the sums placed in the international banking system by a *casa de cambio* who asked no questions. The paper dollars that accumulated in Mexico were then sent to Wachovia and ultimately to the Federal Reserve. In the space of two years, the CDCs and other foreign correspondents of Wachovia sent almost $14 billion in cash back to the US. Criminal proceedings were brought against Wachovia for allegedly 'willfully failing to maintain an anti-money laundering program', but the case was dropped before it came to court: in the end, the bank paid $160 million in fines and forfeiture to the US government to settle the case.

Around the same time, from the early 2000s to around 2007, HSBC also got into trouble in Mexico. According to court documents filed by the US Department of Justice in 2012, at least $881 million in drugs money had been laundered through HSBC Bank USA by a variety of cartels, including the famously brutal Sinaloa in Mexico and Norte del Valle in Colombia. In a wiretap, a trafficker was heard recommending HSBC as the place to take your hard-earned cash, and, according to US authorities, the cartels even 'designed specially shaped boxes that fit the precise dimensions of teller windows' at the bank. HSBC eventually paid a record fine of $1.9 billion to the US treasury and agreed to improve its compliance department. As with Wachovia, no charges were brought against individuals, and nobody went to jail.

The second lesson from *Dima*'s story is that banks come in all shapes and sizes. High street banks tend to be under a relatively higher level of scrutiny, especially in large financial hubs such as

London. Private banks are a different kind of beast. Catering to 'high-net-worth individuals' and embedded in a culture of confidentiality, they provide basic banking services as well as investment management, insurance, management of companies, trusts and foundations. Usually requiring a minimum opening deposit and minimum average balance, ranging from tens of thousands to millions of pounds, they are particularly valuable to people from outside the US and the European Union. While many private banks are based in Switzerland, other EU countries, most notably the UK, have their fair share. In 2013, the 119 private banks and wealth management firms in the UK employed almost 23,000 people and paid £1.2 billion in taxes, generating £1.15 billion of profit. But private banks continue to be a weak link in the anti-money-laundering system: a 2014 Financial Conduct Authority report stated (perhaps with some understatement) that within this sector 'issues remain around client assessment and enhanced due diligence'.

Central to *Dima*'s activities is the use of corporate accounts. A proficient laundry man (or woman) should set up companies. *Dima* conducts his operations through corporate accounts belonging to a 'company' that is little more than a shared office and a two-page document naming directors and outlining some crude rules for the creation of share certificates. Anybody can establish such a company quickly for a minimal fee. Companies are legal entities that can contract, own assets and open bank accounts. They bestow a degree of formality on activities that, if conducted by an individual, might look suspicious, and they allow people to hide behind a name and an address that is often overseas. In addition, a company may be owned by another company, so that the ultimate beneficiary is able to reside in a jurisdiction that does not require disclosure of his or her name. The roles of both director and secretary can be performed by another company. Deregulation since the period in question has made it even easier to create these shell companies, thereby allowing the overall owner anonymity.

Nowadays, one can simply 'buy' directors, an address, secretaries and nominee shareholders. Agents can sell you 'shelf companies' that have existed (on paper) for a number of years, giving a new operation a veneer of respectability. A *Guardian* investigation published in 2016 lifted the lid on a smart London address, 29 Harley Street, from which an organisation known as Formations House operates. A stone-fronted terraced house not far from Oxford Street, this is currently home to 2,159 companies, each of which is nothing more than a prestigious address and an answerphone. Someone called Edwina Coales is or has been an officer at 1,560 of the companies registered at this address.* Of course, there are a variety of perfectly legal reasons someone might want to do this – owning, hosting or selling one of these companies is not *de facto* evidence of criminality. But they are vital to mafia financiers: a 2012 academic study of company formation agents, entitled *Global Shell Games*, concluded that 'organised crime and terrorism depend on financial secrecy. Untraceable shell companies are the most important means of providing this financial secrecy.' And this creates a role for service providers like *Dima*. Mafiosi would not sign up directly to a website to create a shell company. They need trusted fixers who will do that work for them – something that has been made easy by deregulation.

Once a company has a legitimate corporate account, it can rent it to those who need to deposit dirty money, as *Dima* did regularly for the Solntsevskaya men in Europe. If you peruse the most active criminal cyber forums in the Russian Underground (the portion of the Russian internet where cybercrime takes place), you come across individuals willing to offer corporate accounts to anybody who wants to launder earnings. Such a service is expensive, however, and can cost up to 50 per cent of the sum in question. The accounts are usually in the US, Germany and the UK.

Although they might compete for power, different Mafia groups seem happy to pool capital when there's a clear benefit to be had. *Dima* received money from groups all over Russia, but the idea wasn't his: it has a long provenance. In the 1930s, when the Italian Mafia was coming under intense pressure from law enforcement, it decided to move its riches outside the US. They had noted Al Capone's conviction for tax evasion and needed a way of making

---

* Formations House are not doing anything illegal, and I do not imply that that companies registered by this firm have been involved in organised crime.

their earnings appear lawful. Meyer Lansky, who was known as the 'Mob accountant', struck a deal with the Cuban dictator Fulgencio Batista, giving him $3 million up front and guaranteeing an additional $3 million every year. As with the Russian Mafia investments through *Dima*, Lansky pooled the funds of various Mob Families and split the casino and hotel concessions in Cuba among those who contributed to the consortium. Mobsters could receive profits into their American bank accounts and claim that their lavish lifestyle was the product of legitimate investments.

But the relationship between a service provider and his client is as fragile as it is complex. By March 1996, the Solntsevskaya had fallen out with *Dima*. First, *Dima*'s house is searched by a special unit of the Italian police, who find several fake passports, undeclared guns and lots of cash. The police have been called by a Russian couple who were visiting *Dima* in an attempt to recover money the woman's late father, a prominent member of the Solntsevskaya, had lent him a few years back. *Dima* and his associates have no intention of returning the money and threaten to rape the woman and kill them both before they managed to escape and call the police. As a consequence of the house search, the premises of *Dima*'s company are also searched and documents emerge linking him to Solntsevskaya's operations in Europe. Frantic conversations are exchanged between Solntsevskaya bosses and associates. They discover that *Dima* has been engaging in arms trafficking on the side without informing them.

By the summer of 1996, a Solntsevskaya boss is heard saying several times: '*Dima* has stolen money from half of Russia.' The consummate fixer has turned out to be a liability. Their discovery exposes how money laundering is more than a logistical problem for the mafia. It is undertaken by highly skilled fixers who pose a challenge for Mafiosi: How can they trust that someone who is specialised in complex commercial transactions will tell them the truth? If a deal does not materialise, or the money gets lost somewhere in the ether sphere, how can they be sure that they haven't been cheated? If a transaction is legal, several mechanisms exist to reduce this risk. These include contracts, an effective court system, easily traceable information, and the good name of the service provider. None of these mechanisms is perfect, however, and risk is never eliminated entirely: written contracts may be incomplete, and resorting to the courts is a costly process. Trusting others always requires a leap of faith, even in the context of legal transactions.

Some of the mechanisms at work in the legal sphere also operate in its illegal counterpart, although they are less reliable. Reputations can be built among actors operating informally and illegally, but information on past behaviour does not flow easily in the underworld. People change name, disappear and need to hide from the police. One might find a degree of 'honour among thieves', yet as the wealth of a given customer grows in size, the temptation of bankers and financial wizards to cheat Mafiosi also increases. If I have billions of dirty money to hide and invest in the legitimate financial system, my 'banker' will have to construct a complex structure that ultimately only she can unlock, and I end up being highly dependent on her. Even the most powerful Mafiosi are at risk of being cheated by underworld service providers, as Antonio Calderone, the underboss of the Catania Mafia Family, recalled in his autobiography: 'For a certain length of time we had a treasurer, but then we fired him because he wasn't honest; he took money from the cash box.' In 2005, Sicilian boss Bernardo Provenzano is also forced to sack the man in charge of keeping the accounts of his Family because he is suspected of cheating. These men might be thought to have got away lightly: a report by the Austrian police recounts how in May 1995 one Solntsevskaya boss threatened to kill their banker, because he had failed to deposit US$5 million into the organisation's account. These individuals must know that, if caught, punishment will be swift and cruel, yet they think they can get away with it. Perhaps they reason, since they are breaking the law themselves, why not cheat other law-breakers, too? Most of the time they are probably right to trust their instinct, but occasionally their plans founder.

On 11 September 1996, *Dima* travels from Rome to Moscow in order to settle some outstanding business, and to pursue some scams of his own. He has reason to feel worried. The Solntsevskaya is starting to think that they have been scammed on several financial transactions he has performed for them. By April 1996, a *Brigada* (a sub-unit of the group) starts to suspect that *Dima* is cheating them. By August, they are certain. The deputy head of the *Brigada* and his crew are trying to meet or speak to *Dima* in Rome, but he manages to give them the slip. They are nevertheless able to reach one of his associates. This is what he reports back to *Dima*, in a conversation fifteen days before his trip to Moscow.

> *Dima*: Any news?
>
> Associate: Yes, he came with his team today. The deputy and his *Brigada*.
>
> *Dima*: I wanted to call them later, they tried to contact me yesterday and I wanted to go and see them with you. Well, I am late now …
>
> Associate: So a serious team of 'boys' arrived. They were in their forties, not kids, serious people. I told them that there are no problems, everything is all right, all these headaches are not helpful to anybody, let's fix a meeting in fifteen days, so nobody gets hurt and everything is clear.
>
> *Dima*: So you had a normal conversation?
>
> Associate: Yes, normal, we sat down, we had something to drink, they left their numbers, it will be no problem to solve all the issues. I told them 'try to understand me', they understood the matter and that we offer guarantees.

Dima's associate is clearly shaken by the encounter, and they are both in no doubt that they are in danger from 'the roof', the jargon word for Mafia protectors. *Dima* decides to travel to Moscow in order to reassure his partners.

Intent on covering his tracks, *Dima* takes a roundabout route to reach Moscow: travelling on a false passport, he flies from Rome to Milan, then crosses the Swiss border in a rented car, and finally takes a plane from Zurich to the Russian capital. While in Moscow, he carries a gun at all times. But by the end of his week in the Russian capital, *Dima* feels confident. He has reassured all the partners involved. Despite fears voiced by his family before the trip, nothing bad has happened. He can relax and spend the last few nights in his native city in style. He rents a suite at the Tverskaya, an upscale hotel located a few yards from Red Square on the central Tverskaya Street, which runs north-west towards St Petersburg. On the night of 23 September, he is sipping a pre-dinner drink at the bar on the fourth floor when two men enter the hotel looking for him. Even with the hotel's closed-circuit television system and its heavily armed security guards, entry is not difficult. The men show a bogus hotel pass and board the lift to the fourth floor. They walk past the gaggle of heavily made-up women gathered around the bar, and stop in front of *Dima*'s table. They extract two TT pistols complete with silencers. Their victim is hit in the head by four bullets (some reports say five). The killers, who are seen on the CCTV camera, calmly take the lift back to the lobby, walk on to busy Tverskaya, and climb into an old Zhiguli that is waiting for them. They are in the hotel for no more than six minutes, between 6.55 and 7.01 p.m.

In the meantime, some 1,500 miles away, a special unit of the Italian police is picking up a lot of chatter on the several telephone lines currently being tapped. More details on the murder emerge. *Dima*'s brother, who lives in Vienna, had joined him and is sitting on the same sofa when *Dima* is shot. At 7.51 p.m. Moscow time, *Dima*'s wife receives a call from her brother-in-law from the police station where he is being interrogated. Her husband is dead. At first she thinks it is a joke, but then she asks if it was a 'Georgian' who has shot *Dima*. 'It happened very fast, but the man was dark-skinned', she is told. The next day *Dima*'s wife speaks again with her brother-in-law. She cannot comprehend how the murder could have happened in one of the best hotels in the city, in front of so many people, with no reaction whatsoever from the hotel 'security'. Her brother-in-law is more realistic: 'The police say that the murder has the hallmarks of a professionally planned operation, with the intention of sending a clear message to others as well. Believe me, there is no chance the culprits will ever be found.'

When a Solntsevskaya boss hears of the untimely death of *Dima* in the Moscow hotel, he is unsurprised: 'He should not have cheated so many people.'

While it might have been easy to identify *Dima* as an unreliable schemer and possible cheat, *Andrei*, the man from the Russian Far East, has been a dependable problem-solver for the Solntsevskaya.

Yet, in such a world, surprises can come out of nowhere. *Andrei* has handled several transactions adroitly. In a short time, he is entrusted with ever-larger amounts of money on behalf of the Russian Mob. The last scheme of his criminal career is to invest a large sum in Korea. He suggests opening a casino or, alternatively, buying a fishery. As improbable as it might sound, *Andrei* has contacts in the country through the ethnic Koreans he knew back in Sakhalin. The mafias of Russia, from Magadan to Moscow, are convinced by the plan and give him US$10 million. But shortly after landing in Korea, *Andrei* disappears off the radar. He stops answering calls, changes hotel, and does not pick up multiple faxes. He has vanished. We will never know if he has tried to embezzle funds in order to spend them in the casinos of South East Asia, or whether he has been conned himself. Even laundry men may be victims of somebody else's scheme. In any case, he has made a terrible mistake: 'he should think twice before deciding to cut loose from his own friends', says his Solntsevskaya boss with icy understatement. The Mob is furious and a crew is quickly dispatched to Korea to find him. Eventually, they track him down and escort him back to a European city, where he is imprisoned in the basement of a house. *Andrei* enters hell. He is repeatedly tortured. A conversation overheard on the wires records this of his ordeal:

> Solntsevskaya boss: I am going crazy ... I took a bottle and
> smashed it on *Andrei*'s head ...
> Solntsevskaya enforcer: Tell *Oleg* to come and break his skull.
> Solntsevskaya boss: I will do that myself.
> Associate: We must finish him off.

Both *Andrei*'s wife and secretary are repeatedly threatened. A plan to kidnap the latter is discussed. The gang decides to put *Andrei* on a plane bound for Moscow, accompanied by a 'jailer'. Yet while in captivity in Europe, *Andrei* manages to tell his wife of his imminent arrival in Moscow. She in turn contacts a police officer friend, who arrests *Andrei* as soon as they land in Russia. The arrest is just for show. *Andrei* is whisked away and the Mafia jailer is left empty-handed. *Andrei* is finally safe, and starts to make plans to join his wife and run away, far from his life of crime. But the Mafia has its ways, the police betray him and shortly afterwards he meets his destiny. We do not know whether he suffered. His body has never been found. Somebody who knew both *Dima* and *Andrei* is heard saying on the phone: 'Are they both dead? Well, these people kill each other all the time ...'

Methods and techniques to hide money may change over time – though some techniques, such as Meyer Lansky's consortiums, remain popular. But what does not change is the need for Mafiosi to trust service providers who might cheat them. And as our financial systems become ever more complex, Mafiosi find themselves both on the threshold of new opportunities, and at risk of becoming the victims of crime, as the stories of *Dima* and *Andrei* remind us.

5

LOVE

Via Meli, Palermo, 2004: Nicola, Amalia, love and ritual

Nicola lives with *Amalia* in a luxury apartment on Via Meli, Palermo (we encountered them already, in chapter 2). They are in love. They share everything, successes and worries. He calls her 'my love'; she is protective of his well-being. They call each other several times a day, and go on holiday together. They are inseparable. She is beautiful, while he is slightly chubby and bald, but a woman could not ask for a more loyal and devoted partner. Nicola was born in 1968 to a Mafia heavyweight. Although Nicola already belonged to Mafia aristocracy, he earned the trust of top boss Bernardo Provenzano, who put him in charge of no fewer than five Families to the east of Palermo city, with a 'distinguished' history dating back hundreds of years (Bagheria, Ficarazzi, Villabate, Belmonte Mezzagno and Misilmeri). Yet Nicola does not behave like an old-time Godfather, avoiding conspicuous consumption in order to reduce resentment among fellow mobsters. He belongs to a new generation: he gambles at the Saint-Vincent casino and travels first class only. He is also more open-minded. Nicola wants to share Mafia secrets with *Amalia*, but he knows that he is breaching Cosa Nostra rules. And yet he tells her everything. (Little does he know that the police have planted a listening device in the flat.) When Nicola becomes the boss, he cannot resist telling his woman:

Nicola: Although it is not known yet, I rule over Villabate [*a small town outside Palermo*] now. What I say, they do. Do you understand?

In another exchange, he explains to *Amalia* that he is involved in recovering debts. At first *Amalia* does not understand why he should be concerned over somebody else's debt.

Amalia: Are you directly involved in this matter?
Nicola: No, I have nothing to do with the debt.
Amalia: So are you going to gain something by getting involved?
Nicola: My love, when these things arise, when they have trouble recovering money, it is normal for me to be involved, and I get in the region of 15, 20 million [lire], do you understand?
Amalia: Twenty?
Nicola: Yes, this is the way it is! Always!
Amalia: So much money?
Nicola: What do you think, of course!
Amalia: You get so much money every time?
Nicola: Always …

There is more. Nicola is so madly in love that he wants to share with *Amalia* the most important event of his Mafia life. The most sacred rite for the organisation, the admission ceremony, is only open to men. *Amalia* is excluded by definition. Nicola accepts the official rule, yet deep inside he finds it impossible to agree with it. He wants to break it, at least symbolically. He arranges for *Amalia* to undergo the ritual, in their home. The age-old rule excluding women from Cosa Nostra is momentarily breached. *Amalia* enters a circle officially beyond her reach on account of her gender.

The ritual normally starts with the recounting of a fictitious tale on the origins of the Sicilian Mafia. Then, the boss recites the rules of the organisation. They have not changed since Antonio Calderone's own ceremony, narrated in chapter 1. After the rules are recited, those to be 'made' are given the option to leave. If they don't, there is no turning back. At this point the future Mafioso selects a guardian who has cast a protective eye on him for a while already, and has introduced him to Cosa Nostra. Nicola now plays the part of the guardian and tells *Amalia* what to do.

Nicola: Take the image of the Saint ...
Amalia: What do I do with that?
Nicola: I'll show you.
Amalia: Yes! Do I have to prick my finger and spill blood?
Nicola: Have I already told you that we need to spill blood?
Amalia: Yes!
Nicola: Did I tell you that as well?
Amalia: Yes!
Nicola: OK.
Amalia: Yes, you did!

Nicola is amazed at how much of the secret ritual he has already revealed to his partner. The conversation continues:

Nicola: Have I already told you all the details?
Amalia: I prick my finger, spill my blood and we pass around the image of the Saint.
Nicola: And then what do we do?
Amalia: Now I can't remember what we have to do ...
Nicola: You toss it around, take it and set it on fire. You move it from one hand to the other and, as it burns, you repeat three times: 'If I betray Cosa Nostra, my own flesh will become ash like this image.' Repeat the same sentence three times. And, at the very end ...
Amalia: What else?

At this point in the home-made ritual, Nicola's mind wanders off. He is reminiscing about the high number of people who have breached the oath by defecting to the state and informing on the Mafia. (The Sicilian Mafia has the highest number of members who have turned state witness – 6.9 per cent of the membership – compared to 2.6 and 2.8 per cent respectively for the two other major

Italian organised crime groupings, 'Ndrangheta and the Camorra.) *Amalia* fully shares Nicola's view that informants are pure scum.

> Nicola: I am just thinking about how people have turned against Cosa Nostra ...
> *Amalia*: Almost everybody, the vast majority ...
> Nicola: Yes, the vast majority ... Well, recently a little less, but there was a time, between '95 and '96 ... It was a disgrace.
> *Amalia*: Yes, but even now [there are many of them] ... Because they know that only by becoming state informants can they have an easy life ...

Nicola reveals to her that his sources within the police have just informed him of another defector.

> Nicola: They have just told me about a new one ... Another one has defected ...
> *Amalia*: Who?
> Nicola: It is not yet official, but I have been told ...
> *Amalia*: So, who is he?
> Nicola: I am not worried about his defection. The police arrested him [name mentioned] this summer ... I am not worried because what he could say he has already said ... He talked about the time we were all in Jamaica together.

When the oath is over, one is supposed to kiss all the men of honour attending the ceremony on the lips ('without the tongue', points out a Palermo Mafioso in his court testimony) and then everyone greets the new member. He has become a man of honour. Normally, the ritual is repeated for the other men present at the event. And then the Family throws a grand party. Nicola and *Amalia* also celebrate, and kiss.

Women appear to play an increasingly important role in criminal organisations, yet they cannot acquire independent positions of leadership in the five mafias discussed in this book because they are not allowed to undergo the initiation ritual and therefore, by definition, cannot be full members of the club. Thus we have to address two issues. Firstly, why women continue to be formally excluded. And secondly, under which conditions they might acquire greater informal power.

Why have females never been admitted to the organisation? There are plenty of historical reasons. In nineteenth-century Sicily, Japan and Hong Kong, women were excluded from most professions, and were absent from politics, religious institutions and the top of businesses. In some cases, they were not even allowed to inherit property. As voting rights were extended, women were the last to be granted suffrage, and in these territories only in the middle of the twentieth century. The Italian-American Mafia grew out of its Sicilian counterpart and, unsurprisingly, adopted its mindset. While the Russian Mafia emerged in full after the fall of the Soviet Union, a regime which at least in principle was committed to eradicating gender inequalities, the *vory-v-zakone* criminal fraternity was modelled on the rules of the Russian Orthodox Church in the early twentieth century, and in stark opposition to the Soviet regime. Then, as now, women were not allowed to enter the priesthood. In sum, mafias grew out of structurally sexist societies and institutions and are themselves slow to change.

Yet discrimination against women has been reduced in these societies over the past century and a half.* We are a far cry from equal participation in the workforce or at the top echelons of many professions, but women are formally allowed to enter almost any career and are granted full legal equality. Why are mafias lagging behind? These organisations have shown that they are able to embrace change and adapt to technological innovation. They have moved

---

* Italy ranks 41st in the 2015 Gender Gap Index, with a score of 0.726. The ratio of female-to-male presence among 'legislators, senior officials and managers' is 0.36, which is above the sample average, while the female-to-male ratio of labour force participation is 0.72. This means that out of 100 men we find respectively 36 and 72 women in those categories. Over the past ten years, Italy's position has improved (it used to rank 77th, with a score of 0.646 in 2006). Japan has a greater gender gap than Italy (rank 101/score 0.67), and it is similar to Russia (rank 75/score 0.69) while the US is the best positioned (28/0.74).

into new markets and taken advantage of innovations like Skype, online banking and chat rooms. The organisational structure has also evolved over the centuries. The assembly of Mafia bosses, the Commission, is a relatively recent innovation for the Sicilian Mafia (it dates from the late 1950s). At the time of the Castellammarese War in 1930–31, American Mafia families opened up their ranks to people born outside Sicily, most notably Neapolitans. The Italian-American Mafia changed its rules on admission in the 1970s, so that it is now sufficient to be of Italian origin on one's father's side only rather than on both sides. Yet no Mafia goes as far as admitting women. Why?

An often-stated explanation is muscle: after all, women continue to be excluded from combat roles in most armies because of concerns about their capacity to fight at the same level as men. It is crucial that a Mafioso is able to deploy violence in a convincing way: a credible reputation is vital. And yet violence does not rest solely on physical strength. Mafia women are as capable of cruelty as any man, and may be as good a shot. Moreover, women are allowed to serve in combat roles in seventeen professional armies, including those of South Korea, the US, the UK, Serbia, Sweden, Turkey, Israel, Germany and Canada. One of the most successful snipers in history was Roza Georgiyevna Shanina, one of 2,000 female snipers who served in the Soviet Army during the Second World War. Praised by allied newspapers for her fifty-four confirmed kills, she had legendary precision and was awarded the Order of Glory, before being killed in action in 1945 aged twenty.*

A recent review of research into female terrorists indicates that in left-wing groups fighting for state independence and liberation women feature in all roles, including those of 'warriors', 'leaders' and 'dominant forces'. Kurdish female soldiers engaged in the fight against the Islamic State in Syria are no less effective – or brave – than their male comrades. In any case, mafias could employ female members in roles that would require less reliance on violence, and

* Svetlana Alexievich, winner of the 2015 Nobel Prize for Literature, is the author of *War's Unwomanly Face* (Moscow: Progress Publishers, 1988), where she interviews hundreds of women who fought with the Red Army during the Second World War.

Roza Georgiyevna Shanina (1924–45), a Soviet sniper during the Second World War who was credited with fifty-four confirmed kills. She was awarded the Soviet Order of Glory.

greatly help the organisation by infiltrating areas where men would find it hard to reach. The 'violence' argument has never entirely convinced me.

As we saw in chapter 1, there is an intimate connection between the established churches and the mafias. At the time of their birth, mafias borrowed from religious institutions for their rituals and overall values (twisting them for their own purposes, of course).

As there were no women in the ranks of the Church, it would have been odd for mafias to allow women to undergo the ritual. Since women *continue* to be excluded from Church hierarchies, mafias are under no pressure to reconsider their position. Unsurprisingly, the progressive egalitarianism championed by the feminist movement in the twentieth century has hardly touched the mafias; quite the contrary, feminist movements are natural allies of grass-roots anti-Mafia organisations. Women campaigning for equal rights certainly do not champion the opening up of Mafia ranks, but rather support the female relatives of Mafiosi who break away from their families.

In sum, there are good historical reasons for the exclusion of women. Yet mafias have developed a deep suspicion of women, which might explain why they continue to be excluded. Love poses a serious threat to these organisations. It is a threat to any project that demands total dedication to a cause, as the characters in George Orwell's *1984* know only too well. In Orwell's dystopian society, the Party quells all physical sensations of love, including filial and maternal love, and sex is just a duty. It is harder to persuade people in love to fight for abstract causes as their loyalties are divided by the duty they feel to their loved ones. Love permits no lies: secrets are revealed, emotions laid bare, and courage is found when we believed we had none. Love impels people to do things that are not responsible or respectable. As the anarchist manual *Days of War, Nights of Love* states, 'true love is irresponsible, irrepressible, rebellious, scornful of cowardice, dangerous for the lover and everyone around them, for it serves no master.' Love also engenders other unstable emotions: jealousy, desperation, obsession.

The Mafia – like the Party in *1984* – demands that its members put the organisation above everything else: 'It is the Member's duty to be available for Cosa Nostra at all times, even if a wife is about to give birth,' recites one of the Sicilian Mafia's commandments. Marriage is a formality, a duty devoid of love. Like unions among royalties, marriages in the Mafia seal alliances between different Families. Marriage is always strategic, never the culmination of a genuine passion. Felicia Impastato, whose son was murdered by Cosa Nostra in 1979, recalled how the Mafia interfered in people's choices: 'My cousin was attracted to a young man, who was also well off, but the Mafia opposed it [...] the wedding was not allowed. [In another instance], the daughter of a Mafioso wanted to marry an honest man, but the Mafia was against it.' Sexual attraction is scorned. Indeed, as a Sicilian saying goes, 'For women and wine, a man makes himself a swine.' The greatest crime of all for a Cosa Nostra member is to covet the women of other members. If a member romances the wife of another Mafioso, it is an affront to the latter's reputation and he would have to respond, potentially leading to an endless sequence of violence.

It is not just romantic love that frightens the organisation. Antonio Calderone, underboss of the Catania Family, makes the following point:

When a woman's deepest feelings are affected, she no longer reasons. *Omertà*, the Mafia code of silence, no longer applies; there is no more Cosa Nostra, no arguments or rules that can hold her back. Women become crazy if their sons are touched, because there is no greater love than that of a mother for her son.

If her son is killed, she 'loses her mind [...] and the pain makes her do and say the unthinkable', continues Calderone, referring to the women who testify in court against the organisation.

Serafina Battaglia (1919–2004) was one such woman. She witnessed the murder of her partner, a Mafia member who had been expelled from the organisation in 1960. At the trial, she testified against the killers, who nevertheless went free. Overtaken by grief, she began to encourage her son, Salvatore, to avenge his father. Each morning she reminded him of his mission: 'Get up, get up, they have killed your father! Get up and kill them!' Although reluctant, the boy eventually hired an assassin to kill the two brothers responsible for his father's murder. But the Mafiosi got wind of the plot and killed both the boy and the hired assassin. During the trial over her son's murder, Serafina testified again, but the Mafiosi were freed, again owing to insufficient evidence. Her campaign against the Mafia did not stop there, however. Although she was unable to find a lawyer willing to represent her in court, she went on to be a witness in several trials across Italy, becoming the first female state witness. In the interviews she granted to Italian TV, she appeared possessed, as if speaking from the netherworld, and always dressed in black, with her head covered by a scarf. She carried a gun at all times. 'I keep it to defend myself, but my only gun now is justice,' she used to say. Likewise, Giacoma Filippello, whose husband was killed by a rival Mafia group on 7 May 1990, expected at first that his Family would exact retribution. When she realised that no action was forthcoming, she grew incandescent, shouting at one mobster: 'My fortune will be your misfortune. Tell them. While I have courage and a breath of life in me, I will do everything to break the chest and to eat alive the heart of those who murdered [my partner].' The emotions of Serafina and Giacoma do not fit neatly into the ordered, controlled world of the Mafia.

The prospect of wives and mothers turning state witness is so dangerous to the Mafia because men tend to confide in them: though technically excluded, women connected to the organisation can know nearly as much – or more – as full members. Information such as a member's whereabouts is very sensitive because it could reveal criminal plans if divulged. One of the crew tasked to kill judge Giovanni Falcone, arguably the Mafia's highest-profile murder, was eased out of the plan because, according to the boss in charge, 'we had started to suspect him: we were convinced he was talking to his wife.' Precisely because they are loyal to a husband above the organisation, wives can be trusted with such sensitive information by their life partners. Serafina Battaglia knew a great deal about her partner's activities: 'My husband told me everything; this is why I know everything.' Another wife of a Mafioso said that 'I was like a sponge. If you ask a direct question to your husband, he might not answer, but if you stay quiet and silent, they confide in you, in order to feel important.' If Serafina and the others had been full members rather than external observers, the damage to the organisation would have been incalculable. Yet knowing so much is dangerous too. The story of Damiano Caruso proves it. Caruso was a member of Cosa Nostra's Riesi Family. The boss Luciano Liggio hated Caruso because he believed that he was responsible for the murder of a young man that he liked a lot. When Liggio met Caruso in Milan in 1973, he had him killed. Liggio knew that

Caruso confided in his lover, who in turn had a teenage daughter with whom Caruso was also sleeping. Liggio asked the two women to join him, telling them that Caruso was wounded and in need of help. 'The women came immediately,' recalls Calderone in his autobiography. 'Liggio killed the mother and fucked the daughter, who is maybe fifteen or sixteen, then he killed her too.' There are no rules against killing women in the Sicilian Mafia.

It is no surprise that both the Sicilian and the Italian-American Mafiosi encourage members to spend a lot of time together and in the absence of women. Since eating is a crucial part of entertainment, the men are good cooks and prepare lavish multi-course dinners. Indeed, the ritual of admission into the Mafia is invariably followed by 'grand gorges', as former Cosa Nostra boss Giovanni Brusca told an Italian journalist in 1999. Convivial occasions are a key feature of the life of Mafiosi in Sicily, Brusca explains, and women are never allowed:

> The grand banquets, great feasts in the countryside were the principal occasions for socialising … Women were never admitted … Different men brought different dishes: baked pasta, meat, fish, cakes and sweets … we had some excellent cooks … they cooked for all their comrades when they were in prison.

In his memoirs, Brusca continues:

> When everything was ready, we sat down and there began a game of offering food and drink … We also talked about women … The banquets almost always ended in general bacchanalia, with the men throwing around sacks of water and plates and glasses going flying …

On these convivial occasions, women are mocked and generally made irrelevant. This is a society of men who are deeply suspicious of the opposite sex. In Sicily, the acceptable social world of Mafiosi is defined by hunting parties and grand banquets while in the US socialising takes place in bars, nightclubs, casinos and strip joints, where the women present are prostitutes.

Yet police pressure in recent years has led to women assuming greater responsibility within the Sicilian Mafia. With so many bosses and soldiers behind bars, women can become crucial and trusted cogs in the organisation. Wives, daughters and sisters are less likely to defect to the state than are fellow male Mafiosi. For instance, the only remaining high-profile fugitive of Cosa Nostra in Sicily, Matteo Messina Denaro, trusts only his sister, Patrizia, with key information about his whereabouts. So far, he has managed to avoid arrest. In some cases, women have taken up more significant roles. In 2014, the girlfriend of the boss of the Arenella neighbourhood, Gregorio Palazzotto, was arrested for involvement in settling a dispute over the ownership of a bar that another Mafioso had claimed as his own. (She was acquitted in 2016.)

Most extraordinarily, in the Brancaccio neighbourhood, the reins of the Family have been taken by the boss's sister since around 2009. Although she had not gone through the ritual, she was authoritative enough to tell the soldiers (in a conversation picked up by police wiretaps): 'Now I am in charge.' Prominent members of the clan were seen entering the bar that she managed in order to give her a percentage of their profits. She kept tabs on protection payments, discussed the management of the money secretly invested in various businesses, and distributed payments to members in prison and their families. A 2009 investigation revealed that in the town of Alcamo, near Trapani, two women were running the Family, while the boss was in jail. They were the recipients of extortion payments and worked out how much each business person was due to pay, with requests ranging from tens of thousands to hundreds of thousands in euros (one pleaded guilty while the other was acquitted). For women to have such a prominent role in the Sicilian Mafia is unprecedented, and it is a direct consequence of the difficulties the organisation now faces.

Italian-American Mafia

Love may weaken the Mafioso's resolve. In 1913, 'Big Jim' Colosimo, the head of Italian organised crime in Chicago, met Dale Winter. She was nineteen years old, from Ohio, and dreaming of a career as an opera singer, under the watchful eye of her mother (her father had died when she was five). She was in town with her mother, trying to make ends meet by singing in the South Park Avenue Methodist Church. A Chicago journalist suggested to Colosimo that he should give her an audition. She was slender, with blue eyes, white skin, and talented. She appeared to come from a world a million miles away from the rackets and the brothels of the Levee, the seediest part of Chicago, where Colosimo, John Torrio (his deputy) and Al Capone were kings. The audition went well and she was hired to perform at Colosimo's Café Lyrical. Soon, she became the main attraction and Big Jim and Dale fell in love. Big Jim started to change: he dressed more conservatively, took elocution lessons and even took up horse riding with her. Colosimo married Dale in 1920. 'This is the real thing,' he told John Torrio. 'It's your funeral,' replied Torrio. According to historian John Kobler, Colosimo started to show signs of weakness. Instead of standing up to extortionists, he paid up readily, most likely because they had also threatened his wife. 'The word went around: "Big Jim's getting soft. Big Jim is slipping."' Love suggests weakness and invites rebellion among the rank and file. On 14 May 1920, while his wife was out shopping with her mother, Colosimo was slain in his office. John Torrio was widely considered to be the organiser of the murder.

Al Capone, who became the leader of organised crime in Chicago after Torrio's death, had the habit of testing his own men's priorities. From time to time, he would expose them to willing, beautiful women. If they failed to show interest, he would grow suspicious, and assign them less responsibility. 'When a guy don't fall for a broad, he is through,' his biographer reported him saying. A gangster who is so attached to his own wife would refuse to betray her; and he is by implication weak and so easily blackmailed or manipulated.

The *vory-v-zakone*

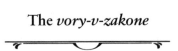

Other mafias also discourage genuine affection towards women. 'A third- or fourth-generation criminal learns contempt for women from childhood,' wrote Varlam Shalamov, the dissident writer who was imprisoned with the *vory* during the early years of the Soviet regime. 'Woman, an inferior being, has been created only to satisfy the criminal's animal craving, to be the butt of his crude jokes and the victim of public beatings.' A *vor* might have had a wife, but any real attachment to her is viewed as detrimental to the member's dedication to the society. While the *vory* code does not preclude monogamy, such faithfulness is seen as a sign of weakness.

Throughout the Soviet period, the wife of a *vor* was allowed practically no social relations with others from outside the criminal world: she was the property of her husband. If he went to prison, she generally cohabited with one of his fellow thieves, while continuing to take an interest in his welfare. Although wives were not as despised as were prostitutes and female citizens not connected with the criminal world, they had no special rights either. Valery Chalidze, a Soviet lawyer who emigrated to the US in the 1970s and published an essay on the *vory* in 1977, wrote that 'the relation of a thief to his wife is that of a master to his slave, except that the slave has voluntarily chosen her lot.' While the wife may have chosen to join the criminal community, she is unable to break away from it. If she fails to meet her obligations, she is warned; if she fails a second time, she is punished. According to Shalamov, there were no *ménages à trois* involving either lawful wives or prostitutes. Both prostitutes and legal wives could be told to satisfy the needs of others, but the understanding is that there is only ever one 'owner'. It follows that the *vory*'s ideology does not encourage paternal feelings.

Time spent in prison engenders camaraderie among the *vory*. They find it quite normal to share the same bed or hotel room. In prison, active homosexuality is acceptable, while passive homosexuality is strictly forbidden. Yet at times of transition or uncertainties, *vory* also rely on women. Italian authorities once heard a Russian boss talking extensively to his wife, who was living with him. He would turn to her for advice on how to deal with members of the clan and a variety of (illegal) matters that arose from their life in Italy. She often gave advice relating to the punishment of members who had defied his authority. It is fair to assume that she would not have had such a role had the boss been on his own turf, but, since he had few people he could fully trust in Rome, his wife became a valued associate.

The Yakuza

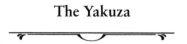

The Yakuza follows other mafias in promoting an ideology of machismo, where women are considered inferior, useful solely for boasting of one's status and wealth. In a study of the role of women in the Yakuza, author Rie Alkemade cites a respondent familiar with the Yakuza underworld:

> Women are merely 'objects'. Yakuza clearly do not respect women. They may lavishly spend money on their young, attractive girlfriends, but this is not out of affection but to make themselves look good; this is one of the girlfriend's 'roles'.

Yakuza men should not feel any sense of attachment to women: being faithful to one's wife is seen as a sign of weakness, as is falling in love with a hostess, a woman whose job is to entertain clients in nightclubs. The son of a Yakuza boss, Miyazaki Manabu, recounted how his father spent all his free time and money on gambling and women. His mother, a small woman, had to follow him around town to grab some cash before he would spend it; many nights the son would not see the father at all. When this man built another house and moved there with his new mistress, the office of the gang moved there as well, although the boss continued to visit his former home.

And yet the peculiar living arrangements of Yakuza gangs mean that women have a significant practical role. The boss and his immediate family live together with the gang members in the same house. The wife of the boss, known as Big Sister,* plays a key role

---

* In Japanese, *ane-san*.

in the organisation of the household, and the gang itself. Not only does she ensure that the daily necessities of her husband's subordinates and those of their wives are met, she also manages the group's finances. The son of a Yakuza boss said in 2013:

> It's the boss's wife who knows how much money the group earns from a day at the construction site, or which of the subordinates have how many children and spend how much on education, who has been feeling ill … The wife is the one who distributes the money to these subordinates when they need it.

He continues:

> The boss's wife is the most knowledgeable on the group's flow of money: how much everyone earns, how many subordinates there are … she probably knows more than the boss himself. If the police investigate the Yakuza group's finances, it will come across the wife's name on their bank accounts, for example. So if they want to go after the money, they'll probably start with the wife.

The female partners of Yakuza often come from the adult entertainment industry and continue to work even when their husbands reach the top position in the gang. Emiko Hamano, a Big Sister, recalls in her autobiography that most of the Yakuza companions work as prostitute masseuses or strippers in order to support their lovers. When the men become bosses, they become Big Sister, and start to earn money in extortion or loan-sharking.

The Big Sister remains the first port of call to discuss household conflicts among the group's subordinates or among them and their wives. The boss, often unaware of the daily relationships among his people, relies on his wife as an advisor and mediator. 'Women,' writes Miyazaki, 'would always be coming to seek the advice [of my mother] about the kind of problems that arise from being married to a yakuza.' His mother would also summon gang members and reproach them for their behaviour. The boy was not allowed to be present at these events but, when he managed to glance inside the room, he saw a big guy 'with the face of a devil' sitting on his knees and cringing in front of his mother, who was scolding him. While the women are not allowed to attend formal events or conferences, they exert informal influence.

Women in the Yakuza are also the myth-makers, the recorders of the gang's exploits. They recount the deeds of the fallen, transforming their lives into folk legends for the consumption of the surviving and future gang members, thereby healing the raw pain of death. Miyazaki Manabu, who grew up in a Yakuza household and became a left-wing activist, came to believe that in such a male-dominated world, women count for a great deal, in both spiritual and material ways. 'I am under the impression that there were many times when my father was dancing unknowingly to my mother's tune.'

Normally women are not allowed to join fights. Miyazaki Manabu narrates that, when the Teramura-gumi faced an existential threat from the attacks of the biggest Yakuza group, the Yamaguchi-gumi, the Teramura boss invoked the help of one of his sworn brothers, Uncle Yamane. While the two of them were strategising with their henchmen, a small middle-aged woman turned up wearing a pair of baggie pantaloons and carrying a Japanese sword in her belt. She is Uncle Yamane's wife. Barely 1.4 metres tall, she was known throughout the organisation for her courage. Several times she intimidated robbers and thieves. On this occasion, she arrived ready for a fight. While her husband sent her away, the very fact that she thought it possible to join the fight suggests that women here have a greater importance even in military matters than they would in any other Mafia.

In matters of power, too, Yakuza women seem to have a significant role. In an extraordinary and unusual turn of events, Fumiko Taoka, the wife of Kazuo Taoka, the third boss of the Yamaguchi-gumi, the largest syndicate in Japan with a current membership of roughly 23,000 people, became the caretaker boss of the entire organisation for three years between 1981 and 1984. Before taking over, Fumiko Taoka was very much part of Kazuo's life. The boss was charismatic and ruthless, known as 'the bear' because he used to claw at his opponent's eyes during brawls. Fumiko was the boss's principal advisor, according to their daughter Yuki:

FUMIKO TAOKA

Fumiko Taoka (1920–86), the caretaker head of the Yamaguchi-
gumi organisation. She took over after her husband,
Kazuo, died in 1981. Her tenure ended in 1984.

When my father was about to become the successor of the
second Yamaguchi-gumi godfather, he discussed it with my
mother. 'These kinds of talks are going on, what should I do.
[...] I have no money, I have nothing, what should I do ...' My
mother said to him, 'I'll take care of the household, whether it's
living expenses or anything else, I will work and take care of it.
You should put all of your effort into the group.'

When the boss died of natural causes in 1981, after thirty-
five years' tenure, the Yamaguchi-gumi agreed that his second in
command should succeed him. However, this man was in prison, so
62-year-old Fumiko Taoka stepped into the shoes of her deceased
husband and took on the role of caretaker head, a position she was
meant to fill for a few months. Never before had a woman taken
such a role. When the designated fourth boss died while serving
his time and the Yamaguchi-gumi could not agree on a new name,
events took a further unexpected turn. Fumiko was allowed to
continue at the very top of the Yamaguchi-gumi hierarchy, as the

primary decision-maker of this enormous syndicate. She never took the formal title of Fourth Boss, but she exercised great influence at a time of near panic among the rank and file (indeed, when a successor was designated in 1984, the gang fell into a state of instability leading to internal conflict and secession). As her daughter Yuki wrote in her autobiography:

> My mother originally came from a 'straight' family so it must have been hard, marrying into such a different world. She had to recognize and learn all the rules, traditions, rituals and norms of a man's world, but also as a woman, a Yakuza wife, and the Big Sister, her own position and role. She did so well in her role that quite often other families would say she was the 'prime model of a woman'.

Fumiko earned the respect of the members for her ability to mediate in conflicts and to take a close interest in the people within the organisation: during her tenure the Yamaguchi-gumi grew in size to a total of 13,346 members. It seems deeply unfair, therefore, that she was not allowed to formally join an organisation that was so much part of her life. Tellingly, pictures of her are not readily available.

6

SELF-IMAGE

Macau, 1999–2014: The Macau 14K boss produces a film about his life

The Hong Kong film *Casino* (1998) charts the rise of Giant, a small-time hood, to the leadership of a vicious Macau Triad gang, as seen through the eyes of an attractive television journalist.* Sitting on a French baroque-style sofa in a tacky chandelier-rich mansion she interviews Giant, capturing his life story on a video camera. The journalist also follows Giant around the island as he discharges his daily duties, such as collecting gambling debts and plotting deadly attacks. Giant is locked in an existential battle to control the casinos' high-stakes VIP rooms against evil rival Ping. As Giant narrates his life, the audience is fed a hearty diet of street fights (including a memorable one in front of Macau's library), praise for Macau's traditional egg tarts, and some predictably trite philosophical lessons for those eyeing up a career in the Mafia. 'If you want to be famous you have to be harder than everyone else' and 'your blood has to be as hot as the sun.' Violence is ubiquitous. As he rises through the ranks, Giant is often beaten up and sports a bloodied face for most of the time. In one scene, he slowly drives

---

* Giant is played by Simon Yam, while the female journalist is played by Kwok Ho Ying.

137

his car over the leg of a woman, while the journalist watches horrified. The film's jagged editing, jump cutting, hand-held cameras and mock documentary style are a nod to the French New Wave and the *cinema verité* of the 1960s. But in fact the film owes as much to 'Broken Tooth' Wan, the boss of Macau's 14K Triad, the man who comes up with the idea, chooses the producer and pays for the film (some US$1.7 million). *Casino* is a piece of self-produced Mafia myth-making that has gone slightly off-message.

The subject matter of the movie is well chosen and the insights into the activities of local organised crime are unparalleled. While in Old Macau one can still savour the graceful lethargy and ease of a bygone era and admire the ruined seventeenth-century Jesuit cathedral, modern Macau is all about gambling. After the handover to China in 1999, Beijing decided to break up the previous gambling monopoly (held by the Grand Lisboa Casino) and so issued new licences. The first Western-operated casino started its operation in 2004. By 2013, the thirty-four casinos in the former Portuguese colony were the most profitable in the world.

The VIP rooms over which Giant battles have always been the backbone of Macau's business model. They are the equivalent of private clubs for high-stake gamblers and are housed inside the most prestigious hotels and casinos. In the best establishments, they offer an oasis of airy luxury, usually comprising several rooms with gaming tables, expensive furniture, sophisticated modern art, flat-screen TVs, a bar, a buffet, obliging staff, and impressive views over Macau. My favourite is Galaxy 33, on the thirty-third floor of the five-star hotel by the same name, which requires a minimum bet per session of 1 million Hong Kong dollars (£99,000/US$129,000). Inside, beautiful women mingle with thuggish-looking bodyguards and wealthy players. Entry is by invitation only but occasionally guests can sneak in. Here, gamblers play baccarat, a fifteenth-century Italian card game favoured by Charles VIII, and by James Bond, who plays it in the 1967 film *Casino Royale*. Players can charge their credit card and regulars have a personal account. The money generated by VIP rooms is enormous: the figure for 2013 was US$29.9 billion, up by 13.1 per cent in year-on-year terms. And, as pointed out by the Chairman of the Nevada Gaming Control Board,

Hong Kong actor Simon Yam poses with Yeung Oi-jing, wife of Macau's boss Wan Kuok Koi, alias 'Broken Tooth' Wan, at the premiere of the movie *Casino*. 'Broken Tooth' Wan bankrolled the film production. The movie was meant to be a biopic of Mr Wan.

A. G. Burnett, such vast profits have attracted the interest of organised crime: 'the operation of VIP Rooms in Macau casinos has long been dominated by Asian Organised Crime, commonly referred to as "Triads".' The Triads are integral to the smooth running of many VIP rooms: they ensure order, punish cheats, discourage operators from stealing each other's clients, and collect gambling debts.

'Broken Tooth' Wan is the most notorious Triad boss involved in the VIP rooms. Born in China, he grew up in a Macau slum and left school at nine, without reaching third grade. After working in a dim sum restaurant, he joined a local gang and was involved in street fights, losing at least one tooth in the process and earning his nickname. In the early 1970s he entered the 14K, Macau's largest and most notorious Triad group. The occasional prison spell in the

1970s and 1980s for loan-sharking offences did nothing to halt the meteoric rise of Wan who, by the 1990s, was the boss. He seemed untouchable: a police officer who arrested him in the 1970s became his advisor, while the former Director of the Central Prison was his lawyer. By the 1990s, he was well connected and rich, driving an iconic purple Lamborghini. As the 1999 handover to China approached, an inter-Triad 'war' broke out over who should control the VIP rooms market, at a time when new players were poised to emerge. The war was especially bitter between Wan's 14K and the Water Room Triad, the thinly disguised arch-rival of Giant in *Casino*, and by the time it ended, twenty people had been killed.

In the middle of the war, Wan took time out to produce the film. When it was finished and ready to be shown to the general public in 1998, Wan organised a private screening in Macao. He invited only a few friends, and his mother. The producer and the director sat at the back. After the credits rolled and the lights were switched on, there was a stony silence. Wan did not say anything. He was furious. He had expected a biopic, and instead was served a rather gritty urban tale of a misguided violent thug, addicted to gambling. The producer admitted in an interview with the *New York Times* that 'for him ['Broken Tooth' Wan], the movie is not grand enough, not epic enough ... Nobody even clapped ... but at least everyone went home alive.' The film went on to become a solid box-office success in Hong Kong and was released in several Asian countries, such as Taiwan, Singapore, Korea and Japan. It is still available on DVD.

Films do a number of things for mobsters. First, they cater to a very human urge, the desire to be remembered: what might well go unrecorded is now fixed in perpetuity. More generally, films give mobsters a sense of purpose – a vindication of their lives. Often the life of a Mafioso is far from glamorous. They spend most of their time being beaten up and shot at, bowing to higher-ups, battling rivals who insist on fighting back, and in jail. As in other professions, when they outlive their usefulness they are pushed aside and forgotten. Often they die poor. Movies give mobsters a sense of dignity missing in their daily lives, a sense of being part of a noble, great enterprise. It makes them believe that their existence is not wasted.

There is a more surprising way in which mafias use cinema – to control and shape their public image. In most jurisdictions, belonging to the Mafia is illegal, so members cannot openly advertise who they are and what they do. Movies help promote the criminal brand to millions of viewers. Veteran Italian film critic Tullio Kezich reports a conversation that he had with a film production manager who was involved in shooting *Salvatore Giuliano* (1962). The producer, he recalls, 'explained to me that organised crime does not mind movies about the Mafia; on the contrary it considers them with a sense of pride, as something that can shed an appealing light [on them], especially if a boss is played by a popular actor.' As Special Agent Joseph D. Pistone (aka Donnie Brasco) was on his way to give another testimony against the Bonanno crime Family in New York, a defendant who knew that a Hollywood movie was in the making (*Donnie Brasco*, 1997) asked: 'Hey, Donnie, who is going to play me in the movie?'

In order to look more credible, real gangsters borrow mannerisms and lines from movies (and from popular culture in general). If people are convinced that the menacing-looking man in front of them truly belongs to a criminal organisation, they will more readily yield to his demands.

Yet a question remains. Which films should the Mafia embrace? The story of 'Broken Tooth' Wan suggests that some stories may resonate with the public but not with people like him.

Yakuza movies loved by the public but not by the Yakuza

The Yakuza films by two great Japanese directors, Satō Junya and Fukasaku Kinji, certainly resonated with the audiences in the 1970s but not with the Yakuza. Working in the early 1960s as young assistant directors at Tōei production company, Satō and Fukasaku changed the Yakuza film genre forever and their early works deserve to be better known outside Japan. What is most astonishing for today's viewer is how much this Japanese 'new wave' resembled, and in many ways anticipated, its American counterpart – particularly with regard to the style of directors coming of age in the 1960s and 1970s, such as John Boorman, Robert Altman, Warren Beatty and, above all, Martin Scorsese. Their films were not the hagiographies favoured by mobsters themselves.

Satō and Fukasaku had direct experience with the vast underground black market that supported the post-war Japanese economy and had seen plenty of gang conflict. They had also witnessed – and at times taken part in – student demonstrations, such as the protests against the renegotiation of the US Security Treaty with Japan in 1959. Satō got the chance to direct his first feature film, which explores the senseless militarism that brought the country to war, in 1963.* By 1967, he had turned his attention to the Yakuza genre, injecting it with a dose of realism. Set in post-war Japan, Satō's Yakuza films portray bosses as manipulative and greedy, often consorting with right-wing politicians.† His third feature, *Organised Crime 3: Loyalty Offering Brothers* (1969), follows a war veteran who becomes a lower-ranking Yakuza. The movie opens with the protagonist defending a Japanese woman from American soldiers who try to rape her, and they later marry. Despite his initial good deed, he is no better than the Americans: he joins other Yakuza and sets up prostitution rings, stealing girls from US-run brothels. The central character teams up with a greedy sociopath and they start to run a protection racket. Their gang even sets up a torture chamber to enable debt collection from reluctant businessmen. At the film's end, the outrageous behaviour of both characters leads to a gang war. As in American gangster movies, the hero is selfish, morally impure and, ultimately, a sick loner.

Fukasaku revolutionised the genre by introducing a new style as well as new themes. In his films, the Yakuza is indistinguishable from any other institution of authority, its members greedy and ruthless in their pursuit of power. The clear-cut struggle between good and evil liquefies. The protagonist of *Street Mobster* (1972) is a loser – born on the day that Japan surrenders to the Allied Forces – who refuses to pay a cut to the local boss and is eventually killed. He is, however, far from being an honourable man; instead, he is a dedicated materialist who starts off by raping young women

---

* *Story of Military Cruelty* (1963).
† *Organised Crime 1* and *Organised Crime 2* (both 1967).

newly arrived from the countryside and selling them to brothels. As he ascends in the criminal world, he strikes up a relationship with one of the women he has sold into prostitution, but he is constantly beaten down by the established gang. Although the boss sympathises somewhat with the protagonist's youthful brashness, he eventually makes sure that the young Yakuza and his woman are killed, in a masterfully shot final scene. The hero's upward move within the criminal world is blocked by the Yakuza hierarchy, which symbolises the greedy new order founded upon American political and social values. Fukasaku's *Battles Without Honor and Humanity* (1973) opens with the atomic bomb blast in Hiroshima, and the gangsters seem to appear right out of the dust and smoke of the mushroom cloud. As in *Street Mobster*, the criminal hierarchy is corrupt and ultimately responsible for the death of honourable people. The protagonist is a lone hero.

In a major departure from traditional films in this genre, these two films of Fukasaku's are based on real-life events. *Battles Without Honor and Humanity* draws on interviews with an imprisoned Yakuza boss recounting the genesis of several post-war Hiroshima 'Families', while *Street Mobster* is based loosely on the life of a real gangster from Fukasaku's home district. The films show old photos, birth certificates and police documents. Dates and names are introduced on screen, while climactic moments are shown as stills. Fukasaku said that his style had been influenced by the newsreels shown in cinemas at the end of the 1960s depicting worker and student protests. 'That's when I was inspired to begin using the hand-held camera,' he explained. 'I believe I first came to use it on [*Street Mobster*]. I myself took the camera in hand and ran into the crowds of actors and extras.'

In an interview given in 1997, Satō looked back at the late 1960s and early 1970s and explained how the Yakuza movies spoke to a wide audience:

As the 1960s progressed, there were more and more students' demonstrations. Many young people thought that the yakuza film characters were almost like student leaders, fighting the system against impossible odds. They took them quite seriously

– both students on the left and the right. And they felt deep empathy for the characters when they would die at the end. There was the aesthetic, too, that saw a terrible beauty in dying this way. In these films, the only way left to make a change in the system is through violence. But the majority of the audience for yakuza films were blue-collar workers who felt virtually at war with the faceless, white-collar, corporate bosses. No one felt they had a system they could depend on. Everyone identified with the individual hero or anti-hero going up against the system.

Yet real gangsters did not quite embrace these depictions. For instance, Fukasaku revealed to a journalist in 1997 an anecdote from around 1973:

> There was the godfather of one gang who is portrayed in one of my films.* He wanted to check it out before it was released, so he set up a screening at Tōei. He came, sat there and watched the film. Afterwards, he remarked that he was a little surprised that his subordinates, some of the men he'd brought with him, were so quiet during the film that they didn't attempt any retaliation in response to what they were seeing on the screen. [Laughs] That was a bit scary.

The experiments by Satō and Fukasaku in radical cinema did not last long and soon their movies offered a more traditional and reassuring view of the Japanese Mafia.† Yet the two directors were never punished for their early, realistic and somewhat critical portrayal of mob life. Another Japanese film-maker, Jūzō Itami, was not so lucky. In 1992 he directed a parody of the Yakuza, *Anti-Extortion Woman*. The action takes place in a hotel lobby where Yakuza conduct their business, including roughing up their victims,

---

* By Tanba Tetsurō.

† See, for example, *Violent Gang Rearms* (1971) and *True Account of the Ando Gang – Story of Attack* (1973) by Satō; *Graveyard of Honor* (1975), *New Battles Without Honor and Humanity* (1974–76) and *Yakuza Graveyard–Jasmine Flower* (1976) by Fukasaku.

which ruins the establishment's reputation. At first the hotel tries to persuade them to leave, offering them money and treating them with great respect. When this does not work, the manager hires a female lawyer (played by Itami's wife), who orders the gangsters around until they are forced to admit defeat. Along the way, the Yakuza are made to look ridiculous and downright stupid – and, at various points, hints are dropped about their dubious sexual dexterity. As noted by film critic Mark Schilling, the film doubles as a 'manual' for businesses on how to deal with the Mafia and has a strong anti-organised crime message. *Anti-Extortion Woman* became the most successful Yakuza movie in many years. In May 1992, some thugs attacked the director while he was entering his home in Tokyo and cut his face. 'They cut very slowly; they took their time,' he recounted later. Five members of the Gotō-gumi, a gang affiliated with the Yamaguchi-gumi, were arrested shortly after. Itami, who recovered, was not deterred and kept up his public campaign against the Yakuza. After the release of his next film, a right-wing activist slashed the screen at a theatre and the distributor withdrew the film without pressing charges against the culprit. In an interview, Itami said: 'If I were to make another film about gangs, it would not be impossible to find a distributor, but it would be difficult.' Under suspicious circumstances, Itami committed suicide in 1997: most observers are convinced that he was murdered by the Yakuza.

Yakuza movies loved by the Yakuza and not by the public

When gangsters have a role in the production of their own image, they do not necessarily make good films. On the night of 31 January 1985, 1,000 members of the Tokyo-based Inagawa-kai, the second-largest Japanese crime syndicate, attended a party in the town of Atami, in Shizuoka Prefecture. They were celebrating the release of a film based on the life of the syndicate's boss. The two lead actors, later interviewed by police, were duly present at the party. When questioned about his link to the Inagawa-kai boss, one actor described the relationship as 'that of a star and a fan'. The film, *A Band of Daredevils*, was released by Tōei.

Tōei is a respected studio that has been at the forefront of the Yakuza movie genre since its foundation in the early 1950s. By 1994, it had produced some 252 such titles. Within the heavily cartelised studio system of Japan, only Tōei was allowed to enter the genre. In fact, there is some circumstantial evidence that former Yakuza had worked for Tōei. The film director Fukasaku recalled that a senior producer, Shundō Kōji, had been in the organisation; and Tōei actors have also come from the ranks of organised crime, most notably Andō Noboru. Born in 1925, Andō formed the Andō-gumi Yakuza group, which he dissolved in 1958 to become an actor for Tōei. In 1965, he appeared in a film about himself, *Blood and Rules*. He later wrote, produced and starred in another series of films about his life and his former gang, the Andō-gumi. Studios often have financial interests beyond the entertainment industry that might bring them into contact with organised crime. By the 1970s, Tōei had diversified into various sectors, such as theatres, hotels, real estate, construction and house decorating. Both real estate and construction are sectors heavily penetrated by criminals, although no direct evidence of connection between Tōei economic activities and organised crime exists.

A Band of Daredevils, like many of Tōei's other productions, portrays a one-dimensional good samurai-Yakuza torn between obeying the criminal code of conduct and helping ordinary people harassed by the authorities and criminals. Plots reinforce the virtue of the absolute duty towards the gang, and, more generally, towards the Yakuza code. They show the gangster as a compassionate human being: whenever he does something evil, he is doing so because corrupt Yakuza take advantage of his devotion to the code. Ultimately, the good Yakuza kills the bad ones and re-establishes the honour of the organisation. The conflict between social obligation* and personal inclination† is the key turning point of the narrative. These films are *excruciatingly* boring, composed of

---

* In Japanese, *giri*.

† In Japanese, *ninjō*.

'litanies of private argot, subtle body language, obscure codes, elaborate rites, iconographic costumes and tattoos', as Paul Schrader, screenwriter of *Taxi Driver* (1976), has pointed out. Not surprisingly, the 1980s saw a general decline in the appeal of these films (most of them were released straight to video) and in 1994 Tōei announced that it was making its last Yakuza movie, *The Man Who Killed the Don*. Although the film was a flop, the studio could not quite give up the genre and it produced two more such films: *Tale of Modern Chivalry* (1997) and *Remains of Chivalry* (1999). Engaging portrayals of the Yakuza in the 1990s were produced outside the Japanese studio system by directors such as Kitano Takeshi, Miike Takashi and Sakamoto Junji. The movies of this new generation of film-makers deal in extreme violence, deadpan wit and deeply felt human dilemmas. They also portray the Yakuza in a less than flattering light.

While Japanese organised crime had some involvement in the studio system that produced Yakuza films throughout the post-war period, allowing for a degree of control over its public image, the final products did very little to further the reputation of the organisation among the general public – unlike the best known of all Mafia films, *The Godfather*.

The Godfather (1972): A movie loved by the Mob and the public

Francis Ford Coppola's *The Godfather* (1972) is based on Mario Puzo's bestselling novel, which was published in 1969. Even before its release, the FBI picked up telephone chatter among Mafiosi discussing the casting of the film. On its release, real-life mobsters watched it endlessly. Louie Milito, a member of the Gambino Family killed in 1988, 'watched the movie six thousand times' according to his wife's autobiography. Ms Milito reports that after seeing the film, her husband and his crew were 'acting like *Godfather* actors kissing and hugging … and coming out with lines from the movie. A couple of them started learning Italian.'

Sammy 'the Bull' Gravano, who instigated the murder of Louie

Milito, was also a fan. He watched the movie in 1972 and was impressed:

> I left the movie stunned. I mean, I floated out of the theatre. Maybe it was fiction, but for me, then, that was our life. It was incredible. I remember talking to a multitude of guys, made guys, everybody felt exactly the same way [...] It was basically the way I see the life. Where there was some honour.

The movie, among other things, even offered Sammy 'the Bull' a justification for killing police officers. Recalling the scene when Michael Corleone guns down NYPD Captain Marc McCluskey, who has helped mastermind the attempt on Vito Corleone's life while the Don is recovering in hospital, he muses:

> Even when Michael says about killing the police captain, that he wasn't just a captain, he had crossed the line into our world. That is true. In Cosa Nostra, it's an unwritten rule. You don't kill news people and you don't kill cops. But we wouldn't think twice about killing a cop or a news guy if they had come in with us.

When talking to John Gotti about a member of his crew, Gravano referred to the man* as 'my Luca Brasi', the slightly dumb hench-man character in the film. John Gotti, the boss of the Gambino Family from 1985, sanctioned Louie Milito's murder and received a sentence of life without parole in 1992 (mostly on the strength of Gravano's testimony). He too loved *The Godfather*. From the moment he saw it, he memorised notable lines, changed his ward-robe and started to behave (outwardly) as if he were Al Pacino.[†] Nick Pileggi, who co-wrote Scorsese's *Goodfellas* (1990) and *Casino* (1995), put it as follows in a 2002 interview: '*The Godfather* gave Gotti a romantic view of his own brutal life. [*The Godfather* films]

---

* Joe Paruta.

† Curiously, in 2011, Al Pacino accepted a starring role in a biopic of Gotti. Eventually the lead role went to John Travolta.

changed the way gangsters thought of themselves. In their heads, they become Brando and De Niro.' Gotti modelled the wedding reception of one of his daughters on the one in *The Godfather*. Thirty tables were booked for Gotti's acquaintances who, one by one, came to pay homage to the boss, as a singer performed love songs.

The movie had a grip even on the children of Mafiosi. Albert DeMeo, son of Gambino Family killer Roy DeMeo, had a steady girlfriend in 1983, the year in which his father was killed. She was kind, sweet, with glossy black hair and a stunning smile, writes Albert in his autobiography. She truly cared about him and sensed that her boyfriend was anxious. As a way of explanation, Albert suggested that she watch *The Godfather* and read the novel. 'That was the closest she could come to understanding my life.'

When Donnie Brasco (the undercover FBI agent Joseph D. Pistone) was sitting with his Mafia mentor Lefty Ruggiero and others at a restaurant in Little Italy, they requested that the strolling guitarist sing the film's score in both Italian and English. Mobsters not only learnt the script by heart, and used the music for their parties, they also got some tips on how to perform their job. In his memoir, Antonio Calderone writes that 'Totò di Cristina has just finished reading *The Godfather* and he has the idea of doing like in the book … They disguised themselves as doctors and killed [a person] in his [hospital] bed.' Most significantly, the movie offered a repertoire of possible messages to send to victims. Even in Sicily, the birthplace of Cosa Nostra, credible threatening messages of intimidation were copied from a fictional representation of the Mafia produced in Hollywood, and the severed head of a horse was found in the car owned by a building firm in Palermo in 1992.

It matters little that the screen representation is not terribly accurate. For instance, Italian Mafia Families are not, in the main, formed by close blood relatives, and bosses are not succeeded by their own sons, contrary to the plot of *The Godfather* (1972), the only notable exception being Gotti himself, who tried to appoint Gotti Junior as his successor. In a memorable scene in the film, the dons are sitting around a table discussing whether the organisation should enter the drugs trade or not, and the younger bosses are pushing the ageing Don Vito to relent. Ultimately, Don Barzini concludes that 'traffic in drugs will be permitted, but controlled.' The notion that there had been a traditional ban on dealing in narcotics is a myth. Firstly, drugs such as heroin were in fact legal until 1924. Secondly, Italian names appear in sixty-five (out of 563) State Department files on 'suspected narcotics traffickers', and included known Mafiosi in the late 1920s. By the end of the 1920s, American Cosa Nostra had pushed Jewish gangsters out of drugs trafficking. Mario Puzo wrote a work of fiction and readily admitted that he had never met a Mafioso in his life when he came to write the book.

The Godfather has travelled further than the US and Sicily. The movie was a favourite of Radik Galiakbarov (nicknamed Radsha), the self-styled Godfather of Kazan, a city in Central Russia with more than a million inhabitants. After the fall of the Soviet Union, Radik's Mafia emerged as the main power in this historic city, controlling firms, factories, shops, restaurants, nightclubs and banks. He even had power over dog fights, a children's publishing house and two cemeteries. His forte was the illegal economy, where he was involved in drugs and prostitution. Sex workers were forbidden to drink and take drugs. Radik kept the most beautiful women for himself, and those who disobeyed his orders were beaten up mercilessly. He fought his way to the top of Kazan's criminal world by duping and murdering internal rivals and leaders of smaller gangs. Scores of people went missing, but their bodies were never found over the twenty-year period of his reign.

A violent and sly man, he liked to portray himself as a wise Don Corleone. He learnt the film's dialogue by heart and recited it to his subordinates. He also did his best to emulate the dress code of Don Corleone, by wearing the types of dark suits, long coats and striped ties seen in the film – over his bulletproof vest. He spoke like Brando. In order to be more credible, he even projected his jaw forward. Finally, Radik was sentenced to life imprisonment in 2002, during a trial lasting two years, and he is now in the toughest prison in Russia, the Black Dolphin.*

---

* As time passes, mobsters have been inspired by movies other than *The Godfather*. When Mafiosi from Calabria fed one of their rivals alive to pigs

What is it about *The Godfather* that appeals to both the Mafia and the ordinary, film-watching public? This form of promotion is indirect. Coppola is not a hired hand in a Mafia-controlled studio and he does not need to be accountable to bosses after the film is finished. Coppola crafted a story of love, honour and death that speaks about universal values. It is the story of a family that aspires to join mainstream society and yet is blocked by a corrupt and greedy system, all too happy to take the Corleones' money but wary of its origins. This element of the story is similar to classic gangster movies, and it is also a strong theme in Satō and Fukusaku's early works. Coppola portrays Vito Corleone as an honourable man, defending age-old values of family love and loyalty. While the basic ingredients of a successful movie loved by both the Mafia and the public are easy to outline, the formula needs something else: talent. The formula fails – not surprisingly – when placed in incompetent hands. This is most obvious in the strange case of Giuseppe Greco, the son of a Sicilian Mafioso who became one of Italy's least successful film-makers.

Giuseppe Greco (1953–2015), the worst Mafia film-maker

Giuseppe Greco (aka Giorgio Castellani) was a mild-mannered man with a boyish look, the son of a feared Mafia boss. He was also fanatically devoted to cinema. The Grecos have for over a century been one of the most influential Mafia families, ruling over the south-east of Palermo, in particular the Ciaculli and Croceverde Giardina

---

in March 2012, observers made the connection to a gruesome scene in the *Silence of the Lambs* sequel *Hannibal* (2001), where disfigured paedophile Mason Verger is fed alive to a herd of wild boars. Simone Pepe, twenty-four years old, who was arrested for the murder, described the killing to a friend in a telephone conversation that was intercepted by police: 'It is satisfying to hear him scream … Mamma mia, how he squealed, but I couldn't give a s—. Someone said a few bits of him remained at the end of it all, but I couldn't see anything, for me nothing remained at all. I said, wow, how a pig can eat!'

neighbourhoods. Known in criminal circles for their involvement in tobacco smuggling and later in drug trafficking, they were accepted into the homes of the Palermo elite, who in turn enjoyed hunting in their Favarella country estate. Giuseppe's father, Michele (1924–2008), known as the 'Pope', was the head of the Palermo Provincial Commission between 1978 and 1986. A cousin of Giuseppe, bearing the same name, became a feared killer. Giuseppe did not fit into the world of Cosa Nostra.

> As a boy, I hated hunting and football: it is all because of a projector that was given to me when I was 8 years old. I dropped out of my law degree to devote myself entirely to cinema, becoming an assistant to director Lucio Fulci. I caught the cinema virus, I am a lover of art. In my life I have bought more books than condoms.

Giuseppe was an only child, particularly attached to his mother, whose maiden name was Castellana. Although he was married, there is no evidence that he felt close to his wife. His relationship with his father was conflicted: Giuseppe knew that he did not have what it took to follow in his family's footsteps. In private, his father accused his mother of having spoiled Giuseppe from an early age, yet all his life he supported his son's artistic aspirations: 'My son was never inclined towards the countryside like I was, and the rest of my family has been for many generations. Never, Giuseppe, never. He has always been inclined towards the artistic life, since he is gifted in that direction.'

In an effort to support his ambitions, his father put up some money to fund Giuseppe's first feature film, the sex comedy *Cream, Chocolate and Pa...prika* (1981). The plot revolves around a clinic where scantily dressed female 'doctors' work alongside crooks, who use the establishment for various illegal businesses. Giuseppe, as well as being the scriptwriter, had a major acting role, and some well-known actors agreed to appear in it too (you can spot Barbara Bouchet, who played Miss Moneypenny in the 1967 version of *Casino Royale*, among others). Apart from Franco Franchi and Ciccio Ingrassia, two of the most beloved comic actors in Italian cinema, who do a decent job with a terrible script, the acting is abysmal. A member of the cast openly admitted that the movie is 'quite horrid'. *Cream, Chocolate* never obtained a general release: only a few Palermo residents saw it and it had a very limited run on local TV stations.

As the film came out, the Anti-Mafia Maxi Trial (1986–7) was being prepared. The trial was dubbed 'Maxi' because some 474 defendants were indicted on the basis of the testimonies of prominent members, such as Tommaso Buscetta and Salvatore Contorno, who turned state witness. In order to accommodate so many defendants, a bunker was specially built inside the prison of Palermo. The trial had huge historical significance, because it confirmed the existence of Cosa Nostra as an organisation directed by a Commission of bosses. Eventually, 360 defendants were found guilty, with nineteen life sentences. Giuseppe found himself part of this event, accused of money laundering, as well as of being a 'made' member of the Sicilian Mafia, because some promotional T-shirts had been found in the hideout of a boss. The prosecutors alleged that the movie had been a way of hiding illegal capital despite the fact that there was no firm evidence, just as there was no proof that Giuseppe had ever formally joined Cosa Nostra, as was being claimed by a former Mafioso. It transpired that a car belonging to a member of Cosa Nostra had been used in a scene in the film, a fact that Giuseppe had admitted at the trial in 1986. Nevertheless, Giuseppe was given a four-year sentence. At the same trial, his father, Michele Greco, was imprisoned for life several times over.

Giuseppe's conviction was overturned on appeal and he left prison after serving only part of his sentence. He came out with his love for cinema undimmed. Adopting a stage name (Giorgio Castellani), he directed *Lost Lives* (*Vite perdute*, 1992). Again, the film was a disaster, and scenes that are meant to be dramatic verge on the farcical. The style is a potpourri of different genres, and it swings from badly filmed violent action scenes to lengthy monologues and periods where nothing happens at all.

Yet it does offer key insights into the way people close to the world of the Mafia see themselves and justify their actions. For this reason, it is an invaluable document. The central character is Rosario

Raito, the boss of a gang of petty thieves who greatly respect him. He never takes responsibility for his actions, because (in his view) he is the victim of a class-based society. Those who come from the wrong side of the tracks are prevented from dating girls from well-to-do families (such as the daughter of the court clerk), giving them a moral justification for taking what they want, robbing and raping. Most revealing is Rosario's religiosity. In a church scene, he launches into a long, disjointed monologue in front of the cross. The movie makes constant references to the Gospels and is full of images of the Virgin Mary and St Rosalia, the patron saint of Palermo.

Death is in the air. Violence is always preceded by a gang member visiting church, taking part in a procession, or at least crossing himself. Politicians – who use people for their own advantage – are the most despised category, alongside police officers and prosecutors, and those who turn state witness. The only true criminals are Romans or Neapolitans, but Sicilians are invariably men of honour; and the women, meanwhile, are either submissive wives and mothers, or whores. The film made no money, although the actors themselves were surprised at being paid in full and on time. *Lost Lives* regularly gets one out of five stars in dictionaries of Italian cinema.

Finally, in 1997, Giuseppe directed what could be considered his masterpiece, *The Grimaldi Family*. The film is the closest the Sicilian Mafia ever got to a self-produced Yakuza-style hagiography. Don Antonio Grimaldi is an ageing boss and landowner opposed to drugs, and the holder of an old-time code of honour. His territory is under threat from a gang involved in international drug trafficking. Don Antonio also finds out that his own nephew, a drug addict, is being blackmailed by his enemies to get at him. He eventually kills the gangsters with his old shotgun, while they try to mow him down using machines guns, in a symbolic enactment of the old against the new. After his arrest, the old boss is released for lack of evidence. The acting is over the top, with people shouting their lines into the camera. A flock of sheep lies dead in a field, supposedly killed by the evil drug traffickers, but the production team cannot keep the sheep lying on the ground and they run away. The movie reworks the classic theme of an old Godfather who upholds the values of honour, loyalty and family against a new generation that betrays the ideals of the Mafia.

The movie is based loosely on Giuseppe's own father, who liked to portray himself as a wealthy landowner and the inventor of a special type of tangerine tree. However, Giuseppe was careful to omit a few details, most notably the fact that his father ran a heroin refinery in his country estate, where a number of Mafiosi were once murdered after a barbecue, their bodies roasted and fed to pigs. Michele Greco was also the man who sided with the ruthless and upcoming faction of the Corleonesi, who started the second Mafia 'war'. The film is thus a deceptive and self-serving portrait of the Mafia, one that would ring false to anyone with the slightest familiarity with the history of the organisation in Sicily.

The Grimaldi Family was premiered in the neighbourhood where Giuseppe's father had been a boss. The Italian journalist and writer Attilio Bolzoni, who was present at the premiere, told me that the audience was made up mainly of curious passers-by. 'Giuseppe Greco cut a rather pathetic figure, I felt pity for him.' The film never received a release and failed to make any money. It is not even registered with the Italian authorities. Just as the Yakuza-inspired movies failed to impress the Japanese public, Castellani's film left barely a ripple.

In April 2016, I interviewed the distinguished director Francesco Maresco, the author of several documentaries on Giuseppe and a person who knew him well.

Q: What kind of person was Giuseppe?
A: He was shy, sad and gentle. I still have the bottle of whiskey that he gave me for Christmas a few years ago. He used to call me often, to suggest improbable joint projects, ideas. Once when I met him, he was accompanied by two tough-looking guys who stayed silent all the time. Giuseppe Greco was utterly devoted to cinema, a person born in the wrong family. His passion for films was akin to a disease.

When I was in Palermo in 2016, I discovered a touching detail about his last days, before his death in 2012. Giuseppe had been suffering from lung cancer. As the disease became more serious, he was hospitalised in order to undergo treatment. Suddenly, his condition worsened – he even suffered a stroke. Giuseppe was about to die. The doctor walked into Giuseppe's room and told him: 'Mr Greco, unfortunately, there is nothing else we can do here for you. If you wish, you can go home and be with your family for the days that you have left to live.'

Giuseppe raised himself on the bed. He wanted to be heard clearly. 'Dear Doctor, please do not send me home. I want to die here.' After a few days, he died peacefully in the arms of the doctor.

Macau, November 2012–2014

In 1999, authorities decided to move against 'Broken Tooth' Wan. The last straw was the explosion of a bomb in the car of the Macau chief of police. They found 'Broken Tooth' Wan holed up in a VIP room inside the Casino Lisboa, watching himself being interviewed on Hong Kong TV.

Thirteen years and seven months later Wan walked out of Macau prison, on 1 December 2012. He had lived in a tiny, windowless cell in a high-security block of the peninsula's only jailhouse. His immediate release was widely announced by the local press, and a small crowd gathered. In the early hours of the morning, a white Lexus LS430 was waiting outside the prison gates. Two thick-necked men got out and waited. At 6.50 a.m., Wan emerged, looking fit and relatively youthful for his fifty-seven years. His hair had the dark colour one expects to see in a much younger man. A 100-table-strong celebration was ready for him at the Sheraton Macau Hotel. Old associates and Wan's elderly mother were to attend. Alas, I was not invited.

Shortly after the banquet, 'Broken Tooth' Wan was back as a VIP gaming-room operator. Speaking in 2012, he said: 'There is no reason for foreign enterprises to occupy the majority of the market in a place that is mostly Chinese.' The entry into the market by US corporations, he added, was 'surely good for development, but Chinese people should have a bigger share'. These seem like the words of a man swimming against the tide of history. His days as the most important

Mafia boss of Macau are long gone. The city that Wan has returned to in 2012 is very different. Large foreign corporations control the best casinos and the Beijing government is aggressively cracking down on corruption. The association between VIP rooms and Triads is becoming increasingly embarrassing for American casino owners, who are under close scrutiny in the US, where they run the risk of losing licences to operate in Las Vegas. As a consequence, some American operators are trying to take direct control of VIP rooms and offering a more diversified, family-friendly experience. Broken Tooth has nevertheless found a job controlling a VIP room at a rather small casino. Yet he might have lost his touch. Reportedly, his establishment was the victim of a serious theft in February 2016, when 1 million Hong Kong dollars went missing.* Broken Tooth now lives in a nondescript high-rise in the Taipa neighbourhood of Macau. His neighbours are middle-ranking government officials, academics and moderately successful business people. When one knocks at his apartment's door, he opens the door himself. No bodyguard is in sight. While 'Broken Tooth' might have lost his earthly power, his cinematic imagine, as depicted in *Giant*, will not be easily forgotten by those who have seen the film he produced.

* £99,000/US$129,000.

7

POLITICS

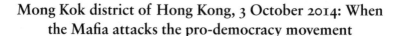

Mong Kok district of Hong Kong, 3 October 2014: When the Mafia attacks the pro-democracy movement

On Friday night, 26 September 2014, several hundred young people took to the streets of Hong Kong to demand direct, universal election of the Chief Executive.* The protest started when some students entered a fenced square near the government headquarters. The police responded by using tear gas to disperse the crowd before arresting demonstrators. The excessive use of force outraged the population of Hong Kong and became instant news around the world. This was the spark that ignited an extraordinary peaceful occupation of three sites in Hong Kong for over two months, starting on the night of 28 September, in the financial district of the city and in the working-class neighbourhood of Mong Kok. Occupy Central – also known as the Umbrella Movement – was born. As I watched the events unfolding on TV, I decided to fly to Hong Kong to observe this remarkable event for myself.

Shortly after landing, I found myself wedged into a crowd listening to a student, not even twenty years old, who was dwarfed by

---

* Breaking an earlier promise, the Chinese government was planning to retain veto power over who is allowed to stand for the post of Chief Executive (i.e. president).

Yvonne Leung Lai-kwok speaks to the crowd during the Umbrella Movement.

The John Lennon Wall in the Admiralty occupation site.

The Umbrella Man, a twelve-foot (three metre) sculpture created from hundreds of wooden blocks, by an artist known only as 'Milk', in the Admiralty occupation site.

gigantic yellow banners hanging from a flyover, a few metres away from the Admiralty metro station. He was crying out for a principle that, in the West, we take for granted: 'one person, one vote'.

The students had created a civilised community of protestors, turning a motorway into a village, protected at the edges by rudimentary wooden barricades. During the day, they did their homework in study areas and makeshift libraries. People from a large cross-section of society joined the students after work, bringing home-made food, books, blankets and water. I saw a carpenter repairing a fence and building furniture while a professor was giving a tutorial in chemistry. Others tended to an organic garden growing on the pavement: nature had reclaimed a small portion of hard concrete. Quotes from Nelson Mandela and Mahatma Gandhi were ubiquitous, but everybody's hero was John Lennon. At the bottom of a concrete staircase renamed after him, students came to take pictures of themselves in graduation gowns, celebrating democracy and degree day. Yellow stickers were plastered on the wall, with the words of John Lennon's song 'Imagine'. The iPad generation was reaching back to an older band of idealistic dreamers.

Every day at around six in the evening, a leader recounted the key events of the day, while the Twitter feed for #OccupyCentral was beamed onto the wall of a government building by a projector. No one was in the mood for grandstanding speeches: any minute the camp might be raided by police or by China's People's Liberation Army. At night, anybody could sleep in one of 2,000 tents, each complete with its own postal address, such as Democracy Lane 1-682. When I tried to offer a donation, the official in charge told me that 'we don't accept money, only useful things like blankets, water, mattresses, food and work.'

During a visit to the occupation sites, I met Yvonne Leung, president of the Hong Kong University Students Union. She had become a well-known figure in the city after appearing in a televised debate about democracy, where she made convincing and pointed rebuttals of the government's position. She had long dark hair, thin black glasses, a studious face and a focused yet timid way of looking at you. Top of her class in law at Hong Kong University,

Anti-Occupy Central protesters attempt to remove a fence erected by
pro-democracy protesters in Mongkok, Hong Kong, 4 October 2014.

she wore tight jeans and a black T-shirt with the yellow ribbon,
symbol of the movement printed on it. She was often to be found
in Mong Kok, a working-class neighbourhood and the roughest
of the three sites of the protest, a very different place from the
elegant Admiralty area, just opposite the government offices, where
the bulk of the students were camped. In Mong Kok there were
no more than 100 occupants at any one time, almost as many as
the watchful police officers that cordoned off the area. I counted
no more than twenty tents, a far cry from the 2,000 at the other
site. Sleeping here at night was less safe: despite the efforts of
Chris Patten, the last British governor of Hong Kong, to spear-
head gentrification projects in Mong Kok, and the presence of a
few high-end hotels and trendy shopping centres (including the
hotel where Edward Snowden stayed before fleeing to Russia), the
criminal activities which have traditionally taken place here simply
moved a few streets away. The local Mafia, the Triads, still controls
prostitution and street hawkers, as well as the red minibuses that
pick up passengers for a few dollars in every corner of the city.
Local shops and restaurants all pay protection money.

The morning of 3 October 2014 started as just another day for
Yvonne and the students in Mong Kok. However, soon after 10 a.m.,

it was obvious that something unusual was going on, as several rough-looking individuals were removing sandbag barriers on the junction of Sai Yeung Choi Street South and Argyle Street.

By just after 2 p.m., minor clashes had broken out between pro- and anti-democracy protestors, with the latter removing tents and fences, and getting into brawls. Around 4.30 p.m., police established a cordon around the sit-in at the junction of Argyle Street and Nathan Road, while anti-Occupy activists were stopped by a chain of police officers as they charged at the cordon. Just before 5 p.m., a student collapsed and lost consciousness where a large group of anti-Occupy demonstrators had encircled some pro-democracy activists. It took several attempts to get him away to an ambulance. The police were no use. A thin line of officers separating opposing sides was stretched to breaking point, and finally gave way shortly after 5 p.m. 'There were not a lot of police when I arrived,' Wing, a TV reporter, told me. 'It was chaotic, individuals who had no face masks joined in while masked thugs were abusing protestors. I did not expect it to be so violent.'

By 6 p.m., Mong Kok had 'descended into violence', according to the *South China Morning Post* reporter on the scene. More pro-democracy supporters rushed there after work. 'We decided to continue the occupation. Our strategy was not to respond to the violence with more violence,' Yvonne told me. 'We stood still, with our arms folded to protect our breast. We tried to smile, and talk. We were pushed, spat at, groped and harassed. In those moments, I saw terrible things and I was scared.'

As the crowd of anti-Occupy thugs grew bigger and the movement's supporters continued to be attacked, no police reinforcement was forthcoming. Many suspected that it was not simply a question of manpower. Mary, a volunteer at a medical supplies station, saw officers watching by the side. Like Yvonne, she was scared. 'The police were deliberately not protecting us,' she told me.

One of the leaders of the movement, Professor Benny Tai, declared at 9.10 p.m. that he suspected Triads of being behind the attack. At 10.15 p.m., the police ordered demonstrators in Mong Kok to leave the site immediately, to no avail. Again, Yvonne and other activists decided to hold the line, whatever the cost. 'It was not an easy decision to take, you have to consider the risk of an escalation. But we knew that the future of the movement depended on us refusing to give in.' By 10.35 p.m., fighting had broken out again, while the police again failed to intervene. Instead, officers formed a line about twenty metres away from the fracas, watching from a distance while guarding the main road junction. The two parties were eventually separated by bystanders. Some evidence of collusion between the police and anti-democracy protestors started to emerge a few hours later. At 12.50 a.m., 21-year-old Wesley Ng saw the police release a man who had allegedly attacked protestors. Yvonne has no doubt that attackers and authorities were coordinating their actions. Ben, a Chinese University graduate, saw the police arresting masked men and escorting them away from the scene but releasing them shortly afterwards: 'The masked men were on a loop, coming and going,' he said.

Amnesty International condemned the Hong Kong police for not protecting peaceful demonstrators. Instead, the police started to target the students. They used pepper spray to disperse a pro-democracy crowd surrounding a man allegedly responsible for violence against the protestors. Students took it upon themselves to chase attackers and hand them over to the police.

By three in the morning, activists had reclaimed a section of Argyle Street leading to the junction with Nathan Road near Langham Place, a shopping complex in Mong Kok behind the main occupation site. By 4.30 a.m., the situation was finally calming down. The anti-Occupy camp had retreated. By dawn, students had largely rebuilt the barricades and raised the tents. As the sun rose over Hong Kong on the morning of 4 October, around 200 pro-democracy students were at the crossroads of Nathan Road and Argyle Street to defend the site. The attack had failed. The thugs had been defeated by peaceful determination and courage. The fight for democracy continued.

During a press conference in the early hours of 4 October, authorities gave their account of the previous day's events. Nineteen men had been arrested in clashes in Mong Kok, eight of whom were believed to have Triad backgrounds. They were facing various charges of unlawful assembly, fighting in a public place, and assault, according to District Commander Kwok Pak-chung. No investigation was launched to establish whether the Triads had masterminded the violence. Who ordered those men to attack students? The police limited themselves to offering a few bare facts. At least twelve people and six police officers had been wounded. Officer Kwok did not rule out more arrests, while emphasising that the police had been fair and did not enforce the law selectively. The anti-democracy attackers arrested on the night of 3 October were immediately released on bail and then cleared of all charges. Only pro-democratic activists were still being prosecuted. On 21 July 2016, a court in Hong Kong convicted three leaders of Occupy Movement, including nineteen-year-old Joshua Wong, one of its public faces.

Was the Mafia attempting to crush a democratic protest and if so why? Answering this question might uncover an important dimension to the relationship between politics, states and the Mafia. Thanks to my local collaborator, I was able to interview dozens of people who had an intimate knowledge of that day's events and of life in Mong Kok. We talked to news reporters, protestors, volunteers at the First Aid Station, academics who had been present on the night of the events, representatives of a local minibus trade union, taxi operators and owners, and business people. We also pored over hundreds of newspaper reports, both in Chinese and English.*

Two members of the Triads with direct knowledge of the neighbourhood and of the events that night agreed to talk to us, provided we did not reveal their real names in print. *Shek*, an affable, perfectly groomed man in his mid-forties, wearing sunglasses, joined the Triads as a teenager and has been active in Yau Ma Tei and Mong Kok (both in the Kowloon area of Hong Kong). He now manages several bars in Causeway Bay and Wanchai. Our second source is *Brick Brother*, a senior-ranking Triad member active in West Kowloon.

Shek knew in advance that an attack was planned. In the early morning of 3 October, he received a text message from his bosses

---

* My co-author, Dr Rebecca Wong, conducted additional interviews after my departure.

and friends asking him to recruit people for the day, and got a second message to that effect in the evening, when the violence had already broken out and the attackers needed reinforcement. He added some information to the profiles of those who joined the fight:

> Most of the people who went were youngsters aged between fifteen and twenty-something. They were nobodies in their Triad groups, so they saw this as an opportunity to prove their strength, to humiliate the police, and to impress their bosses whereas the older ones would want more money.

Brick Brother knew the attackers well:

> I know the people who beat up the students on 3 October, I saw them on television [he mentions several names and laughs]. They received money from their bosses to disrupt the protests. I am not surprised that they are all released after being briefly arrested because the higher command of the police knew they were coming.

When, after 3 October, *Brick Brother* saw some fellow Triads who took part in the attacks, he asked them about the clashes and how much they were paid. He discovered that payments varied depending on experience and seniority. Low-level hooligans were paid HK$800 (US$103). More senior people were offered between HK$1,500 and HK$3,000 for the day (US$133–386), while senior Triads were paid up to HK$10,000 per day (US$1,287).

Shek and *Brick Brother* are not the only Mafiosi to acknowledge infiltration by the Triads. Chan Wai Man, a renowned leader of the 14K Triad (now an actor and wine merchant), admitted to a local newspaper that he knew those involved very well. In an October 2014 interview, he added that the Hong Kong Triads were now ready to protect the government. Everything points to the fact that the attackers were either full members or aspiring members of the Triads, and received cash to harass the students.

Several theories have been put forward about why the Hong Kong Mafia mobilised. One view is that the Triads wanted to protect their businesses in the area, in particular the sex trade, gambling venues, the minibus routes and the various shops that pay protection money to organised crime in Mong Kok. If this were the case, we would expect local Triads to be involved, and the money paid to the rank and file to come from the Triads' own coffers, something which is occasionally reported in the media. Alternatively, the Triads might have mobilised because they were asked to do so by individuals politically opposed to the democratic movement. In this scenario, the attackers might well have come from other parts of Hong Kong, rather than the immediate neighbourhood; to be, in effect, a Mafia for hire.

Local Triads would have mobilised if the economic impact of the occupation had been serious, but it was not. Although the taxi drivers we spoke to were unhappy at the road disruption, which blocked a crucial artery in the Kowloon area of Hong Kong (one of them suggesting to us that the students should instead 'set fire to themselves to get attention and get it over and done with'), the majority of drivers admitted that they had not lost much money during the occupation. 'After all,' one pointed out, 'journeys were longer.' The owner of a 200-strong taxi company told us that although the loss was significant initially, revenue was actually up towards the middle and final phases of the occupation. Owners of taxi companies lodged injunctions to remove the protestors as part of a politically motivated anti-Occupy strategy, but in reality loss of business was insignificant.

One of the sectors to allegedly suffer greatly was that of the private (red) minibuses, known to be controlled by the Triads in Hong Kong. In order for the drivers to pick up passengers, they have to pay a 'station fee' to the Triads controlling their stops. During the occupation, many minibuses had to change routes. The headquarters of one of the minibus trade unions are in the northern part of Mong Kok. The building is run-down and the office far from showy. It is widely understood that the union is a front for organised crime, which controls the minibuses and manages disputes among drivers. The man in the union office is hardly affable, yet after a while he starts to answer our questions. He is a vocal opponent of the pro-democracy movement, as are his drivers. 'Some drivers thought they would lose income during the occupation,' he says. He has anti-democracy posters in the office, to be displayed inside the minibus vehicles. He has also filed an injunction against the Mong Kok protests on behalf of his union. Yet he adds that the drivers, though affected at first, adjusted quickly and found alternative routes. The biggest loss of income was among those stationed on Hong Kong Island rather than at the Mong Kok Occupy site. In the end, he says, his union lodged injunctions with the courts to remove the students from public spaces. The union's reasons were unrelated to loss of income: members were outraged by such brazen defiance of the government.

Shek and *Brick Brother* also acknowledge that the loss of income was minimal. Prostitution and gambling close to the occupied areas were at first affected, but revenue picked up quickly. *Shek* points out that minibuses initially had to avoid the occupied areas and lost some money in the process, but they were soon back in business using different routes protected by the 14K, Sing Wo, and Wo Sing Wo Triads. *Brick Brother* says that since 'the roads were open, why would business go down?'; and adds that many drivers were reassigned to the New Territories during the occupation and none of them was actually out of work.

Given that the Triads' income is not reliant on one source, it doesn't seem likely that they would launch such a high-profile and costly attack as that of 3 October. Brothels, pubs and gambling in Mong Kok lost a little revenue at the beginning of the occupation, but customers quickly returned. Our informants confirm that protection fees are mandatory, and there is no such thing as a discount if business is bad, so income from protection payments was not affected.

A news reporter stationed in Mong Kok maintains that he had never seen the people involved in the confrontation before the night of the attack. They were not local thugs concerned about the disruption. He discovered that anti-democracy protestors had been shuttled to Mong Kok in minibuses and vans. On the morning of 3 October, young offenders were overheard saying, 'We are going to have some fun in Mong Kok because this is what they told us.'

Brick Brother confirms that the attackers were not locals:

The vast majority [of the attackers] are based in Shum Shui Po [an area north of Mong Kok], where they oversee the electronics and wet markets. They went to disrupt the protests and to remove fences. Some came from the New Territories. They belong to the Shui Fong Gang, Wo Shing Wo and 14K Triads.

Shek tells us that some of those who joined the fight 'might have been people of Indian and Pakistani origin because the Sing Wo Triad recruits in these communities, but is based in Hong Kong'. He adds that the local Triad gang were not involved in the attack. Indeed, they had not been informed and were highly upset at what had happened: 'The local guys did not want such a high-profile confrontation; it was against their interest.' In effect, their territory had been invaded.

Why did outside gangs intervene and who paid them? It is not easy to answer these questions with any certainty. A senior reporter from an independent news outlet who followed the occupation very closely told us that 'the people that disrupted the protests were individuals from Hong Kong that wanted to please the central government and to make the statement that they are on China's side.' He went on to explain:

One has to look back at how developers managed to acquire land in the New Territories. According to the regulations, male indigenous inhabitants have the right to build a house on their plot of land. Developers are buying titles of ownership, so local residents asked the government to hold consultation meetings. The tycoons hired the Triads to disrupt these meetings and to put pressure on the government. The government turned a blind eye. The tycoons wanted to pay back the government and funded Triad gangs from the New Territories and Kowloon to intervene.

For him, business interests in Hong Kong were behind the attack, a view that is shared by the pro-democracy academics whom we interviewed. For the Triads, there is, it seems, a tension between assimilation and autonomy. Some gangs were ready to work as hired hands, while other groups resisted outside interference, wishing to retain a degree of autonomy from powerful outside interests. The events of 3 October have brought to the surface a deep dilemma among mafias all over the world: on the one hand, they strive to carve out their own spaces and compete with the state, while on the other they are tempted to strike deals with state structures. Today, the vast majority of Triads are keen to act as a 'patriotic' force within society, taking the side of the state.

This wasn't always the case: until the 1980s, the Triads were fairly autonomous and were even a potential threat to Communist China. In the aftermath of the Tiananmen massacre, as the Chinese authorities were pursuing the leaders of the 1989 student protests, members of the Sun Yee On Triad – which has contacts in Hong Kong's harbour ports – arranged for at least 150 people to escape from the mainland to Hong Kong by speedboat, and then on to France and the United States. Preparing for the island handover to China in 1997, the Beijing government worried that the Triads, and in particular Sun Yee On, the most powerful, would side with liberal political activists and destabilise post-1997 Hong Kong. So they developed a deliberate strategy to woo the Triads into the pro-Beijing camp. The strategy included official statements of support for 'patriotic Triads' and the granting of business opportunities to Triad leaders in China, in exchange for their support in Hong Kong. On 8 April 1993, China's then minister of public security stated that China was willing to work with the Triads if they were 'patriotic and concerned with the stability and prosperity of Hong Kong'. Members of Sun Yee On also met with him in Beijing.

From the early 1990s, China opened its doors to several Triad investments. In May 1992 a boss of Hong Kong's 14K Triad, Huang Jianming, entered China and started a programme of investing 14K funds into Shenzhen, beginning with a restaurant. By 1998, he had acquired thirty-five properties. A nightclub co-owned by the son of the Sun Yee On founder and the minister of public security was opened in Beijing. In August 1993 the vice chairman of one of China's highest political bodies opened a film production centre in China owned by two Sun Yee On leaders. The Sun Yee On also invested in a multiplex to be built in the Nanshan district of

Shenzhen. Nuoquan Chen, a former high-ranking member of the Wo Shing Tong Triad, bought a hotel in Shenzhen, his home town, where he recruited local youngsters and formed his own gang, the Flying Eagle. According to an investigation conducted in the city in 1999, among the fifty-two restaurants and entertainment businesses owned by overseas citizens, thirty-two were associated with outside Triads, making up 62 per cent of the total. The leaders of the Sun Yee On converted the capital they made in China through illegal means in the Hong Kong stock market. Even before the violence of 3 October, the local Mafia had kept its side of the bargain and targeted pro-democracy activists. In February 2014, a critic of the Communist Party and former editor of the outspoken Hong Kong newspaper *Ming Pao*, Kevin Lau, was brutally attacked with a cleaver, an attack allegedly carried out by the Shui Fong Triad.

In any case, the 3 October 2014 attack failed to dislodge the students and was an embarrassing failure for the Triads: their actions made the police look incompetent and raised awkward questions about the connections between the Triads and the police. In addition, it generated tension between the local chapter of the Triads and the invaders. *Shek* told us that after 3 October, local Triad members even hung around the protestors' site in order to ensure that violence did not escalate again, and no serious incident has been recorded since.

In the not so distant future, the Triads might become the main vehicle for enforcing unpopular policies and repressing social movements in Hong Kong. It is certainly the case that the increasing mainland control over Hong Kong is likely to have an effect on the Triads: as a regime becomes more autocratic, the Mafia loses autonomy.

Mafias are private entities that use violence for their own purposes, such as protecting their turf or commercial activities, but, as we've seen, they also deploy violence in cooperation with state structures. Yet these organisations face a dilemma: if a Mafia is highly effective at destroying any opposition to the state, how can it be sure that it will not be next? Lending a supporting hand to state institutions, especially those that are undemocratic and unaccountable, might greatly reduce the autonomy of these groups.

Mafias thrive in democracies. The extension of voting rights allowed them to offer a valuable service to politicians. The first election of a united Italy was held in 1861, with only 2 per cent of the population allowed to vote. By 1919, Italy had universal male suffrage, with women allowed to vote in 1946. The extension of voters' rights and the related increase in power devolved to local authorities (over schools and hospitals, for example) made voting highly significant, and local politicians were quick to enlist the services of the Mafia to manipulate elections.

'Politicians have always sought us out because we can provide votes,' writes Antonio Calderone, from the Catania Family. Sicilian Mafiosi mostly support politicians from the ruling party. According to member Vincenzo Marsala:

> The only party we voted for is the Christian Democrats [the ruling party in post-war Italy]; this is because its representatives were those who had best protected the Mafia ... the rule was that a member could campaign only in favour of the Christian Democrats, while it was strictly forbidden to campaign or vote for the Communists and the Fascists.

Calderone explains the Mafiosi position in relation to the Fascists, the Communists and 'the extreme left parties in general':

> The Cosa Nostra had always opposed the Communist Party and the left. It's against anything leftist [...] We did not like the Fascists [...] While I was in Catania the instructions were to vote only for centrist parties, the 'democratic' parties. [...] If a totalitarian party comes to power, the Cosa Nostra is finished. And which are the totalitarian parties? The Communists, the Socialists, the Fascists. The Christian Democrats were a democratic party, truly democratic. They'd share power. The Mafia could get along with that; it would make it possible to do more.

If politicians depend on the Mafia for votes, they are, of course, more willing to make concessions and to 'share power'. Families expect something in return, such as money, favours, and freedom to pursue their businesses. If a centrist candidate or even a 'democratic' party consistently fails to deliver, it is acceptable to switch allegiance.

The Sicilian Mafia has often targeted labour movements and trade unions because it sees them as direct competition: workers 'protected' by a powerful representative would not be amenable to exploitation by Mafia-backed business people. In 1953, the mayor of Reggio Calabria praised a local Mafia boss for intervening to avert a strike, endorsing the 'simple request', as he had it, of the political authorities of the town.

Similarly, the Japanese Mafia has consorted with both centrist and right-wing politicians. In the nineteenth century, Japan – like Italy – extended the electoral base, opening up a new market for votes, and with it their violent control. While in the 1890 elections, only 1 per cent of the population was allowed to vote, by 1925 Japan had universal male voting rights. The Yakuza, which emerged at the time of rapid transition to a market economy in the Meiji period (1868–1912), consorted with the ruling parties to influence elections and intimidate protestors, amid increasing labour conflicts. Violence and democracy were intimately and inextricably linked in Japan, and the former has been embedded in the practice of modern Japanese politics from the very inception of the country's experiment with democracy. Thugs attacked MPs and even occupied parliament in order to intimidate elected officials. While violence was reduced after the Second World War, the practice of Japanese politics remained dangerous, chaotic and violent. Very much like its Sicilian counterpart, the Japanese Mafia acted in support of a limited number of political actors from centrist and right-wing parties who wanted to halt the growth of socialist ideas. Left-wing movements and radical protests were the main target of Yakuza violence, because they promised to subvert the existing order and to protect workers. Organised crime was used extensively to intimidate and harass workers and strikers, and the Yakuza expected to be rewarded for its support. In 1927–8 the Noda Shōyu food processing company hired the Yakuza to bring a protracted strike to an end. The organisation was also used to break the longest strike in Japan's labour history, at the Miike Coal Mines in Kyūshū in

1960. In a showdown with picketers, a Yakuza killed a striker with a sword.

Russia underwent a similar process, yet even more rapidly than in Sicily and Japan. From 1986 onwards, the country witnessed a spread of property rights that was not matched on the part of the state by the establishment of adequate formal enforcement mechanisms. The transition to the market occurred at the same time as the transition to democracy and a more liberal set of industrial relations. The Mafia quickly started to interfere in the electoral process by supporting candidates from the governing parties and crushing labour protests. In the 1990s, prominent crime figures consorted with centrist politicians, such as Boris Yeltsin. The nationalist and anti-communist Liberal Democratic Party, led by Vladimir Zhirinovsky, has been particularly supportive of the criminal world. Criminals have also been used to crush trade unionists. For instance, in 1997, a gang intervened to stop a workers' strike in the town of Vorkuta, not far from the Arctic Circle. The beneficiary of such action was the company that owns the Vorgashurskaya coal mine.

In his classic study *Organized Crime in Chicago* (1929), John Landesco wrote that 'the relationship of the gangster and the politician becomes most obvious to the public on election day' and went on to examine all the types of electoral fraud that gangsters – Irish and Italians alike – commit on behalf of the politicians they support. The penetration of local politics reached a peak in the case of Cicero, Illinois, a dormitory town of some 60,000 people that in the 1920s and 1930s became the headquarters of Al Capone's gang, whose leader was so powerful that he was able to determine who became mayor. During the Second World War, a secret marriage of mutual convenience was struck between the Mob and the US government. In 1942 the US Navy asked the Italian-American Mafia to spy on Nazi sympathisers and protect the New York City docks against German saboteurs. Joe 'Socks' Lanza, a waterfront racketeer in New York City's Fulton Fish Market, with a criminal record that included homicide, possession of a gun and conspiracy, provided the link between the Navy and Mafia boss Lucky Luciano. The collaboration quickly extended to monitoring and disrupting communist and radical activities by workers not affiliated to the unions controlled by the Mob. In return, Luciano's lengthy sentence for running a prostitution ring was suspended and he was deported to Italy in 1946, where he continued to commit serious crime. In a time of war, security trumps legality and it apparently never crossed the minds of the American navy that the Mafiosi might sell them bogus information (in fact they did, as Luciano himself later revealed).

There is a strong connection between democracy and the emergence of mafias. Totalitarian regimes, such as Stalinist Russia or Nazi Germany, do not allow the emergence of alternative sources of authority, as Antonio Calderone well understood. Indeed, Fascist Italy enacted a severe repression of Cosa Nostra in the 1920s to 1930s. On the other hand, mafias were pervasive during the chaotic years when China was a republic (1912–49), and in the 1990s in Russia. As a regime becomes more authoritarian, the room for manoeuvre is reduced, to the point of being non-existent under a Stalin or Hitler. In such a regime, the authorities don't need the Mafia – they can harass protestors directly.

As a region becomes more authoritarian, criminal control over territories and markets must be negotiated directly with the government from a position of weakness. The Mafia in question, to the extent that it is even allowed to exist, starts to resemble a group of thugs for hire.

When Mafia and state coincide

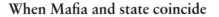

How would a Mafia state look? Surely, both mafias and states value a connection to the sacred. Just as Mafiosi go through a ritual that is deeply related to Church practices, heads of states, politicians and officials plead their allegiance through an oath. In medieval Europe, this was commonly known as the *sacramentum regis,* while the 'oath of allegiance' has its origins in Magna Carta. Even the most radical states, such as the Soviet Union, have tried hard to manufacture the sacred nature of the political bond through newly created rituals. The essence of this bond is non-contractual: God is invoked and the person's physical and spiritual essence is offered to seal the obligation. The bond is permanent and the individual has no right to breach it, no matter what happens.

Like states, mafias can also develop their own ideology and strive for independence. For instance, after the Second World War, the Sicilian Mafia backed the movement for Sicilian independence. The movement was formed immediately after the Allied landings and attracted the support of virtually all of the most consequential Mafiosi at the time. Indeed, the commander of the military arm of the independence movement was a Mafioso. In the end, the movement collapsed when the Sicilian Mafia struck a devil's pact with the Christian Democrats (DC), the ruling party of post-war Italy. The DC would allow Cosa Nostra a degree of autonomy and the freedom to pursue its businesses, and the Mafia would in return provide votes and crush left-wing organisations and trade unions. It turns out that even tax collection was contracted out to a private agency that was owned by Mafiosi. If the Mafia leaders had not accepted the pact, they could have led an independence movement and today we would look at them with different eyes, as heroes of a people's liberation project. When post-war order ended after the fall of the Berlin Wall and a new generation of local leaders (such as Leoluca Orlando) questioned this pact, the Sicilian Mafia had no qualms in starting a terrorist campaign across Italy in order to force the government to reverse a number of decisions related to the fight against organised crime and the harsh prison regime to which Mafiosi are subjected. Members can convince themselves that they are fighting a 'just' war. Gaspare Mutolo, a member of Cosa Nostra responsible for more than twenty murders, said: 'I felt like the soldier of a state. I was not interested in the views of the Italian people … I was interested only in the judgment of my people [*popolo*], and felt at ease with my conscience and with God.' Several Mafiosi in their testimonies use military metaphors to describe their crimes.

What we normally call 'organised crime' is perfectly capable of hijacking legitimate grievances and ethnic identities. In Colombia, for instance, Pablo Escobar, the leader of the Medellin drug cartel, ran for a Senate seat and wanted ultimately to become the president of Colombia. He stood on a platform of 'civic mindedness, nationalism and social, ecological and sports programmes' (his words). His brand of nationalism was meant to reassert Colombian sovereignty in the face of US pressure. Naturally, his political platform was self-serving, as he opposed an extradition treaty with the US, but tapped into genuine popular feelings against the political class and the US. He was a criminal populist. Another example is that of the Mexican cartel La Familia, which invoked the local identity of Michoacán residents against the rival cartel's invasion of their land. Here, the clear-cut distinctions between organised crime, Mafia and insurgency start to become blurred.

When I travelled to Burma, I saw one example of just such a blurring.

Muse–Ruili border, Burma–China, July 2011

Most people have probably never heard of some of the capitals of organised crime: Gioia Tauro (the main entry point for cocaine in Europe in the Italian region of Calabria); Veleshta (the European centre of human trafficking in Macedonia); and Ciudad del Este, in Paraguay, where the black market is legal and goods are not taxed. Arguably the least known is Ruili.

Ruili, with a population of 140,000, is a city in the Chinese province of Yunnan, just across the border from Burma. 'In Ruili, you'll see things you won't see anywhere else in China,' said a taxi driver, who seemed stunned to meet an Italian tourist here. I had flown from Hong Kong to Kunming and then on to the small airport of Dehong Mangshi, a town about an hour's drive away. I arrived late in the evening and took the only taxi left to Ruili. On the way there, we passed through four army roadblocks. Chinese business people cross the border into Burma to buy raw jade, wood, minerals and exotic animals, and gamble in the many casinos that have sprung up near the border. Burmese businessmen come to Ruili to buy cheap electronics on sale in the city's small parking lots, which have been turned into makeshift shops.

The border that these people cross is not an ordinary one and it is not surprising that the Chinese government has sent in the army. Ruili is the gateway into China for a whole range of illegal goods produced in the 'Golden Triangle', a 150,000-square-mile patch of land in the Shan states of Burma. This is the world's second-largest producer of opium after Afghanistan, with heroin and amphetamine refineries scattered across the countryside. Professor Ko-lin Chin, the pre-eminent scholar of the Golden Triangle and a native of Burma, tells me that the laboratories nestled away in the Burmese jungle are now around a hundred strong. Some 45 per cent of the world's heroin is refined in this remote mountainous region. While the world's media chronicle the transition to democracy in Burma, few mention that drug production and trafficking are on the increase, and will have a decisive influence on the country's future. Many Chinese businessmen import heroin and amphetamines from Burma through the border crossing between Ruili and the Burmese city of Muse, itself home to several meth factories. Muse is a destination for drugs produced in several parts of Burma, where they are stocked in warehouses, waiting to be shipped to China, after drugs deals have been negotiated. The merchandise is then moved on towards South China, Guangzhou, Hong Kong and finally to the rest of the world.

Human trafficking is the other large cottage industry. Young Burmese women work in Ruili's hundreds of brothels. Some of them come here looking for a new life, but many have been sold by their own families. Often, Chinese gangs cross the border to kidnap Burmese girls and sell them as wives in China. The first Chinese case of Aids was recorded in Ruili, and the area continues to have China's highest percentage of HIV-positive cases.

After Burma gained independence in 1948, several guerrilla groups were formed, named after the towns where they had established strongholds. By the late 1960s, the guerrilla leaders had agreed to join the Communist Party of Burma. In 1989, as the Berlin Wall collapsed and Eastern Europe was freed from Soviet influence, the leaders of various former communist groups in the border area signed a peace treaty with the government. Under the conditions of the treaty, the three major armed groups in the region – the Kokang, the Wa and the Mengla – were allowed to remain in control of the territory, retain their arsenals and continue their opium trade, while the Burmese leadership directed its attention to crushing the indigenous democratic movement. As a consequence, opium production almost doubled from 1988 to 1997. As the international community started to pay attention to the Golden Triangle, the Burmese government put pressure on the militia to reduce production. Indeed, output decreased between 2001 and 2007. However, progress towards democracy and the relaxation of the oppressive policies of the military junta had the paradoxical effect of allowing yield to increase again, especially after 2009. In a ten-year period (2006–16), the number of hectares devoted to the production of opium more than doubled. A (very) conservative estimate by a 2010 US Congress report indicates that the Burmese drug trade is worth between 1 and 2 billion dollars every year, and is the country's third most valuable export, after jade and natural gas.

In this part of the world, opium cultivation has until recently been legal, and a major source of tax revenue for the local militias. Farmers paid a compulsory tax in opium regardless of whether they grew the plant or not, thereby forcing them to either start cultivation or buy opium to pay the tax. Although now formally illegal, at least 200,000 families continue to work on opium farms.* Heroin and methamphetamine factories also thrive: until 1994, the government collected a 'heroin refinery tax'. Formally at least, the tax has now been abolished, but informally state protection of refineries has not stopped. The continuing production of drugs has had a devastating effect on the local population. Between 60 per cent and 80 per cent of young people in this area are addicted to methamphetamines. A tablet costs between $1 and $3, while a dose of high-quality heroin costs less than a dollar. Entire border cities are inhabited by ghosts addicted to drugs. In Ruili, I was often approached by people showing me four fingers, a reference to heroin, known here as 'four': many visitors to the town are in search of high-quality illegal highs and people assumed that I was one of them.

The most important ethnic armed militia in the region – the Wa

---

* The total population of the Shan State is about 600,000 people.

– is routinely referred to as a drug trafficking organisation, and their leaders dubbed 'drug kingpins', 'drug warlords' and 'drug Mafia'. Like traditional mafias, Mafia states develop a narrative to justify their statehood. In addition, they use the proceeds of drugs to fund infrastructures and state institutions: schools, roads and power plants exist thanks to the black economy. Mafia states are a more sophisticated and 'advanced' form of governance than are mafias. Yet they belong to the same genus. The Wa leadership is trying to build a viable state, even though they do not allow free elections. They have created an elaborate administration, comprising fifteen ministries and seven local administrations. Although there is no Western-style rule of law, even family members and relatives of Wa leaders are arrested if they blatantly break the law. The Wa Army is a professional fighting force, run by a general staff. Granted, the 20,000 soldiers are paid only ten months per year and they have to harvest food for the remaining two months, but it should be kept in mind that this is one of the least developed parts of the world.

The dynamics between drug traders and officials are often based on personal relationships rather than standardised rules. Every businessman in the Wa territory 'donates' part of his profits to state projects, and part to a powerful figure in the army who acts as the businessman's protector.* Typically, a businessman from China asks permission to set up a drug-manufacturing factory and, if granted, troops provide the security. Heroin-related violence is extremely rare, precisely because the army ensures order in the market, as it does for other types of trade and production in the border area. However, it should be noted that the Wa state can be a brutal place, particularly for its ordinary inhabitants: recently, soldiers have killed innocent people 'simply because they inadvertently crossed paths with a heroin laboratory hidden in a remote area', writes Ko-lin Chin.

Even today, when drugs cultivation is nominally illegal, officers in the Burmese city of Muse, just across the border from Ruili, are very careful not to arrest the wrong person. As a drugs enforcement official said recently:

---

* In Chinese, *kaoshan.*

Border crossing between the cities of Ruili (China) and Muse (Myanmar). The author is seen on the left-hand side of the picture.

New recruits in the United Wa State Army.

Before we arrest someone for drug trafficking, we have to take into consideration who is *protecting* the drug dealer [emphasis added]. We know those in Muse who are involved in the drugs business, but we do not dare arrest them. We have to be extremely careful in the process.

The Wa commanders reinvest their profits into the legal economy of several countries. In fact, many of them recycle the proceeds from drugs in Ruili, where they have bought hotels and restaurants: one general, I am told, has recently made a large investment to build a golf course a few miles outside the city centre. He also apparently owns the hotel where I stayed.

A well-known protector of the drugs trade, and also a prominent businessman, is Wei Xuegang, a high-ranking officer in the Wa Army who is wanted by the US. Very few pictures of him exist. An ethnic Chinese born in 1946, he worked first for Taiwanese intelligence before moving to the Wa hills in 1992 with his two brothers. His commercial instincts and international connections were valuable for the Wa leaders and he was asked to join the Central Committee of the Wa party, before being put in charge of the southern region of the Wa state, where he established a number of refineries. From his base near the Thai–Burma border, he ensures that hundreds of millions of speed tablets enter the Thai market every year.

Wei is accused by the US government of having smuggled 600 kilos of heroin into the US in 1987. Thailand blames him for the speed epidemic of the 1990s, and, in 1994, he was sentenced to life imprisonment. In 1998, the US authorities announced a $2 million reward for his arrest. In January 2005, a US federal court in New York charged Wei (and seven other Wa leaders) with drug trafficking. In 2002 the Thai authorities froze assets held in Thailand belonging to Wei worth US$7.8 million.

With the proceeds from the drugs trade, Wei created a business group in 1998 with vast interests in construction, agriculture, jade extraction, minerals, oil, electronics and telecommunications, with branches in China and Burma, including one in the old capital Mandalay, which I visited. Wei has made large donations to support public works in the Wa state, giving millions of dollars to build schools and libraries. The head of the UN office in the Wa area, Jeremy Milsom, said in 2005 that 'Wei has done more to support impoverished poppy farmers break their dependence on the crop than any other single person or institution in Burma, and this has been done by putting drug profits back into the people, as he perhaps tries to move into the mainstream economy.' The Burmese authorities consider Wei an active drug lord in the methamphetamine trade, but they are wary of antagonising him for fear of reprisals from the Wa Army.

Mafias and states are similar beasts. They both impose governance on people. They claim control of a territory where individuals reside, and want to impose order. When mafias operate within a state's borders, they have negotiated a pact that allows them a degree of autonomy. Politicians 'share power' with the criminal organisation, as noted by Calderone. Mafiosi who strike this deal have concluded that this strategy offers greater prospects of success than does engaging in a frontal war with the state. One can take this logic to its extreme and conclude that mafias are forms of governance that have chosen to operate within existing state formations. Insurgencies have taken their struggle for autonomy a step further, and have developed more formal state-like structures than those we observe in mafias. An example would be the pseudo-states of northern Burma, but other insurgent groups – such as the Indonesian Free Aceh Movement and the National Liberation Army in Colombia – behave in the same way and impose their system of taxation on the population living in their territories. Until recently, the FARC (Revolutionary Armed Forces of Colombia) controlled an area of some 42,000 square kilometres. In this territory, it carried out regular censuses and established a specific 'tax' rate for each member of the community under its control, and it also protected coca plantations and laboratories. After the Calì and Medellin cartels were dismantled in the early 1990s, the FARC began to provide protection to smaller trafficking groups. There is evidence that the protection offered by the FARC was genuine and that a rudimentary judicial system was in place, including complaints offices hearing all types of cases. Reportedly, there was a degree of popular support for these tribunals. (As of 2016, the FARC demobilised and signed a peace agreement.)

Somali piracy is another hybrid. Anja Shortland and I have shown that in Somalia there is a fundamental difference between piracy and the protection of piracy. Extracting a significant profit from boarding a ship requires a secure land base. A complicit land-based state or Mafia would be very helpful. At sea, ships can be looted of their valuables, such as tools, crew possessions and petty cash. However, without access to a land-side infrastructure, pirates cannot unload the cargo or give a ship a new identity, so at best they are restricted to kidnapping crew members and stealing goods which can be transferred to their own (small) boats and for which there is a local market. The big money is in hijack for ransom, which allows pirates to extract an additional premium from the owner for the crew, cargo and ship. However, it also requires a great deal more organisation and infrastructure than on-the-spot extortion. Establishing a 'fair price' often takes several months, sometimes in excess of a year. A 2012 study shows that the highest ransoms are paid after four to eight months of negotiations. Pirates therefore need to keep the ships under their control for significant periods of time. Yet Somali pirate groups do not control the territory and do not have access to shipping lanes. Essentially, they are 'gangs of thieves', who rely on the services of local protectors for safe anchorage, safe passage and access to supply lines, and to enforce internal agreements and settle disputes.

Those who protect piracy in Somalia provide important local governance functions in a country where the central government does not project power in the regions. Clan elders and Islamist militias facilitate piracy by protecting hijacked ships in their anchorages and resolving conflicts within and between pirate groups. Pirates pay a fee to the 'protectors' and are no different from those criminals who pay protection money to a Mafia in order to ensure a degree of security from competitors, other criminals and from domestic and international police forces. As in the case of mafias, clans protect theft and appear to be a rudimentary state formation.

The 'anchorage fee' is in the region of US$100,000 to US$300,000 – payable at the moment of entry rather than at the conclusion of the ransom negotiation, according to analysts based in Somalia interviewed in 2012. This fee is normally funded by the investors, who also supply the capital for the attack crews. The provider of security is guaranteed an income regardless of the outcome of the negotiation. There also appear to be significant payments to regional authorities. The United Nations, in a 2010 report, documents extensive links between the Somali state of Puntland and various pirate groups, with one pirate leader claiming that 30 per cent of the final ransom was paid to the Puntland government. In exchange the government tolerates piracy, guarantees the free movement of known pirates in the main cities, and ministers intervene on behalf of pirates to ensure their release from local and foreign jails. Even diplomatic passports are available to well-connected pirates. Those who control coastal territory in Somalia extract substantial financial gain from protecting pirates.

Al-Shabaab is the Al-Qaeda affiliated jihadist militant group that controls southern Somalia. Although it is against Islamic law to profit from theft and ransom, our evidence suggests that Al-Shabaab is paid for tolerating the local clan's protection of piracy in Harardhere (it is also illegal for Western companies to pay ransoms that end in the coffers of terrorist organisations). Bloomberg maps of the trajectory of ships after hijack between 2010 and 2012 show that the vessels were stationed in the direct vicinity of Harardhere, an area controlled at the time by Al-Shabaab. Local sources indicate that an Al-Shabaab representative takes a cut of each ransom payment. A report in *Suna Times* (5 May 2011) specifically mentions a 'head of relationship with pirates' in the organisation's leadership, while Al-Shabaab leader Ahmed Godane has referred to pirates as the 'mujahedin of the sea' who were 'at war with non-Muslims', according to one of our interviewees. Pirates are asked to pay a 'community development fee' of 20 per cent of the final ransom, we are told.

Just as insurgent groups, terrorist groups and local clans behave as rudimentary states, so too do many of the so-called Latin American drug cartels. Increasingly, Mexican cartels operate as states within the state, having evolved into governance structures in many parts of the country. Some 85 per cent of legitimate businesses in the Mexican state of Michoacán were forced to pay the local cartel, La Familia (now disbanded). Estimated revenues from extortion in Mexico are between US$2 billion and US$7.5 billion. When the owner of the Casino Royale in Monterrey refused to pay protection money to the criminal syndicate Los Zetas in 2011, a commando killed fifty-two customers. Pharmacies, bars and funeral services, even medical practices and schools, are victims of Mafia extortion. The mayor of Ciudad Juárez describes the spread of extortion as a 'major concern'. Eduardo Guerrero-Gutiérrez has compiled a dataset containing 1,029 instances of violence collected from local and national newspapers in Mexico between December 2006 and March 2011. He uses the data to estimate the level and type of violence in the country. He finds that 'drug-trafficking-ridden' violence predominates along the American–Mexican border, while 'Mafia-ridden' violence is most common in central Mexico. Cartels are known to offer services of dispute resolution and cheap loans to businesses. In addition, they have developed a quasi-political message of resistance and struggle against injustice, often conveyed through songs extolling their actions (the *narcocorridos*). The Mexican gangs control a territory, have an ideology (and occasionally rituals of their own) and have taken on many functions of the state. These organisations are political entities standing in between traditional mafias and states.

Many observers argue for a fundamental distinction between mafias on the one hand, and insurgencies and states on the other. Curiously, and for completely different reasons, something similar has been articulated by elites and state agents who have consorted with mafias. Organised crime is often considered a lesser evil in the fight against ideological enemies, most notably against communism in the twentieth century. Secret services and centrist politicians have come to terms with mafias, on the understanding that they would ultimately support the established order rather than subvert it. More recently, American commentator Thomas Friedman has suggested that the American Cosa Nostra should be enlisted to fight Islamic extremists on US soil. As we've seen, some forms of organised crime can indeed morph into quasi-states and challenge legitimate institutions as much as ideological enemies do. It is a mistake to ignore their potential for statehood.

In some cases, the process is reversed: former insurgent groups turn into organised crime. The IRA and paramilitary groups have in the past functioned as agents of local governance, kneecapping drug dealers and joyriders and demanding payments to local communities. Many former paramilitaries continued to demand protection money from local communities even after the Good Friday Peace Agreement of 1998. Some police estimates suggest that they control as much as 80 per cent of the protection business. However, they are now categorised as 'organised crime'. A 2015 UN investigation has suggested that the Taliban leadership are 'increasingly acting more like "godfathers" rather than a "government in waiting"'. This underscores the profound similarities between groups that aspire to control territories, regardless of how they are labelled. Once you lose the ideological veneer, you become simply 'organised crime'. Most observers fail to understand that some organised crime groups are structurally akin to the state, in that they provide governance. A state might have within its territory effective alternative providers of protection in the shape of mafias, gangs, insurgents, private armies or clans – some with a relatively high degree of legitimacy.

But one should not take the similarities between states and mafias too far. Insurgent and terrorist groups, and powerful Mexican cartels, can be understood as lying on a continuum from Mafia to state, as long as they aspire to govern territories and markets. What distinguishes them is the set of mechanisms that makes those in charge accountable to the people: in a country based on the rule of law, citizens can appeal to an independent judiciary if the state breaks its own laws. Those who live in a democratic country can even elect their representatives. But mafias are wary of elections, even of bosses. They would never allow the people that live under their 'jurisdiction' to express their choice of ruler. This is why those who inhabit a Mafia territory or live in a Mafia state are not citizens but victims of a tyrannical power. As St Augustine once said, 'Without justice what are kingdoms but great bands of robbers?'

Hong Kong, 2015–2016: The end of the occupation; Yvonne returns to the classroom

Yvonne has now stepped down as president of the Hong Kong University Students Union. She has also refused any other leadership position. Is this an admission of failure? After all, the occupation ended in December 2014 with no concessions from China and no tangible political change in Hong Kong. There will be no universal suffrage for the election of the next Chief Executive of Hong Kong. The strategy of the Hong Kong government has succeeded: it let the students wear themselves out, until internal disputes and fatigue emerged. In addition, business associations such as taxi drivers and the minibus trade unions lodged civil injunctions against the occupation of public spaces. This soft strategy had an effect and on 18 December bailiffs started to clear part of the camp in Admiralty. Some students refused to leave, while the vast majority decamped voluntarily: the 79-day occupation was over.

I spoke to Yvonne again at the beginning of February 2017. She has now returned to the classroom. I asked her about the most recent developments. She was pleased that at the Legislative Council elections on 4 September 2016, three pro-democracy candidates were elected, including Nathan Law, one of Yvonne's friends: he obtained some 100,000 votes. Yet, since his election, there has been an attempt to disqualify him. 'This is a very serious act. We are facing a constitutional crisis in Hong Kong,' she tells me. 'The Umbrella Movement has not reached full democracy for Hong Kong, as we hoped. While I am not pessimistic about the future, I believe that there is still a lot left to do.' The point is not just to fight for a more competent Chief Executive, but also to have a fully democratic system. We talked, too, about her own future. Yvonne is in the fifth, and final, year of her law degree. After she graduates, she will still need to obtain an additional qualification in order to practise. 'I expect to be fully qualified in two or three years.' What kind of law would you like to practise? 'Public law or criminal law, I have not decided yet. But in any case I want to contribute to the struggle for democracy and human rights as a future lawyer. We need people to be protected against harassment. I now work closely with volunteer lawyers who act pro bono for activists who are incarcerated unjustly. This will be my contribution.'

8

DEATH

Via Michelangelo, 24 September 2005, 10.23 a.m.

Antonino Rotolo, the boss of the Pagliarelli Family in central Palermo, grooms his anointed successor, Gianni Nicchi, by transmitting to him his most valuable knowledge. Among other things, he teaches him how to kill.

Antonino: With whom are you planning to do this job?

Gianni: It is just two of us, we do not need anybody else.

Antonino: Will you take a gun each?

Gianni: Yes.

Antonino: Make sure you test the guns beforehand. Shoot always three times and do not get too close.

Gianni: Of course, I know. We have already talked about this.

Antonino: There is no need to make a lot of mess. One shot to knock down the guy and, when he is on the ground, aim for the head. Mind that when aiming at the head, he can spurt blood, so you have to move away …

Gianni: I will put on shoes that have nothing to do with the ones I wear normally, oilskin trousers with side buttons that are easy to take off, and a raincoat. I will keep my helmet on at all times, and I am all set!

Antonino: And the gloves?!

Gianni: I use latex gloves like the ones nurses wear.

Antonino: But have you tried to hold a gun in latex gloves?

Gianni: Yes, I have done everything, I checked if it slips, as you
had already explained to me.

Antonino: Then everything that you wear must be burnt …

The conversation continues with additional advice. 'Use chemical fertiliser to hide traces of gunpowder from your hands.' The plan is ready. Gianni is not just the shooter. He is in charge of the execution. The young man shows no remorse, no hesitation, no fear. This is what Antonino admires most in his pupil, who is mildly annoyed at the repeated advice of his over-protective Godfather.

After ordering the umpteenth murder of his career, the ageing boss reflects on his own trail of blood. 'I have done things,' he admits to one of his interlocutors. He expects the descendants of those who have been killed during the Mafia war of 1980–82 to seek revenge. 'They were children at the time, but they have now grown up, they are now thirty-something. If these people regain their authority, they cut our heads off.' The shadow of death hangs over Rotolo's conversations. It pushes life away and informs future strategies. I imagine him squeezed next to his interlocutor yet talking to himself, the sounds coming from the other houses, the vitality of children playing in neighbouring gardens, the sense of being sealed off. He is unfazed. This is his life.

Mafiosi need to be prepared to kill and need to be relatively good at it. The notion that there is a division of labour within mafias, whereby somebody can limit himself to a role that does not involve violence (such as accountancy) is bogus. Giovanni Brusca, a boss allied to Antonino Rotolo and later turned state witness, writes in his autobiography: 'The Mafia is made up of people who from the start have to kill, and have to know how to kill.' Any member can be asked to kill, and he cannot refuse. Mafiosi kill both outsiders and their own.

When they kill non-members – such as police officers, judges, journalists and activists – the Mafiosi follow their victim, study their routine and then act. The execution is in plain sight and the body is left on the pavement. Normally, Mafia killers do not act alone: a team is hiding in the background, ready to intervene if necessary. Usually they wait in a car nearby, with their guns easily visible, the thinking being that the display of firepower will make the police reluctant to intervene. According to a Cosa Nostra killer, the most reliable gun is a .38-calibre revolver. Automatic pistols jam more easily, causing distraction, whereas a revolver with a drum does not jam or miss a shot. But the more protected the victim, the more likely it is that the Mafia will resort to extreme means, including bazooka, flame-thrower rifles, and explosives. Typically, this is how security-conscious prosecutors are killed.

Mafiosi also kill those of their own who have fallen out of favour, are caught in a power struggle or have breached the organisation's rules. Revenge is a powerful motive. Relatives might be killed in order to blackmail members, or because, it's believed, they know too much. Mafiosi also kill in the paranoid expectation that they will be murdered themselves. When they kill their own, they normally set a trap.* The murderer will know his target well. As a friend and long-time partner in crime, his victim will agree to meet, take a drive with him or even welcome him into his house. Occasionally the Mafioso senses that he is going to his death. Roy DeMeo, the leader of a murderous crew attached to the Gambino Family, suspected that he was being set up when he agreed to attend a certain meeting. He told his son: 'This is the life I chose, and this is just part of that life. I can't be a rat, and if I stay, they'll ruin all your lives.' While he had planned to fake his own death and escape to the Bahamas, he understood that doing so would put his wife and children in mortal danger. The Family would come after them in order to find him. He knew this because this is what he had done himself in the past. When his son opened a drawer in Roy's desk a week after his disappearance, he found, neatly lined up in a row,

---

* Clearly, there are exceptions. Especially during a 'war', mobsters would be cautious about accepting a rendezvous in a secluded place, so they are more likely to be murdered in plain sight: Salvatore Inzerillo was killed in a flurry of Kalashnikov bullets in 1981, during the second Mafia 'war', as he stepped into his armoured car.

Roy's diamond watch, his wallet, his wedding ring and his gun. He also saw a small Catholic Church brochure from the local parish. Roy had gone to confession.

Once the victim is lured into the trap, the Mafia prefers methods that are not too noisy or messy. Sicilian boss Giovanni Brusca – reputed to have killed between 100 and 200 people – describes in great detail how he used a thin nylon rope: 'Two of us are holding the poor soul by the arms, two by the feet and one, behind, pulls the rope … after some ten minutes, death arrives. How do you know that? Because tissues start to relax, and the person pees and shits in his pants …' Torture is added in the elaborate system of goat-tying.* With the victim facing down, the killers loop a rope around his neck and feet, which are pulled up behind his back, like goats when they are slaughtered before Easter. When the muscles of the legs stretch, the rope tightens around the neck, causing a slow death by self-strangulation. Yet, claim many Mafiosi, the torture is unintended. This is simply the most effective way to transport the victim in the boot of a car.

The next step is to dispose of the body. The best way is to dissolve it in acid but the killers have to be confident that the person is definitely dead. If the victim is still moving while immersed in acid, the splashes could hit those standing around. The substance is the same as that employed to purify silver, and to refine heroin. For a while, it was easily available in Sicily until the authorities realised what it was used for and imposed restrictions on sale (although it is still possible to buy it from construction workers, who use it to clean bricks). It is also stockpiled when available and stored for future use. It takes a lot of acid and some time to dissolve a body: at least fifty litres over a three-hour period. Occasionally, a gas burner flame is also enlisted, to increase the heat and speed up the process. The body dissolves slowly, eventually leaving only the teeth, while everything else, including the skull, becomes deformed. The pelvis keeps its shape the longest. After a good three hours, virtually nothing is left, and the remains are picked up and thrown in a field or in a river. In 2002, Nicola Mandalà, the boss who appears in several chapters

---

* In Italian, *incaprettare*.

of this book, was seen transporting the body of a local businessman to a marble quarry on the outskirts of Palermo. There he personally saw that the body was dissolved in acid. The victim had become a nuisance. As testified by his accomplices, 'the man was putting up an air of importance and was a pain in the ass.' He had to disappear. Without leaving a trace.*

It takes some technical expertise to use acid. This rather advanced method was favoured first by the more educated Palermo Families, such as the Inzerillo. Up to the early 1980s, Families from the countryside just burned the bodies on specially made grills – a more primitive and time-consuming process. One has to start early in the morning and it takes until the following dawn to fully dispose of just one body. During those hours, one needs to keep the fire burning, so piles of logs must be used. Others use gasoline. Lea Garofalo, the 35-year-old daughter of a murdered boss, decided to break away from the Calabrese Mafia and to testify against her own partner in 2002, yet her information was not sufficient to secure a conviction. A few years passed and she decided to exit the witness protection programme. When in 2009 her ex-partner suggested meeting in Milan to discuss the future of their daughter, she agreed, hoping that the presence of their daughter would prevent the man from harming her. She was wrong: on 24 November 2009, Lea was picked up by four people in Milan, thrown in a van and delivered to her killers. In a remote location on the outskirts of the city, she was interrogated, beaten up and then shot. To dispose of the body the gang used gasoline. It took three days for the body to burn. In the end all that was left of Lea was a pile of 2,800 bone fragments weighing one kilo and 300 grams, which was found by the police together with a necklace and a braided bracelet in yellow and white gold. This murder shocked Italy and led to a high-profile court case in Milan in which Lea's daughter was called to testify and pointed the finger at her father, who was convicted of Lea's murder.

The least advisable method of disposing of a body is simply to bury it in the ground: as the number of Mafiosi turned state

---

* In Italian, the process of destroying a body is the so-called *lupara bianca* (white shotgun).

informants in Sicily increased dramatically from the 1980s, they could direct police to where bodies were buried, lending additional credence to their testimony. Yet occasionally a crew has no access to acid or a grill. In those instances, it is advisable to dig as deep as possible, up to fifteen metres, ideally using a powerful digger.

Italian mafias have also used dismemberment. In the early years of Italian organised crime in Chicago, bodies were just dumped in a clay hole or rock quarry. Later in the twentieth century, policing of organised crime in the US became more effective and mobsters had to devise smarter ways to evade probing investigations. In New York City, the crew led by Roy DeMeo lured their target to the apartment on the top floor of their headquarters, at the Gemini clubhouse. Once there, the victim was shot in the head with a silenced pistol, and immediately the wound was wrapped in a towel to halt the blood flow. Another member of the crew stabbed the target in the heart. 'That stops it from pumping blood,' Roy DeMeo explained to a new member of the team. The scene must have been surreal: the killers were in their underwear because they did not want the blood to spill on their clothes. With the man dead for sure, the body was stripped and put into a bathtub. It took some forty to forty-five minutes for the blood to congeal. So they waited. They had a drink or got a pizza. Dismemberment was the next step: the body was placed on plastic sheets and cut up. The parts were then put into garbage bags, placed in cardboard boxes and sent to the Fountain Avenue dump in Brooklyn, where tons of garbage were dropped each day.

Murders can be used to send a message. This is a high-risk strategy as it may allow law enforcement to get hold of vital clues, including the body, and open a murder investigation. Yet occasionally the message is crucial and might result in scaring others into submission. Of course, messages have to be decoded and understood properly (recall the old joke: 'What does a post-modern Mafioso do? He makes you an offer you cannot understand'). On a cold morning in January 1982, a state police officer found the body of a Sicilian man in the boot of a Cadillac in the car park of the Hilton Hotel, Mount Laurel, New Jersey. The body, with head thrown back, was wrapped in a plastic bag, and the officer could see that a bullet had gone through the skull. He was also faced with a peculiar spectacle: a wad of cash was wedged into the man's mouth. More dollars were found with his genitalia, which had been cut off. The message was: the victim is 'half a man' who has 'eyes bigger than his stomach'. He and his allies 'wanted to eat too much, leaving only crumbs for the other Families. Now they can choke on their money.' Stuffing somebody's mouth with dollars – or pressing a nickel into his hand – is a relatively easy message to decode, and it has the same meaning regardless of the victim. When a body is found goat-tied, the inference is that it is a Mafia murder, regardless of the victim. Over time, other signature methods have emerged and then faded out of fashion. Sicilian gangs in Brooklyn, for example, used to disfigure an enemy, particularly an informer, by slitting his face from eye to ear. Nowadays, nobody would recognise that method as typical of Cosa Nostra. In other cases, the message is specific to the person or context, as when an informant is killed and dumped in front of the FBI headquarters or in the territory of the Family he has been informing on.

Sometimes certain imagery is imposed by an outsider and becomes an authentic sign of a mob murder. In the 1960s, a Sicilian photographer who specialised in taking pictures of Mafia murders used to carry with him prickly pear leaves* typical of the Sicilian countryside, a Cosa Nostra hotbed. Whenever he was called to take a picture of a murder, he placed the leaves next to the body, suggesting a Mafia hit. Newspapers would not buy the pictures unless they had this signature. In due course, such symbolism became associated with organised crime murders in Sicily. Naturally, no one has a monopoly over symbols, or effective ways to monitor how they are used. Those who want to confuse the police may try to pass off an ordinary murder (or a killing undertaken by non-Mafia gangs) as a Mafia hit by goat-tying the victim or slashing his face 'Mafia-style'. The novels by Andrea Camilleri, set in Sicily and featuring the world-famous Inspector Montalbano, are replete with instances where respectable people or low-level criminals try to muddy the

---

* In Italian, *Pala di fico d'india*.

water by exploiting symbolism traditionally associated with Cosa Nostra.

Murder methods in other mafias

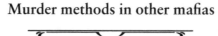

Other mafias also have their signature methods of torture and murder. In the 1990s in Perm I was invited to the house of a businessman who had borrowed money from a loan shark. His plans had foundered, he told me, and he could not pay it back in time. The Mafia group sprang into action and kidnapped him. He was chained to a radiator for a week, and repeatedly tortured. The gang used a hot iron to mark his torso and stomach, and inserted a hot stick into his rectum. In other cases, he told me, the gang used a hair-dryer. In capable hands, this everyday appliance can burn the lungs if inserted in the mouth, and can be used to brand the face. While the businessman was imprisoned, a member of the gang moved into his flat, harassing his wife and creating a menacing presence for their young daughter. When I met him, this hapless businessman was cowed and unresponsive: he had sold his house to pay the debt and lived with his family in a single room on the periphery of town. He could hardly look me in the eyes. Those who knew him said that he was a shadow of his former self. His wife awkwardly offered me tea, as their daughter played around us. A degree of normality had returned to their life. At first, I was not quite sure why he was telling me his story, then I understood: the group wanted people to know what happens to those who do not pay. In the depth of Russia, the local Mafia was sending a message, and I was part of the audience: do not mess with us or else. Curiously, members of the same group had offered to lend me money and I had promptly refused.

The Russians had developed peculiar ways to dispose of the bodies. Like other gangs, they would chop up a body and scatter the remains in a field or a forest, where it was unlikely that the police would find them. Yuri I. Pigolkin, Chair of the Forensic Medicine Department at I. M. Sechenov First Moscow State Medical University, recently recalled the system of 'double burial' used in the

1990s. 'Killers removed a coffin and dug further down. They placed the new body [in the ground] and covered it with the old coffin.' In the 1990s, gangsters went to the trouble of hiding bodies in only 30 to 35 per cent of cases, but today that figure is up to 85 per cent, and law enforcement agencies struggle to find evidence. Pigolkin mentions another change: criminals are now trying to get rid of witnesses, including children. This was not the case before. As law enforcement in Russia becomes more effective, we expect to observe more elaborate and sustained efforts to hide evidence.

The knife is the weapon of choice of the Hong Kong Triads. In 2010, a high-ranking member of the Harmoniously United Society Triad made a call. He ordered the murder of a dealer at Macau Sands Casino. The dealer had been helping a patron win HK$100 million from a high-stake VIP room. The plan was to chop off his arms and legs with meat knives before killing him and dismembering his body. The gambler would face the same end. Previously, members of this gang had been convicted for decapitating a victim with knives. 'Watching a person's head being chopped off is so exciting,' said a young Triad to an undercover cop. Acting on a tip-off from one of the would-be murderers, officers of the Hong Kong police raided the gang's hideout, where they found guns, steak knives, a Japanese dagger, balaclavas, handcuffs, and a notebook with details of gambling debts. A comprehensive study of Triad-related homicides in Hong Kong over a ten-year period (1989–98) found that firearms were used in only 11.5 per cent of instances. Chop knives, melon knives and beef knives were the favoured weapons in the majority of cases, the author reports. A police expert suggests that the use of knives is a cultural preference – knives are also used, for example, to sever the head of a chicken during the Triad ritual. However, there might be a more mundane reason: possession of guns is tightly controlled in Hong Kong. Those found in possession of a firearm without a licence can face a prison sentence of up to fourteen years, even if the gun is not used. Necessity might be at work here, rather than culture. Mafias adapt.

While Triads use knives, Japanese Yakuza use swords. In 2016 a 41-year-old executive of a Mafia gang tried to kill a rival. The weapon used was a seventy-centimetre-long samurai sword. Since medieval times, the Japanese nobility and its warrior class, the samurai, have venerated swords, and they despised guns when they appeared in the nineteenth century. Yakuza claim to be descended from the samurai and to have embraced the warrior's sense of duty and honour, including the cult of the sword. (The real origin of the Yakuza is more likely to be in the gamblers who loitered around open markets in the late nineteenth century.) In mainstream Yakuza movies, the Yakuza abide by the code of honour and dispatch enemies to their death using a sword, never a gun. As with the Triads, cultural and historical explanations are invoked to account for this. But again, a more practical interpretation may be in order. Until the 1980s, jail time for a fatal shooting was between twelve and fifteen years. Under the 1995 Firearms Law, anyone found in possession of a gun and matching bullets can be charged with aggravated possession of firearms, with an average prison sentence of seven years. If the gun is fired, the perpetrator can receive a jail term of up to life imprisonment or even the death sentence, regardless of whether anyone is injured or killed. In addition, a 2004 ruling by the Supreme Court established that bosses are liable for criminal acts committed by their men, such as violations of firearms laws. A Yamaguchi Godfather went to prison for six years after one of his bodyguards was found to be carrying an illegal firearm. Not surprisingly, guns have since been banned by many bosses. A low-level Yakuza interviewed by *Japan Times* in 2013 said: 'Having a gun now is like having a time bomb. Do you think any sane person wants to keep one around the house?' Indeed, shootings by Yakuza gangsters have declined sharply in the twenty-first century, to seventeen in 2010, down by five from the previous year. In 2000, there were more than 200 incidents recorded.

The death of the Mafia

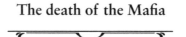

Italian prosecutor Giovanni Falcone said that mafias are a human phenomenon: they emerge, evolve and eventually die. How can we prevent the emergence of a Mafia or accelerate its end? To find an answer we can run through the journey taken in *Mafia Life*. When I arrived in Russia in the late 1980s, the country was engulfed in a chaotic transition to the market economy. State planning had ended and capitalism had arrived, almost overnight. The Soviet state was not capable of dealing with this massive transformation. Many people in a position of power were stealing state assets and it was not clear who was legally entitled to challenge them. At the time, I met a manager at a research institute. He had manoeuvred himself into position as the recognised owner of an instrument used to conduct space research, which he then quickly sold to a foreign country. He pocketed $200 million and has lived off that money ever since: he is a small-time oligarch. The state at this time was not equipped to defend the common property of the people. When disputes arose among property owners or if somebody wanted to challenge crooks, courts were not much use. Even if a court passed judgement on a firm, when the bailiff reached its premises the office would be as empty as the company's bank account. Officials lacked legitimacy and so people looked for alternative sources of protection. Those who were in a position of power within the state system used their influence to enrich themselves and their friends. Those who had no friends in power and wanted to do business had to deal with gangsters. Members of the fraternity of the *vory*, former Red Army soldiers, Afghan veterans, unemployed sportsmen – all were ready to organise rackets and put themselves up as alternative sources of power. Western advice was focused on privatising the economy as quickly as possible, instead of helping to strengthen the institutions that make a market economy work, such as clear laws and an effective and impartial court system. The downsizing of the Soviet state had a further negative effect: people skilled in violence were suddenly unemployed and ready to be hired by organised crime. At the time of such transitions, great care should be taken to ensure that people trained in violence are not unemployed and state institutions are not weakened.

The story of Russia in the 1990s mirrors that of other places where mafias grew out of a similar set of circumstances. Italian sociologist Diego Gambetta has shown that the Sicilian Mafia emerged during the flawed transition to a market economy in the nineteenth century. The Italian state was not a credible and effective enforcer of justice and law in Sicily, and individuals trained in the use of violence found themselves suddenly unemployed: field guards formerly working for the landowning barons, disbanded soldiers who had served the defeated King of Naples, and the occasional thug always ready to pick a fight. Similarly, the Yakuza emerged in Japan when the country changed from an agrarian, feudal society to a modern, industrialised economy in the Meiji period (1868–1912). For the first time, Japan was a unified country, rather than a loose collection of autonomous fiefdoms. Overnight feudalism was abolished, property ownership (mainly in land) spread and the government enacted Western-style legal reforms – including land reform (1873–6), a written constitution (1889), and a French-style civil code (1898). Because of the spread of ownership, disputes increased, both between individuals and the state (mainly over the levels of taxation) and between individual owners. The state, however, was not equipped to provide new property owners with ways to settle their disputes efficiently. At the same time, the end of feudalism led to a crisis for the large and economically useless warrior class, the samurai, who had been in the service of feudal lords. While some samurai turned to thieving and rebellion, others began selling protection services to villages and market towns. People trained in violence but outside the scope of the state started to act as providers of order, giving rise to the modern Yakuza.

Russian gangsters, Sicilian Mafiosi, Yakuza: they all emerged in societies undergoing a sudden and late transition to the market economy but lacking a legal infrastructure that reliably protected property rights and settled business disputes. The best way to prevent the birth of such groups is to ensure that capitalism is properly regulated and managed by an effective state, which is capable of legitimate (and ultimate) governance.

Sometimes, mafias emerge when a large and illegal market is created. Italian Mafiosi arrived in New York City from the very end of the nineteenth century. Some were escaping prosecution in Italy, while others were in search of a better life. At first, these criminals engaged in petty crime and crude extortion, such as sending letters to fellow immigrants demanding money (this is the so-called *La mano nera*). When, in 1920, the authorities banned alcohol consumption and manufacturing, a vast illegal market was created. Mafiosi stepped in to protect truckloads entering the city from the New Jersey coastline ('Rum Row') and large stills in upstate New York. They were also instrumental in the creation of spaces where suppliers could meet distributors and prices could be set. The Italian Mafiosi were independent of both suppliers and distributors, offering their services to both. During and after Prohibition, the Italians were active also in managing prostitution and gambling. The transition to a capitalist economy was not what gave rise to the Italian-American Mafia; rather it was the existence of a demand for some illegal goods. And yet there is a profound similarity in both scenarios: in the 1920s, the state gave up protecting a large market, and buyers and sellers turned to other sources of order, namely gangsters. Governments should be careful when they outlaw a commodity that is in high demand, such as alcohol or drugs. (I myself am strongly in favour of legalising marijuana, and draining revenues from organised crime.)

Mafias aspire to look legitimate. They portray themselves as moral institutions. The induction ritual (described in chapter 1) is meant to convey the message that mafias are honourable fraternities, devoted to the well-being of their members. They borrow imagery and wording from established religions, such as the Catholic Church, the Russian Orthodox Church, Shintoism and Buddhism. Religious leaders should take a firm stand against this association. Antonino Rotolo was particularly bruised by John Paul II's condemnation of the Mafia in Sicily. And while John Paul's successors, Pope Benedict XVI and Pope Francis, have continued to distance the Catholic Church from the Italian mafias, some lower-level clergy continue to permit religious processions to be sponsored by known Mafiosi, even allowing processions to stop in front of their houses as a sign of respect.

Effective state repression can go a long way towards bringing about the death of mafias. As discussed in chapter 2, bosses in Sicily are today mostly in jail or under house arrest, their phones constantly monitored, their assets confiscated. It is impossible for a gangster to govern a territory, to collect the 'neighbourhood tax', if he cannot walk freely in the streets. The Sicilian Mafia appears to be under more police pressure than the Salford gangs have ever been. Arguably, effective policing increases internal disputes, and the willingness of victims to report crimes. As it becomes harder to operate, the Mafia will be less effective in providing genuine protection to entrepreneurs, who will start to think that they are paying for nothing, become less scared, and be more willing to report Mafia harassment to the authorities. When the hierarchy is no longer able to pay the salaries that will fund their members' lifestyles, disputes within the organisation will rise. Recall the story of the Mafioso who was forced to return a car when his Family stopped paying the monthly fee. He is now under investigation for allegedly organising the murder of the boss's brother.

An effective fight against organised crime involves not just crude repression but the formulation of appropriate incentives for members (and victims) to come forward. In both Italy and the US, Mafiosi who collaborate with authorities can reduce their sentences significantly. Such 'prizes' are controversial and end up rewarding cold-blooded killers. For instance, Sammy 'the Bull' Gravano reduced his life sentence to five years for testifying against John Gotti and the Gambino Family. After serving his time, Gravano went on to commit other crimes. Yet without incentives for members to defect, the fight is much harder. The testimonies of state witnesses have to be confirmed by additional evidence, but they are invaluable.

Several unintended structural changes in the world economy have weakened the mafias. In Sicily, the effects of the 2008 economic crisis have been particularly severe and have reduced the organisation's revenues. More generally, technological innovations that lessen the need of some businesses to be located in a physical territory have undermined mafias. Corner shops are most vulnerable to extortion. As we increasingly obtain films online, the old video and DVD stores have disappeared, and so a potential victim is gone. Yet such changes might have other consequences, such as reducing city centres to wasteland and fostering the rise of large conglomerates. Globalisation might increase crime more generally, while reducing the ability of the Mafia to control it. For instance, innovation in the transportation and selling of illegal products makes it harder for the

Mafia to monitor sellers and buyers but might lead to an increase in the overall supply of illegal goods. Although it is still a small section of the market, it is now possible to buy drugs online and get them delivered by mail to the doorstep. Broad social changes have seen the arrival in Sicily of migrants from Africa and Asia, a phenomenon that has increased diversity and challenged the status quo. Some have become tough competitors of Cosa Nostra in illegal markets, while others have withstood criminal harassment and refused to pay extortion. In both instances, they have made the life of the organisation harder.

Sustained police investigations and arrests have made it particularly difficult for mafias to coordinate *across* Families and to devise common strategies to deal with the outside world, especially politicians (chapter 3). It took a long time for Merab to organise a Gathering, in great part because he had to change venue, from Calabria to Rome and eventually to Dubai. Every time, he was chased by the police. The Commission in the US has not met for twenty-five years, while the Commission in Sicily operated fully for only a few years.

Mafiosi need to hide their money, and they rely on the providers of financial services to do so (chapter 4). And when it comes to hiding capital, complicit bankers are key players. Untraceable and anonymous shell companies are illegal and help crooks of all kinds to hide assets. International standards require certified IDs when creating a shell company. But, as documented by the 2014 study *Global Shell Games*, it takes only a few hours to create anonymous shell companies without offering any proof of identity, and indeed it is easier to do so in OECD countries, including the US, than in tax havens. Yet Mafiosi find it hard to trust providers of complex financial services: if money goes missing they never know whether they are being cheated or not. Sustained police scrutiny of service providers like *Dima* is a sure way to fight money laundering.

Love can have a devastating effect on mafias (chapter 5). The bond that some women create with their Mafia partners erodes the integrity of the organisation. In some cases, as we've seen, women may step into the shoes of their men in order to manage Mafia Families or businesses, invariably because they are trusted more than fellow Mafiosi. Those same bonds can lead to the formation of family firms, which are difficult to break up, since the loyalty that binds them is harder to dent than that among people who have taken an oath of allegiance to a criminal fraternity. Not surprisingly, there are more defectors to the authorities among Sicilian Mafiosi than among members of the Calabrese`Ndrangheta, a criminal organisation largely based on blood ties.

Mafias are very sensitive about their public image (chapter 6). When they have taken control of their own cinematic representation, they have often failed to impress. The best publicity is indirect, as in *The Godfather* movies. Indeed, positive representations of the Mafia abound, starting with the first gangster movie ever produced, *The Musketeers of Pig Alley* (1912), a seventeen-minute film directed by D. W. Griffith. Most films have continued to depict Mafiosi either as people with a respectable moral code, or as bloodthirsty evildoers. Both representations end up enhancing their reputation. Jūzō Itami chose instead to portray the Yakuza as low-rent buffoons with an uncertain sexual identity. The mobsters were furious, and it is rumoured that they were responsible for the director's death. In Italy, the movies by Palermo-based directors Ciprì and Maresco, such as *Lo zio di Brooklyn* (1995) and *Totò che visse due volte* (1998), have portrayed Mafiosi as unpleasant dwarfs and perverts, constantly farting, in a style that borrows from the radical poetics of Pier Paolo Pasolini, Carmelo Bene and Luis Buñuel. They use parody and farce to describe the world around Cosa Nostra (see, for example, their film on producer Enzo Castagna, *Enzo, domani a Palermo!*, and the one on Giorgio Castellani, *Vite Perdute*). Ciprì and Maresco put the stench that comes from Cosa Nostra up on screen, and the hypocrisy of those in Palermo who accommodate it. Works of art that demystify the Mafia help to undermine it.

Mafias have thrived in electoral democracies (chapter 7). They help politicians obtain votes and, in return, carve out spaces of autonomy and secure favours. Not all electoral systems are equally vulnerable to organised crime, however. Systems that allow a candidate to be elected on a list with a few preference votes through proportional representation (PR) are more vulnerable to Mafia penetration than systems based on large constituencies and a single winner (first-past-the-post). It is difficult for a Family to control thousands of votes and their influence can be negligible in large constituencies. After all, Massey was not elected in Salford when he ran for mayor. On the contrary, in small towns in Italy a handful of (preference) votes for a candidate can secure election to the city council. A second lesson to be learnt from chapter 7 is the interest that mafias have in devolution. The Sicilian Mafia backed away from supporting Sicilian independence after the Italian government (through the Christian Democratic Party) assured significant devolution of power to Sicily. The budget of the regional government of Sicily was large and easily influenced by criminals in Palermo. It would have been much harder to influence Rome. Yet once Cosa Nostra was able to sponsor its candidates to the National Assembly, it had a role in decisions taken at the national level. Such a role was possible only because they were powerful in a most significant and rich region of Italy. The more that decisions are devolved to a local level, the higher the risk of corrupt practices, the potential for inadequate oversight, and, ultimately, the likelihood for alternative sources of governance to take root. This is a vulnerability that should be considered – and addressed – when setting up mechanisms to devolve powers from central to local authorities. See, for instance, the recent decision by the UK government to devolve the NHS budget to the local authority of Manchester. Such a decision might be welcome for several reasons. However, it also increases the opportunities for corrupt exchanges at the local level, something that has been ignored by the public debate on this issue (Transparency International published a report in October 2013 warning of the 'mounting risks' of corruption in local government in the UK). Localised governance entails risks that are generally ignored.

Three strategies are crucial in order to defeat a Mafia in a democratic state. First, legitimate institutions of authority must dispense justice quickly and fairly. They must be superior to criminal 'justice'. If citizens do not trust officials, the fight against organised crime will never succeed, something that is just as true in Salford as it is in Palermo. The organisations I have discussed in this book are at their best and most pernicious when they are able to settle disputes among business people who cannot wait eight years for a decision (the Italian average). Since helping business people to reduce competition is a criminal activity of mafias, strong anti-trust and competition laws can help push mobsters out of the legal economy.

The second ingredient is social integration and opportunities for all. The *vory* are disproportionately non-Russians, while ethnic Koreans and members of the *burakumin* minority make up the vast majority of the Yakuza. As social integration grows and racial discrimination is reduced, the Mafia will find recruiting members in multi-ethnic societies more difficult. Indeed, the Italian-American Cosa Nostra is short of Italians, who are no longer discriminated against in the legitimate job market. Racism pushes people into the hands of organised crime. As political leaders target particular groups, such as Muslim citizens in the US or Europe, the ranks of organised criminality increase. Recent studies have shown that law-breakers can then move from crime to terrorism.

Finally, the fight against evil must have heroes – those who have the courage to lead from the front. They remind us that Mafiosi are merely human, and liable to be scared when confronted by determined citizens. The following example illustrates better than any other the power of ordinary people.

Giuseppe Impastato was a young left-wing activist in the small town of Cinisi, Sicily, in the 1970s. Every day, through a local radio station, he exposed the illicit activities of the local boss and his political allies, often by way of irony and parody. Eventually his voice grew too powerful and he was killed by the Mafia in 1978. On the day of the funeral, his mother, Felicia, was at home with relatives, waiting for the procession to reach them so that they could lead the coffin to the cemetery. At the time, Impastato was ostracised in the town and it was far from certain that anyone would show up for the funeral. Among Felicia's kin was a man known as Sputafuoco (his real name was Impastato). Like several other relatives on her husband's side, Sputafuoco was a member of Cosa Nostra. In an interview recorded in 1984, Felicia told two academics what happened next:

As the funeral was about to take place, so many of Giuseppe's comrades were due to join the procession. [Sputafuoco] was sitting alone, with his back to the wall. At one point, my niece Maria rushed into the room and said: 'Felicia, come here, have a look, there is a sea of people, and more are coming.' At that point, the face [of Sputafuoco] turned white, like that of a cadaver, and he said: 'It might well be that now somebody smashes a chair on my head.' He was scared to death and asked for a glass of water.

Civil society terrifies the Mafia.

The Impastato funeral offers a glimpse of how far a community has to travel to stand up against organised crime. It recalls the rather different response to the death of Paul Massey in Salford in 2015. Although Massey was a violent criminal who once left a man for dead after stabbing him outside a nightclub, hundreds turned up to pay their respects on the day of his funeral. He had been murdered a few days before, so it was not surprising that armed police were on standby to ensure that no further violence took place. Mourners quietly lined the streets as a pipe band led his carriage, pulled by four white horses, followed by eight black limousines. He was a 'legend', said the words in the floral tribute attached to the carriage. The horses were wearing the flags of Manchester United, Massey's beloved local football club. A pub near St Paul the Apostle Church had home-made banners on display, bearing the words 'RIP, Respect'. One sheet had been spray-painted in huge red letters reading, 'Simply The Best P.M'. Many mourners wore white shirts and jeans, as requested by the boss's family, and had arrived in a variety of cars, including a chauffeur-driven black Rolls-Royce. This scene could be straight out of *The Godfather* but happened in a very English town. The cortege left the Ordsall area of Salford, where Massey was born and had made his name, and travelled the short distance to St Paul's for the service. Hundreds of people had gathered at the entrance and applauded when the coffin was lowered from the carriage.

9

POST-MORTEM

In November 2016, I decided to travel back to Russia. I had not been back since 1998, almost twenty years. Flying at night over Moscow offers an impressive view. The city lights were glowing, as I had never seen before. As you approach, you can make out the Kremlin in the distance. Domodedovo is as glitzy as any Western airport, and a very efficient train takes you to the centre of town. When I walked out of my hotel on Tverskaya the next day, a crowd marching towards the Kremlin swept me away. I joined in. This was a very different street demonstration from those I had witnessed in the past, like the crowd that protested against the August 1991 coup and welcomed the restoration of democracy. This orderly sea of people, on 4 November 2016, was celebrating Unity Day, a holiday created by Putin in 2005 to commemorate the 1612 uprising against the Polish occupation. The marchers were well dressed, civilised and enthusiastic. The man next to me holding a flag of St George chanted, 'Unity! Motherland! Freedom! Putin!' For a moment I felt part of a popular, street-level plebiscite for the new Russia. We ended up not far from the Kremlin, where the president unveiled a new, giant monument of Prince Vladimir, the Christian ruler of the proto-Russian state. The crowd stopped a few hundred metres away from the statue, and we were offered a concert. Some 80,000 people took part.

Despite my enthusiasm, I did not feel brave enough to listen to state-sponsored pop music. I left the crowd and headed for a cemetery. I was in search of those grand mobsters' graves that supposedly litter Moscow cemeteries. Since I left Russia, journalists have made a great deal of these graves, reading them as a symbol of the Mafia takeover of the sacred. I headed off to the prestigious Vagan'kovskoye cemetery in northern Moscow, only a few metro stops from my hotel. I had discovered that there is a hierarchy among Moscow's cemeteries. Red Square and the Kremlin wall are the top spots: this is where the heroes of the revolution and many party leaders have been buried. Second on the list is the Novodevichy cemetery, behind the monastery of the same name, where you can find the graves of Raisa Gorbacheva, Boris Yeltsin and Anton Chekov. Vagan'kovskoye is third in the pecking order. Still, it is a highly sought-after burial place for the Moscow elite. Just outside the church is the grand monument of Viktor V. Tikhonov, the coach of Russia's national ice-hockey team.

As cemeteries are a maze, I arranged to join a tour. I thought that, if I were lucky, the guide would direct me to the burial place of Vyacheslav K. Ivan'kov, a notorious mobster who had served time in the US and tried to mediate between Grandpa Khazan and Merab's clan, but ultimately appeared to have taken one side and was killed by the other in 2009. Sure enough, the guide eventually took us to his grave: plot 26. He is buried next to his mother. The monument is fairly grand, but by no means grander than others we had seen of admirals, fighter-jet pilots, and an assorted cast of artists and singers. He sits with hands in his pockets, looking as old as his mother, his shirt open, and with a barely visible golden chain against his chest. The black slab behind him has two scenes. One depicts the Mother of God with a baby Jesus, a traditional Orthodox icon that signals the deceased's faith – Ivan'kov was known to be deeply religious and was a collector of antique icons. As I brush the snow away, I see another image, one of prison iron bars opening onto an empty black landscape. The effect is both impressive and sobering. The sculptor is the renowned artist Alexander Rukavishnikov, who has created several statues around Russia honouring political leaders, artists and writers. Ivan'kov's grave is remarkably similar to the Soviet-era graves of people of importance. Indeed,

The grave of Vyacheslav Kirillovich Ivan'kov in the
Vagan'kovskoye cemetery, Moscow. The author of the monument
is the renowned sculptor Alexander Rukavishnikov.

it is quite measured and restrained compared to some I have seen.
Many sculptures have the deceased sitting or standing next to the
objects of their trade, a tank, an aeroplane, a musical instrument.
For Ivan'kov, it is prison.*

As I lunch and dine my way through a city I no longer recognise, I meet a range of people: diplomats, expats, business people,
minor oligarchs and government officials. Invariably, they tell me
that politics trumps economics. While Russia is not a Western-style
democracy, it is a functioning state, one to be reckoned with, they

---

* Curiously, Ivan'kov's name on the grave is misspelt, missing the apostrophe
(it should be *Ivan'kov*).

say. The bureaucracy works relatively well, taxes are low and people appear to be polite: I notice how, in the underground, they hold the heavy doors open for you now. Western advisors and greedy oligarchs manipulating an often drunk president are a feature of the past. But something does seem unchanged: business people still have a protector, yet he (or she) is invariably an official, a person of authority who can obtain contracts, navigate the system and even get their children into university. This might be a corrupt society, but the Mafia is kept in check, confined to illegal markets such as prostitution and drugs trafficking. Street rackets are long gone. When I suggest to a diplomat that Mafiosi might be used as thugs to carry out the dirty work of state agencies, he retorts: 'Not even that. Warlords are there for these kinds of jobs.' As in Hong Kong, the authoritarian regime has made the life of mafias very difficult.

Most conversations in Moscow end as follows: 'Just do not get involved in politics and life in Moscow is wonderful.' Back in my hotel, I read that the first person to be sentenced under a new law criminalising 'repeated violation of protest laws' has managed to get a letter out of the sub-Arctic IK-7 prison: 'If they subject me to torture, beatings, and rape again, I will not last another week.' In other news, a librarian is under house arrest for having put Ukrainian nationalist books on open shelves. She protests that it was her duty and that she could not simply bin state property.

As always in Russia, however, life in the provinces might be different. Once more, I pack my bags and travel to Perm. This time, I fly with S-7, an airline that is part of the Star Alliance and a partner of British Airways. As I land in the town where I lived in the 1990s, I find familiar places and much that has changed. I hang around Café Paris, which serves excellent coffee and has a speedy Wi-Fi connection. I give up on cyber paranoia and happily surf the net. The economic crisis and the drop in oil exports are having an impact on the city. Several banks have closed down, and so have some businesses. Yet the city has improved massively in the past twenty years. IMAX cinemas stand tall in clean streets, next to fancy apartment blocks. I walk around the central market, where I used to interview Tajik and Kazakh traders. The traders are still there, but now they are housed in warm large pavilions, where customers can admire the display of merchandise. Super-markets are called 'Giper-markets'. They are enormous and so well stocked that one is left speechless. It appears that the 2014 sanc-tions to punish Russia for the annexation of Crimea had no effect whatsoever. I find Galbani mascarpone, Barilla olives and Chianti Riserva in the supermarket next to the Gorny Krustal' restaurant. At the checkout, a UniCredit cashpoint dispenses dollars, euros and roubles. Among the languages in which you can conduct your transaction are Italian, English and German.

Finally, I decide to go to Perm's necropolis, the last journey of *Mafia Life*. The place is outside the city, and is so large that one would be lost without a guide. It's not possible to walk there but a kind soul takes pity on me and drives me. I am in search of Zykov's grave. When I arrive, the burial site is covered in snow: it is early November after all. A full-sized slab of black marble reproduces an image of his small figure. His gaze appears uneasy, as if he does not enjoy being on display for everyone to see. His hands are tucked in the pockets of his jacket, the same type of jacket I had seen on Ivan'kov's grave, and his shirt is open at the neck. The image is fading, the dates hardly visible – I can just make them out. A low marble fence surrounds the monument. On one side stands a mini-ature table, and on the other side of the perimeter there is a large white cross. Fresh red flowers crawl out of the snow and are in full view. Next to them is a tiny sturdy glass. Traditionally, those who come to pay their respects to the dead pour a glass of vodka on the grave, and drink a shot.

One feels inclined to pay tribute when in front of a grave, to distil a few sentences into some kind of obituary. Russia has entered a new period of authoritarian rule, and characters like Zykov – small pawns in a game they no longer control – are bound to be losers. As we've seen, mafias are intimately connected to free markets and democracy, and the challenge for democratic regimes is to fight them following due process. And while democracies often come up short in this battle, one cannot win by losing one's soul. Authoritarian regimes, however, will not tolerate independent sources of power, including that of the mobster. Usually, we feel generous towards the dead: they belong to the past and will soon be just a memory. And while the pain caused by the likes of Zykov can never be condoned, I am aware that a different kind of suffering stays with those who continue to live in a country where freedom is slowly but surely being eroded. Democracies struggle to eradicate organised crime, but there is no other system I would want to endorse.

GLOSSARY

The Mafia, and/or country of reference, is given in square brackets.

artel' (plural *arteli*) [Russian Mafia]: guild of ordinary thieves, nineteenth century.

baltagya [Egypt]: thugs.

Cosa Nostra [Sicilian, American mafias]: the name used by insiders to refer to the Mafia.

fenya [Russian Mafia]: criminal language.

gulag [Soviet Union]: the administration of Soviet forced labour camps (lit. acronym of 'Main Camp Administration').

incaprettare [Sicilian Mafia]: a murder technique used by the Sicilian Mafia involving looping a rope around the neck and connecting it, behind the back, to the feet, which are raised up, like goats when they are slaughtered before Easter (lit. goat-tying).

ikka [Yakuza]: the basic crime unit of the Yakuza (lit. a family, a household).

kanonieri qurdebi [Georgia]: Georgian expression to refer to the *vory-v-zakone*.

kaoshan [China]: informal protector.

kleimo [Russian Mafia]: jargon word for tattoo (lit. brand).

klichka [Russian Mafia]: the name given to the new *vor* at the ritual (lit. nickname).

kobun [Yakuza]: novice.

lupara bianca [Sicilian Mafia]: the process of destroying a body without leaving a trace (lit. white shotgun).

made [Italian-American and Sicilian mafias]: full member.

mesata [Sicilian Mafia]: the monthly salary of made members (lit. monthly salary).

mettersi a posto [Sicilian Mafia]: the process of paying protection money (lit. to settle the matter).

obshchak [Russian Mafia]: the communal criminal fund.

omertà [Sicilian Mafia]: code of silence.

oyabun [Yakuka]: boss (lit. father).

pizzo [Sicilian Mafia]: protection money (lit. the beak of a bird).

ponyatiya [Russian Mafia]: Code of Conduct (lit. understanding).

progon [Russian Mafia]: the act of letting people know that new *vory-v-zakone* have been inducted into the fraternity (lit. announcement).

regalka [Russian Mafia]: jargon word for tattoo (lit. regalia).

reklama [Russian Mafia]: jargon word for tattoo (lit. advert).

raspiska [Russian Mafia]: jargon word for tattoo (lit. writing).

skhodka [Russian Mafia]: Gathering (lit. meeting).

tama [Yakuza]: bullet.

tebori [Yakuza]: process to carve tattoos by hand (lit. to inscribe by hands).

vor-v-zakone [Russian Mafia]: the top rank in the Russian criminal hierarchy (lit. thief-in-law; plu. *vory-v-zakone*).

APPENDIX: SYNOPTIC TABLE OF MAFIA RULES

Norms/ Mafia	Sicilian Mafia	Italian-American Mafia	Yakuza	Triads	Vory 1920–1950	New Vory
Norms related to mutual help and obedience:	Remain forever loyal to the Cosa Nostra Family.	Do not fail in obedience to superiors.	Don't disobey, or cause a nuisance to superiors.	Do not betray fellow members.	Be honest and helpful to one another and always tell the truth to fellow members.	Be honest and helpful to one another and always tell the truth to fellow members.
	Avoid disputes among the group.		Don't fight with fellow members or disrupt the harmony of the gang.		Avoid conflict with other *vory* and do not undermine each other's authority.	Settle disputes in a just and 'fair' way.
	Do not steal from each other.	Do not withhold money from the gang.	Don't embezzle gang funds.		Share all you have with fellow *vory*.	Raise sources of income to support the communal criminal fund, the *obshchak*.
	Offer refuge to each other.				Never leave the fraternity.	Be a bonding element for other criminals.

217

Norms/ Mafia	Sicilian Mafia	Italian-American Mafia	Yakuza	Triads	Vory 1920–1950	New Vory
	Members must be executed by other members only on reasonable grounds.				Accept the rulings of the *vory*'s tribunals.	Accept the ruling of the *vory*'s tribunals.
					Acquire a leading role in the camps, rule over criminals according to the *vory* rules and search for recruits.	Be devoted to the *vory*'s tradition.
Norms related to sexual behaviour:	Do not covet each other's women.	Never violate the wife or children of another member.	Don't touch the woman of a fellow gang member.	Do not become involved with wives of other members.	A *vor* might have a wife.	
					Passive homosexuality is strictly forbidden.	
Norms regulating interactions with outsiders and the authorities:	Never pass any information about Cosa Nostra to outsiders.	Never reveal secrets of the organisation.	Don't betray your gang or your fellow gang members.	Do not disclose the secrets of the organisation.	Never work for the state or join the Red Army; never pay taxes or work in the camps.	

Norms/ Mafia	Sicilian Mafia	Italian-American Mafia	Yakuza	Triads	Vory 1920–1950	New Vory
	Never report a crime to the police.	Do not appeal to the police or law.		Do not become a police informant.	Have no connections with law-enforcement agents.	Have no connection with law-enforcement agencies, but use them for own ends.
	Never introduce yourself to other members.				Never get involved in political activities and, upon entering the fraternity, sever all links with society, including familial ties.	
	Always behave properly.					
Additional norms:	Do not protect prostitution.	No personal involvement with narcotics.			Show contempt towards the accumulation of assets.	

APPENDIX: SYNOPTIC TABLE OF MAFIA STRUCTURE

The basic units of all five mafias are organised hierarchically. Ordinary members, who have gone through the ritual, are grouped into the Family's subunits and carry out the day-to-day operations of the group. In every Mafia there is a boss chosen from among the leaders of the subunits. Honorary roles such as underboss and advisor are found in most mafias, but their relative power differs depending on context. As police pressure eases, the roles become more formalised and the structure more elaborate. Yet it is remarkable that, despite geographical distance and cultural diversity, Families show such a similar structure.

English equivalents	Sicilian Mafia	Italian-American	Russian Mafia	Japanese Yakuza	Hong Kong Triads
Inter-Families Coordination Body	Commissione	Commission	Skhodka	Kanto	Headquarter system/ 'Central Committee'
Crime group	Famiglia	Family	Gruppirovka	Ikka	Branch Society
Boss/Leader	Capo Famiglia	Boss/Father	Avtoritet/ Pakhan	Oyabun	489 Cho Kun
Deputy Boss	Sottocapo	Underboss	–	Wakashira	438 Assistant Mountain Lord
Advisor to the Boss	Consigliere	Counselor	Sovetnik	Hosa/ Komon	–
Heads of Internal Groups	Capi-decina	Capi	Brigadir	Dai-kambu/ kambu	426 Red Pole
Ordinary members	Soldati	Regimes/ soldiers	Boeviki/ Torpedy	Kumi-in	49

A word on the Triads. A full member is known by the number '49'. The Triads have a passion for numerology and each role is defined by a number starting with four, a reference to the four oceans surrounding China in ancient times. The number 49 refers to the oaths the new recruit must swear before joining: there are 36 (4 by 9). Ordinary members answer to a Red Pole, also known by the number '426'. A Red Pole is the leader of a subgroup, organising the activities of the members and carrying out the orders of the boss. A council of Red Poles presides over the group as a whole, with one of the Red Poles being elected as Dragon Head (occasionally a treasurer is also elected). The Dragon Head is responsible for the organisation as a whole, including arbitrating in conflicts between various Red Poles, and for charting the group's strategy.

Above each Family stands the Commission. The Hong Kong Triads and the Yakuza have their own version of the Commission. In Hong Kong, until recently it was called the 'headquarter system' and has been in place since the beginning of the twentieth century. Today, the 'Headquarter system' is called 'Central Committee', possibly an indication of the growing importance of Communist China. Mafia groups in Japan are large and, as one might suspect, highly complicated to manage: as mentioned before, the quasi-legal nature of the Yakuza makes it easier for the groups to grow. Indeed, they have a higher degree of codification and standardisation of roles, and a highly detailed formal structure. For instance, the core members of the Italian-American Cosa Nostra are just 10 per cent of their Japanese counterparts. Crucially, these Yakuza groups are a coalition of smaller, highly independent entities, the equivalent of the Hong Kong 'branches', or the Mafia 'Families' in Sicily. The Yamaguchi-gumi and the Sumiyoshi-kai are national-level alliances of autonomous gangs, who elect a president from among the gangs' leaders. The role of the high-level bosses is to mediate and resolve conflicts among individual Families. The top management of each alliance is consulted when a gang decides to change its boss or expand in certain territories or markets, and when there are complaints regarding abuses. Yakuza groups have even formed loose inter-alliance associations comprising all major groups, called *Kanto*, to promote peaceful co-existence and to ensure that conflicts do not escalate. The *Kanto* is the equivalent of the Regional Commission of the Sicilian Mafia, which comprises Families operating beyond the province of Palermo.

LIST OF ILLUSTRATIONS

While every effort has been made to contact copyright-holders of illustrations, the author and publishers would be grateful for information about any illustrations where they have been unable to trace them, and would be glad to make amendments in further editions.

ACKNOWLEDGEMENTS

I have the great fortune to be able to draw upon a band of friends who, at short notice, are happy to take time away from their busy lives and read my work. Maurizio Catino, Luke Harding, Paul Howard, Ole Jann, Agnes Kovacs, Chiara Medioli, David Skarbek and Galina Varese have all read drafts of the manuscript. I am extremely grateful for their ever so helpful comments. Paolo Campana has also read several versions of the text and accompanied me to some of the places I describe. My sincere thanks. Liz David-Barrett, Vittorio Bufacchi, Jonathan Lusthaus (who also suggested the title), Julian Roberts, Teresa Smith and George Smith have given me detailed comments on an almost final version of the book. As always, David and Jane Cornwell have been supportive of this project. Antonio Nicaso has been generous to a fault: he has given me his views on various matters related to several mafias, including the `Ndrangheta. He has also provided me with valuable judicial documents. Alexander Sukharenko, director of New Challenges and Threats Study Center, Vladivostok, has kept me updated with developments in Russia. I had great fun organising an event with Paolo Veronesi in Ferrara, Italy, in 2012, when I first experimented with some of the ideas contained in this book.

Some of the material in this book was produced first as reports for *La Stampa*. There I worked closely with Mario Calabresi and Cesare Martinetti, who have always encouraged (and published) my endeavours. Paolo Palazzo has been a good friend and a valuable expert with whom I have discussed issues related to my work.

Cecily Gayford at Profile has read several versions of the text and her comments have greatly improved it. My agents Andrew Franklin, Marco Vigevani and Alberto Saibene have been supportive of this project from the beginning. On behalf of Profile, Susanne Hillen has copy-edited the text superbly, and has been kind enough to add last-minute changes. I was lucky to find in Penny Daniel a most brilliant and untiring production editor.

The Department of Sociology at Oxford University and the John Fell Fund have supported some of the trips I have taken for the book. My heart-felt thanks. Nuffield College has been generous as always for giving me a space to work. The Warden, Sir Andrew Dilnot, has made me welcome at Nuffield and supported me at crucial moments.

I have received help in relation to specific chapters:

Introduction. Neal Keeling of the *Manchester Evening News* has read and commented on a version of the Introduction. I have also spoken at length to him about Salford. After talking to him, I felt I knew all that I needed, although he should not be held responsible for any mistakes that remain. Anja Shortland has pushed me to expand on my experiences in the field. Heather Hamill also suggested some crucial improvements.

2. Work. I benefitted from a conversation with Piergiorgio Morosini. Leoluca Orlando and Salvatore Orlando were wonderful hosts during my visits to Palermo. Salvatore in particular was an invaluable guide. Antonio La Spina has read and commented on a version of this chapter and has suggested useful references.

3. Management. Several people helped me greatly while researching this chapter, including Ellada Larionidou, who has given me extensive comments. She also allowed me to read her groundbreaking dissertation. Giuseppe Puzzo read the text and gave me invaluable comments. He also has been extremely generous with his time in Rome: I am very grateful. Gianni Santucci and Ombretta Ingrascì have also been extremely generous in sharing material. My special thanks to Elisabetta Pugliese and Giulia Romanazzi for sharing their knowledge with good humour and impeccable grace. It was a privilege to meet them. To all those who hosted me in Bari and made me feel so welcome: *Grazie.* I will be back!

5. Love. Valeria Pizzini-Gambetta has read a version of the chapter and given me most valuable suggestions. Toshihiro Abe has translated key passages from Japanese for me. My thanks also to Heather Hamill for a conversation on this topic.

6. Self-image. Peter Thomas Zabielskis has been a generous host in Macau. I hope to be back. As always, Ray Yep has welcomed me in Hong Kong. I am grateful to Attilio Bolzoni and Francesco Maresco for granting me an interview and for sharing with me their knowledge of Giorgio Castellani, cinema and the Mafia. Giuseppe Lo Bianco was also present at the interview with Maresco and offered his insights into the history of Cosa Nostra. Francesco Guttuso and Emiliano Morreale have also been helpful.

7. Politics. The section on the Occupy Movement is a joint work with Rebecca Wong. Rebecca has offered me invaluable advice and has accompanied me to several places described in this chapter. She has also conducted some of the interviews cited in the text after I left Hong Kong. The papers on Somali piracy were written with Anja Shortland. She has been extremely patient waiting for this book to be finished so that we can get back to our planned additional research.

8. Death. Eiko Maruko Siniawer has pointed me to relevant sources related to the Yakuza.

REFERENCES

Introduction

pp. 1–2. Data on Salford gangs, including children in fear of death, is cited in the BBC *Panorama* programme 'Gangs, Guns and the Police', 8 February 2016; available at: http://www.bbc.co.uk/programmes/b07ornw4.

p. 2. On the police operation against illegal parking see, for example, 'Police smash Manchester United match day illegal car park racket', at: http://www.manchestereveningnews.co.uk/news/greater-manchester-news/police-smash-manchester-united-match-679255.

pp. 2–3. Peter Hook, *The Haçienda: How Not to Run a Club* (London: Simon & Schuster, 2010), describes the role of gangsters at the iconic club. The quote is from p. 257.

p. 3. Paul Massey's death has been reported widely by the British press. See, e.g., Helen Pidd, 'Funeral for Salford's "Mr Big" takes place with armed police on standby', *Guardian*, 28 August 2015, available at: http://www.theguardian.com/uk-news/2015/aug/28/funeral-salfords-mr-big-paul-massey-armed-police-on-standby.

I interviewed Don Brown, a former Greater Manchester police officer and leader of Project Gulf, in London on 6 April 2016. I also interviewed a journalist and a community activist in Salford on 21 April 2016. They prefer to remain anonymous. PMS is no longer in operation and any reference to any existing company with the same name or initials is purely coincidental.

p. 3. The importance of reputation in the underworld was first highlighted by Peter Reuter, *The Value of a Bad Reputation: Cartels, Criminals, and Barriers to Entry* (Santa Monica: Rand Corporation 1982). See also Diego Gambetta, *The Sicilian Mafia* (London: Harvard University Press, 1993), pp. 43–6, especially p. 44.

pp. 4–5. The murder in the pub is that of Lee Headman. His mother and Nazir Afzal, Chief Crown Prosecutor, North West of England (2011–15) discuss it in the BBC *Panorama* programme, 'Gangs, Guns and the Police' 8 February 2016; available at: http://www.bbc.co.uk/programmes/b07ornw4.

p. 5. On the 'Salford Firm' and on gangsters as alternative authority figures more generally, see Peter Walsh, *Gang War: The Inside Story of the Manchester Gangs* (Preston: Milo Books, 2006), pp. 130–32.

p. 5. Results in 2012 Salford mayoral election: https://www.salford.gov.uk/elections-2012.htm.

Salford is not unique in the UK. Some gangs in London, according to a recent study by James Densley, 'protect community residents from violence and exploitation, provide them with financial sustenance, organise recreational activities and otherwise "serve" the community, much like certain larger US gangs' (James Densley, *How Gangs Work: An Ethnography of Youth Violence*, London: Palgrave Macmillan, 2013, p. 65). The Fujianese communities in Britain are also victims of local rackets (see Jack Dees, 'Claws of the dragon. Chinese organised crime in the UK', *Papers from the British Criminology Conference*, 12:61–78. http://britsoccrim.org/volume12/pbcc_2012_Dees.pdf). In 2014, the chief inspector of constabulary, Tom Winsor, maintained that some communities in Britain rarely, if ever, call the police to report a serious crime. Residents, he said, 'administer their own form of justice ... It could be anything from low-level crime right up to murder'. 'Tom Winsor, "Some parts of Britain have their own form of justice"', *The Times*, 18 January 2014; and 'Communities "taking law into their own hands", says police chief inspector', *Guardian*, 18 January 2014.

I have expanded on the connection between organised crime and communities in: Paolo Campana and Federico Varese, 'Interpreting Organised Crime: Illegal Governance and Communities', 2016, paper under review.

pp. 6–7. Some of my reflections on ethnography have already been published in Federico Varese, *The Russian Mafia* (Oxford: Oxford University Press, 2001, 2005), pp. 9–13, especially pp. 11–12. On the systematic use of police wiretaps see Paolo Campana and Federico Varese, 'Listening to the Wire: Criteria and Techniques for the Quantitative Analysis of Phone Intercepts', *Trends in Organized Crime*, 15(1), 2012, pp. 13–30. 'A tiny observer of enormous world,' wrote W. H. Auden in a poem in May 1929.

On the use of the judicial evidence for historical research, and its 'truth value', see the classic statement by Carlo Ginzburg, *The Judge and the Historian: Marginal Notes on a Late-Twentieth-Century Miscarriage of Justice* (London: Verso, 2002). Timothy Garton Ash, *The File: A Personal*

History (London: Flamingo, 1997) is a subtle and inspiring exploration of the tension between official records and personal memories.

The human desire to tell one's story is also noted by Massimiliano De Simone, a priest who became a confidant of a prominent Mafioso turned state witness. See Alessandra Dino, *A colloquio con Gaspare Spatuzza. Un racconto di vita, una storia di stragi* (Bologna: Il Mulino, 2016), p. 18.

p. 10. See Giovanni Falcone with Marcelle Padovani, *Cose di Cosa Nostra* (Milan: BUR, 1992), p. 83: 'If we want to fight the mafia effectively, we should not turn it into a monster ... We should admit that it resembles us.'

1. Birth

Zykov in Perm, Russia, 1993

p. 12. On Russia in the 1990s, see my book *The Russian Mafia*. On the early period of the Russian transition, I also consulted David E. Hoffman, *The Oligarchs: Wealth and Power in the New Russia* (New York: Public Affairs, 2003, 2011); the recent project coordinated by Irina Prokhorova, '1990: opyt izucheniya nedavnei istorii', published by the journal *Novoe literaturnoe obozrenie* (2007); and Cesare Martinetti, *Il padrino di Mosca* (Milan: Feltrinelli, 1995).

p. 13. A. Vaksberg is cited in F. Varese, 'Is Sicily the Future of Russia? Private Protection and the Rise of the Russian Mafia', *Archives Européenes de Sociologie*, 35(2), 2009, p. 224.

pp. 13–16. I present here some material on the *vory*'s history and rituals already published in *The Russian Mafia*, where one can also find information on Maximilien de Santerre (whose words quoted here can be found on pp. 145–6); full references to the essays by Varlam Shalamov on the criminal world; and information on Zykov.

p. 13. For the translation of the expression *vory-v-zakone*, Serio and Razinkin suggest 'thieves professing the code'. See Joseph D. Serio and Vyacheslav Razinkin, 'Thieves Professing the Code: The Traditional Role of *vory v zakone* in Russia's Criminal World and Adaptations to a New Social Reality', *Low Intensity Conflict and Law Enforcement*, 4(1), 1995, pp. 72–88. More generally, see Mark Galeotti (ed.), *Russian and Post-Soviet Organized Crime* (London: Routledge, 2002). Galeotti is the author of the first scholarly paper on the Russian Mafia, published in 1992.

p. 14. The *vor* who became a minister in Shevarnadze's government is Dzhaba Ioseliani (1926–2003). The leader of the Mkhedrioni militia, he led the coup against President Zviad Gamsakhurdia and was instrumental in Eduard Shevardnadze's ascendency to the presidency.

p. 15. For Pasternak's description of Yuryatin/Perm, I have used the new translation of *Doctor Zhivago* by Richard Pever and Larissa Volokhonsky (New York: Vintage Books, 2011). On today's Perm, see *Perm': Kniga-fotoal'bom* (Senator: Perm', 2014).

p. 18. The Soviet historian is Dmitri Likhachev (cited in *Russian Mafia*, p. 150).

pp. 18–20. For a study of *vory*'s tattoos see the three-volume work by Danzig Baldaev, Sergei Vasiliev, Alexei Plutser-Sarno and Alexander Sidorov, *Russian Criminal Tattoo Encyclopaedia* (London: Fuel, 2003–8). I draw upon Plutser-Sarno, 'The Language of the Body and Politics: The Symbolism of Thieves' Tattoos', vol. 1, pp. 26–53. On p. 31 he discusses the various names of tattoos (*reklama, advert, regalka, raspiska* and *kleimo*). I also consulted Sidorov, 'The Russian Criminal Tattoo: Past and Present', vol. 3, 2008, pp. 16–43. *Vory*'s punishment for those who acquire illegitimate tattoos is also mentioned in Emmanuel Carrère, *Limonov* (London: Penguin Books, 2014), p. 49.

p. 20. The *vor* who talks about the importance of prison is Merab (see chapter 3).

p. 21. A discussion of the Obama Administration strategy to combat transnational organised crime can be found at: https://www.occrp.org/index. php/ccwatch/cc-watch-indepth/1015-us-attempts-to-combat-dark-side-of-globalization. The official statement is at: https://www.whitehouse. gov/sites/default/files/microsites/2011-strategy-combat-transnational-organised-crime.pdf.

See also 'Treasury Designates Key Members of the Brothers' Circle Criminal Organisation', 20 December 2012, at: https://www.treasury.gov/press-center/press-releases/Pages/tg1811.aspx.

p. 21. On the estimate of *vory* active in 2015 by PrimeCrime.ru, see Yekaterina Sinelschikova, '"Thieves-in-law": Russia's close-knit criminal corporation', *Russia Beyond the Headlines*, 21 July 2016.

Nino Calderone joins Cosa Nostra, Catania, Sicily, 1962

pp. 22–5. For Antonio Calderone's description of the ritual, I draw upon: Pino Arlacchi, *Men of Dishonor: Inside the Sicilian Mafia* (New York: William Morrow & Co., 1993), chapter 5. Direct quotations are on p. 63, p. 65 and pp. 66–70. See also Giovanni Brusca's 1976 initiation in Saverio Lodato, *Ho ucciso Giovanni Falcone* (Milan: Mondadori, 2006) pp. 32–5.

pp. 25–7. Elements of my discussion of the ritual draw upon Letizia Paoli, *Mafia Brotherhoods: Organized Crime, Italian Style* (New York: Oxford University Press, 2003), especially chapter 2. In particular, Paoli stresses the emotional dimension of the process, and uses Weber's discussion of 'status contracts' to criticise those who interpret the ritual as either a 'contract' or the equivalent of entering a professional guild. Some citations are also taken from Paoli. See also the remarks on rebirth by Fabio Armao in *Il Sistema Mafia* (Turin: Bollati-Boringhieri, 1999), pp. 74–5. I have also consulted Diego Gambetta's discussion of the ritual in his *The Sicilian Mafia* (London: Harvard University Press, 1993). In particular, he makes the point that entry into the Mafia gives the recruit access to the collective reputation of the organisation and that it confers certainty in a context of mistrust and confusion (p. 152).

Nicola Gratteri and Antonio Nicaso are the authors of seminal works on organised crime. In their recent *Acqua Santissima* (Milan: Mondadori, 2013, pp. 37–46) they show that the Calabrese `Ndrangheta ritual shares many features with the one we find in the Sicilian Mafia. Both mafias call it 'baptism'. They also report how the thumb of a member of the `Ndrangheta, Luciano Piccolo, was cut in the shape of a cross (p. 42). See also Gavin Slade, who reminds us, among other things, that the *vory* ritual is known as baptism (*natvla*) in Georgian (Gavin Slade, 'No Country for Made Men', *Law and Society Review*, 46(3), 2012, p. 633).

Two important analytical papers on criminal rules and rituals are: David Skarbek and Peng Wang, 'Criminal Rituals', *Global Crime,* 16(4), 2015, pp. 288–305; Maurizio Catino, 'Mafia Rules. The Role of Criminal Codes in Mafia Organizations', *Scandinavian Journal of Management*, 31(4), 2015, pp. 536–48. Most recently on the connection between the Catholic Church and the Mafia, see Isaia Sales, *I preti e i mafiosi. Storia dei rapporti tra mafia e Chiesa cattolica* (Soveria Mannelli: Rubbettino 2016).

p. 25. State witness Gaspare Mutolo's words are cited in Paoli, *Mafia Brotherhoods*, p. 65.

p. 25. The quote from Gravano ('You are born as of today') is from Peter Maas, *Underboss: Sammy 'the Bull' Gravano's Story of Life in the Mafia* (New York: HarperCollins 1997), p. 140.

p. 25. The Mafioso who recalls his initiation on 7 April 1941 is Serafino Castagna, a member of the `Ndrangheta. See Serafino Castagna, *Tu devi uccidere*, ed. Antonio Perria (Milan: Editrice il Momento, 1967, p. 31 and p. 35).

p. 25. Max Weber has a relevant discussion on status contracts in *Economy and Society* (Berkeley: University of California Press, 1978), p. 672. See also the discussion in Paoli, *Mafia Brotherhoods*.

p. 26. The quote from Giovanni Falcone is taken from *Cose di Cosa Nostra*, p. 97.

p. 26. On the 1997 planned ceremony in Madonna di Campiglio, see Cesare Martinetti, 'Scacco matto alla mafia russa in Trentino', *La Stampa*, 18 March 1997.

pp. 26–7. My discussion of Genesis 15:5–12 and 17 is indebted to remarks by Ignazio Schinella, cited in Nicaso and Gratteri, *Acqua Santissima* (p. 43) and Robert Alter, *Genesis: Translation and Commentary* (New York: W. W. Norton & Company, 1998), p. 65. Illuminating remarks on the oath in Western culture are in Giorgio Agamben, *Il Sacramento del Linguaggio. Archeologia del Giuramento* (Rome-Bari: Laterza, 2008); and Paolo Prodi, *Cristianesimo e Potere* (Bologna: Il Mulino, 2012). Jean Sybil La Fontaine remarks on the equalising effect of (Mafia) rituals in *Initiation* (Harmondsworth: Penguin Books, 1985), p. 45.

Sakai joins the Yakuza, Southern Japan, 1978

p. 27. For the meaning of the word 'Yakuza', see Peter B. E. Hill, *The Japanese Mafia: Yakuza, Law, and the State* (Oxford: Oxford University Press, 2003), p. 36; Andrew Rankin, 'Recent Trends in Organized Crime in Japan: Yakuza vs the Police, & Foreign Crime Gangs – Part 2', *Asia-Pacific Journal*, 10(7), no. 1, 20 February 2012, note 35.

p. 27. Data on the Yakuza are taken from the National Police Agency, *Crime in Japan in 2010* (Police Policy Research Center National Police Academy, 2011), p. 12. According to official data, the number of affiliates has been decreasing steadily since the mid-1960s. See Andrew Rankin, '21st-Century Yakuza: Recent Trends in Organized Crime in Japan – Part 1', *Asia-Pacific Journal*, 10(7), no. 2, 13 February 2012, p. 2. In 2014, the Yamaguchi-gumi launched its own website, available at: http://mjyouka. web.fc2.com/.

pp. 27–8. The estimate of the Yamaguchi-gumi monthly fees is mentioned in Jake Adelstein, *Tokyo Vice* (London: Constable, 2010), p. 97.

pp. 28–34. Sakai's story is contained in the as yet unpublished PhD thesis by David Harold Stark, 'The Yakuza: Japanese Crime Incorporated' (University of Michigan, 1981), pp. 97–109. This work remains one of the best ever written about organised crime, let alone the Yakuza. Junichi

Saga, *Confessions of a Yakuza: A Life in Japan's Underworld* (Tokyo, New York, London: Kodansha International, 1991) is also fascinating.

pp. 28–9. The description of the Yakuza ritual is taken from David Kaplan and Alec Dubro, *Yakuza: Japan's Criminal Underworld* (London: Robert Hale, 2003), p. 9. For a slightly different rendering of the words, see Hiroaki Iwai, 'Organized Crime in Japan', in Robert Kelly (ed.), *Organized Crime: A Global Perspective* (London: Rowman & Littlefield, 1986), p. 215.

p. 30. Words by Calderone are taken from *Men of Dishonor*, p. 37. Also cited in Gambetta, *The Sicilian Mafia*, p. 153.

pp. 31–2. The discussion of tattoos in Yakuza is based on Stark, 'The Yakuza', pp. 116–17. For a current estimate of the cost of a body suit tattoo, see Clarissa Sebag-Montefiore, 'Horihide still practices the dying art of hand tattoo', *Los Angeles Times*, 24 June 2012. More generally, see Takahiro Kitamura and Katie M. Kitamura, *Bushido, Legacies of the Japanese Tattoo* (Atglen, PA: Schiffer Publishing, 2000).

p. 33. The text of the expulsion letter is in Stark, 'The Yakuza', p. 106. For another wording of the Yakuza expulsion letter, see Hill, *The Japanese Mafia*, p. 76. Sakai's expulsion is narrated in Stark, 'The Yakuza', pp. 106–10.

George Cheung enters the Triads, Fulham, London, 1992

pp. 35–41. The story of Wai Hen Cheung can be found in the *Independent*, 16 October and 21 October 1992; 4 December 1992; *Courtnewsuk*, 2 November 1992. I draw mainly upon Tony Thompson, *Gangland Britain* (London: Coronet Books, 1996), pp. 251–80. Direct quotations come from *Gangland Britain*, pp. 270–75. I have also consulted Yu Kong Chu, *Triads as Business* (London: Routledge, 2000), a confidential report by the Met on Chinese organised crime in London; and the *South China Morning Post*, 24 February 2013.

p. 38. The estimate of Yakuza ethnic composition is cited in Andrew Rankin, 'Recent Trends in Organized Crime in Japan: Yakuza vs the Police, & Foreign Crime Gangs – Part 2', *Asia-Pacific Journal*, 10, no.1, 20 February 2012, p. 8.

p. 38. On the ethnic distribution of *vory* in the Soviet period, see Varese, *The Russian Mafia*, pp. 176–8. Georgi Glonti and Givi Lobjanidze, *Vory-v-zakone: Professional'naya Prestupnost' v Gruzii* (Tbilisi: Transnational Crime and Corruption Center, 2004), point out that some 35 per cent of the total recorded *vory* in 2004 were born in Georgia, despite the fact that Georgia is home to only 2 per cent of the Soviet population. See also Gavin Slade, *Reorganizing Crime: Mafia and Anti-Mafia in Post-Soviet Georgia* (Oxford: Oxford University Press, 2013), p. 99, for the distribution of *vory* within Georgia.

p. 39. The quote from Gravano on the non-racist Mafia is in Maas, *Underboss*, p. 134.The Italian-American Mafia had been recruiting beyond Sicilians since the time of Giuseppe 'Joe the Boss' Masseria. See C. Alexander Hortis, *The Mob and the City: The Hidden History of How the Mafia Captured New York* (Amherst, NY: Prometheus Book, 2014), p. 55.

p. 39. Another former Mafioso whose relatives were murdered by Cosa Nostra as a punishment for his collaboration with the Italian state is Francesco Marino Mannoia. The mother, the sister and the aunt were killed while stepping into a car (*La Repubblica*, 25 November 1989).

p. 39. Joseph D. Pistone with Richard Woodley, *Donnie Brasco: My Undercover Life in the Mafia* (New York: Signet, 1987).

2. Work

Key sources for this section are four investigations conducted by prosecutors in Palermo:

Gotha. 2008. Sentenza di rito abbreviato. N° 1579/07 Reg. Not. Reato N° 800165/07 Reg. Gip, Tribunale di Palermo, Sezione dei giudici per le indagini preliminari (judge Piergiorgio Morosini).

Old Bridge. 2008. Provvedimento di fermo N. 11059/06 R. mod. 21 DDA PROCURA di Palermo (prosecutors Guido Lo Forte, Giuseppe Pignatone, Michele Prestipino Giarritta, Domenico Gozzo, Maurizio de Lucia, Antonino Di Matteo, Roberta Buzzolani).

Grande Mandamento. 2005. Fermo di Indiziati di delitto. N. 3779/03 RGNR DDA N. 1855/04 R.G. GIP. Procura della Repubblica, Direzione Distrettuale Antimafia, Tribunale di Palermo. 28 January.

Villabate. 2009. Requisitoria seconda parte. Nr. 3779/03 R. MOD. 21 DDA PROCURA di Palermo.

I have also consulted the following court documents:

Old Bridge-USA. 2008. United States District Court, Eastern District of New York against Joseph Agate et al. (Assistant US Attorney Daniel D. Brownell).

Addiopizzo–Lo Piccolo. 2009. Sentenza Adamo+50.

Dalla Chiesa. 2002. Sentenza di Primo Grado. Proc. nr. 25/99 RG Corte di Assise, nr. 07/02 Reg. ins. sent.N. 2867/96 R.mod. 21 DDA Corte di Assise di Palermo, sezione seconda.

p. 42. The shed conversations of Antonino Rotolo are mainly reported in Gotha (2008) and Old Bridge (2008). Extracts of Gotha (2008) have been published in Piergiorgio Morosini, *Il Gotha di Cosa Nostra: La Mafia del dopo Provenzano nello scacchiere internazionale del crimine* (Soveria Mannelli: Rubbettino, 2009). I found Morosini's discussion of Cosa Nostra's 'fiscal system' particularly insightful. See also Enrico Bellavia and Maurizio De Lucia, *Il cappio* (Milan: BUR, 2012).

p. 43. Totò Riina was a resident at Via Bernini 52, Palermo, from 1987 to 1992, under an assumed name. On Riina's arrest, see Lodato, *Ho ucciso Giovanni Falcone*, pp. 124–35.

p. 43. 'How is it possible that when we talk about something, cops know about it next day?!?' is cited in Gotha (2008), p. 187.

p. 43. The data on fugitives and number of inmates is cited by Antonio La Spina in, 'The Fight against the Italian Mafia', in Letizia Paoli (ed.) *The Oxford Handbook of Organized Crime* (Oxford: Oxford University Press, 2014), pp. 603–5. See also Antonio La Spina, *Il mondo di mezzo: Mafie e antimafie* (Bologna: Il Mulino, 2016).

pp. 43–5. Information on Antonino Rotolo's life is contained in the above court files. See also: Franco Coppola, 'Ora vi racconto come funziona il supertraffico dei narcodollari', *La Repubblica*, 27 November 1986; 'Mille sistemi per beffare le microspie nel box di lamiera il bunker del boss', *La Repubblica*, 21 July 2006; Giuseppe Cerasa, 'Corso dei Mille, il più feroce dei clan', *La Repubblica*, 20 October 1984. On Rotolo in English, see Attilio Bolzoni and Giuseppe D'Avanzo, *The Boss of Bosses: The Life of the Infamous Totò Riina, Dreaded Head of the Sicilian Mafia* (London: Orion, 2015), pp. 281–8.

p. 44. On the Mafia 'war' of 1981–3, see Saverio Lodato, *Dieci anni di Mafia* (Milan: Rizzoli, 1992) and Falcone, *Cose di Cosa Nostra*, p. 24.

p. 45. The information on Gianni Nicchi is contained in the court documents cited above. See also Riccardo Arena, 'Mafia, Campanella racconta "Così il Killer si fece Boss"', *Giornale di Sicilia*, 2 November 2006.

p. 46. Nicchi refers to extortion/protection payments as the 'neighbourhood tax' (*la tassa di rione*) in a conversation cited in Gotha (2008), p. 221.

p. 46. Francesco Bonura's discussion of racketeering is in Gotha (2008), pp. 230–31.

pp. 47–8. The Mafia ledger is found in Gotha (2008), pp. 233–4. See also Giovanni Bianconi, 'Ecco i conti che portano a Provenzano', *Corriere della*

Sera, 14 May 2005; 'Ha sborsato? Chi nega chi ammette', *La Repubblica,* 14 May 2005.

p. 49. On the chain of retail shops discussed in the text see Gotha (2008), p. 244. Bosses forcing entrepreneurs to hire their protégés is a well-known practice, already mentioned in Arlacchi, *Men of Dishonor.* See also Gotha (2008), p. 248.

p. 49. The size of Palermo Families in 2013 are estimates by Italian Ministero dell'Interno reported in *Salvo Palazzolo,* 'La "nuova" Cosa nostra ha un esercito di 2 mila affiliati', *La Repubblica,* 16 December 2013.

p. 49. The studies alluded to in the text include Peter Reuter, *Disorganized Crime: The Economics of the Visible Hand* (Cambridge, MA: MIT Press, 1983); Filippo Sabetti, *Political Authority in a Sicilian Village* (New Brunswick, NJ: Rutgers University Press, 1984); Gambetta, *The Sicilian Mafia;* Yiu Kong Chu, *Traids as Business;* Varese, *The Russian Mafia;* Hill, *The Japanese Mafia;* and Varese, *Mafias on the Move* (London: Princeton University Press, 2011).

p. 50. On the smaller size of firms in Sicily, see Mario Lavezzi, 'Economic Structure and Vulnerability to Organised Crime: Evidence from Sicily', *Global Crime,* 9(3), 2008, pp. 198–220.

p. 50. Antonio La Spina, Giovanna Frazzica, Valentina Punzo, Attilio Scaglione, *Non è più quella di una volta* (Soveria Mannelli: Rubbettino, 2015) is an excellent study of recent development in extortion practices in Sicily by Cosa Nostra. In particular, I have found very useful the contributions by La Spina, 'Le estorsioni in Sicilia. Una realtà che resiste e cambia' (pp. 7–29); and Valentina Punzo, 'Le nuove dinamiche del fenomeno estorsivo. Tra crisi economica e mutamento organizzativo' (pp. 97–135), both of whom highlight the current difficulties of Cosa Nostra in Sicily and cite relevant evidence. I draw upon their work in this chapter.

p. 50. La Spina, 'The Fight against the Italian Mafia', p. 606.

p. 50. The two brothers punished in the 1980s for unauthorised extortions were Enzo and Leonardo di Cascio. See Gotha (2008), p. 242.

p. 51. The Santa Rosalia story is mentioned in La Spina, 'Le estorsioni in Sicilia', p. 20; and Riccardo Lo Verso, '"Le estorsioni? Colpa degli sbirri", la strategia dei boss di Pagliarelli', 27 June 2015, at: http://livesicilia. it/2015/06/27/Mafia-estorsioni-palermo-pagliarelli-cosa-nostra_642860/.

p. 51. The trucking company mentioned in the text is Autotrasporti Cuffaro. See Old Bridge (2008), p. 196, p. 213, pp. 218–34.

p. 51. The trick with the euro–lira exchange rate is in Old Bridge (2008), p. 197.

p. 52. Giovanni di Giacomo's comments on the lack of victims for extortion are cited in A. Ziniti, 'Il nuovo pizzo in tempo di crisi', *La Repubblica*, Edizione Palermo, 20 April 2014. This is also discussed in Punzo, 'Le nuove dinamiche', p. 101. Data on Sicily's GDP is taken from Nino Amadore, 'Svimez: La Sicilia ha perso 11 punti di Pil in cinque anni. Bruciati 86mila posti di lavoro', *Sole 24 Ore*, 8 November 2013, cited in La Spina, 'Le estorsioni in Sicilia', p. 25.

p. 52. Official statistics on extortion in Sicily are cited in La Spina, 'Le estorsioni in Sicilia', p. 23.

p. 52. Allessandra Ziniti, 'Il nuovo pizzo in tempo di crisi', *La Repubblica*, Edizione Palermo, 20 April 2014, mentions the practice of asking only twice a year for protection money. Also in Punzo, 'Le nuove dinamiche', p. 102.

p. 52. On the 'austerity budget' see: S. P., 'La Spending Review del clan dietro il delitto di Giacomo', *La Repubblica*, Edizione Palermo, 21 May 2015; A. Ziniti, 'La Mafia si arrende alla crisi, il pizzo si pagherà con lo sconto', *La Repubblica*, 20 April 2014. See also La Spina, 'Le estorsioni in Sicilia', p. 14.

p. 53. The 3 per cent charge on the public contract is mentioned in Gotha (2008), p. 913; and see p. 920 for the story of the University of Palermo contract. On the use of the courts as opposed to the Mafia 'tribunal', see Old Bridge (2008), p. 104.

p. 53. The extortion of Chinese shopkeepers is discussed in Gotha (2008), pp. 228–9.

p. 54. P. Perez, 'Falsi euro cinesi, Napoli base del traffico', *Il Mattino*, 13 December 2014; see discussion in Punzo, 'Le nuove dinamiche', pp. 118–19.

p. 54. The cases of the Romanian thieves is discussed by Punzo, 'Le nuove dinamiche', pp. 117–18. See also Riccardo Lo Verso, 'Banda di rumeni razziava le case. Il boss: "Rompiamogli le gambe"', *LiveSicilia*, 14 May 2014.

p. 55. On Yusapha Susso, see http://palermo.repubblica.it/cronaca/2016/04/04/news/rissa_con_sparatoria_tra_giovani_di_ballaro_e_del_gambia_un_fermato-136868284/; Ismail Einashe, 'Meet the migrants who are helping Italians take on the Sicilian mob', *International Business Times*, 14 October 2016; Laura Anello, 'La rivolta contro il pizzo degli immigrati di Palermo', *La Stampa*, 24 May 2016. Emanuele Rubino is awaiting trial and has denied the accusation.

p. 55. S. Palazzolo, 'La nuova Mafia di Ballarò. Ecco i boss nigeriani che controllano il mercato di droga e prostituzione', *La Repubblica*, Edizione Palermo, 12 November 2014; Punzo, Le nuove dinamiche', p. 116.

*Gianni Nicchi and Nicola Mandelà scheme to make
the Sicilian Mafia re-enter the drugs trade*

p. 56. How a short time horizon leads to an increase in violence has been discussed by Gambetta, *The Sicilian Mafia*, and modelled by Alastair Smith and Federico Varese, 'Payment, Protection and Punishment', *Rationality and Society*, 13(3), 2001, pp. 349–93.

p. 56. The Turkish trafficker working with Rotolo was Yasar Aunì Musululu, while the Swiss-Turkish trafficker was Paul Waridel. See 'Trial is told drug suspect received millions in cash', *New York Times*, 1 April 1986; United States of America, Appellee, *v*. Filippo Casamento *et alii* 887 F.2d 1141 (2d Cir. 1989), US Court of Appeals for the Second Circuit, 887 F.2d 1141 (2d Cir. 1989), argued 26 January 1989. Decided 11 October 1989.

p. 59. On the rise of non-Italian mafias in the US, see Peter Reuter, 'The Decline of the American Mafia', *Public Interest* 120, 1995, pp. 89–99.

p. 59. I have taken the price of cocaine from Scott Stewart, 'Mexico's Cartels and the Economics of Cocaine', *Stratfor Security Weekly Report*, 3 January 2013, at: https://www.stratfor.com/weekly/mexicos-cartels-and-economics-cocaine.

p. 60. On Nicola Mandalà, see Gotha (2008).

p. 60. Up until 2006–7, three prominent Mafiosi – Bernardo Provenzano, Salvatore Lo Piccolo and Antonino Rotolo – were *de facto* managing Cosa Nostra and taking key decisions. See, for example, a letter from Provenzano to Rotolo, dated 5 August 2005 ('Al momento risolviamo le cose con la responsabilità di tutti al momento ricordo che siamo tre. Voi. Lo Piccolo e io'), cited in Old Bridge (2008), p. 117.

p. 61. On Frank Calì, see Gotha (2008), Old Bridge (2008), Old Bridge-USA (2008) and Grande Mandamento (2005). I have also consulted Attilio Bolzoni, 'Franky Boy, the invisible boss, who wanted to have Palermo back', *La Repubblica*, 8 February 2008; Jeff Israely, 'The case of the exiled mobsters', *Time* magazine, 7 February 2008; 'Staten Island mobster takes Gambino leadership: report', *New York Daily News*, 21 August 2015.

    It is not unusual for US mobsters to host dinners for visiting Sicilian Mafiosi and invite their lovers. Giovanni Brusca, who was invited to such a dinner in New Jersey, was shocked. He writes: 'Such a thing would be inconceivable in Sicily.' (Lodato, *Ho ucciso Giovanni Falcone*, p. 83.)

p. 63. The cocaine deal with Venezuela is in Gotha (2008), p. 109. It is quite common for Mafia families to pool money to finance drug ventures. See, for the Italian-American Mafia, Hortis, *The Mob and the City*, p. 142.

p. 63. Data on Venezuela as the main transit country for cocaine are in the UNODC Report 'The Transatlantic Cocaine Market', April 2011, especially, p. 25. See also Roberto Saviano, *Zero Zero Zero* (London: Allen Lane, 2015), p. 291.

pp. 64–7. The conversations between Nicola and *Amalia* are contained in several court documents mentioned above. See also 'Cocaina e hotel di lusso *Amalia* col pancione ha evitato le manette', *La Repubblica*, 27 January 2005. On the effects of cocaine on the brain I have consulted the government website: http://www.drugabuse.gov/publications/research-reports/cocaine/how-does-cocaine-produce-its-effects. See also Saviano, *Zero Zero Zero*, pp. 57–8.

p. 68. On the arrest of key bosses, see: Andrea Cottone, 'Omicidio Geraci: confermati gli ergastoli', *LiveSicilia*, 29 October 2009; Salvo Palazzolo, '"Addio pizzo", 13 condannati e 4 assolti ai boss Lo Piccolo trent'anni di carcere', *La Repubblica*, 22 January 2010; Riccardo Lo Verso, 'Processo Gotha. Definitivi due secoli di carcere', *LiveSicilia*, 12 November 2012. On the new structure of the Pagliarelli Family and drugs trafficking, see, e.g., 'Mafia, ritorno alla droga: 39 arresti una donna gestiva il traffico', *Corriere della Sera/Corriere del Mezzogiorno*, 26 May 2015.

3. Management

Greece–Milan–Bari, 2010–2012

I had access to the following documents:

DZHANGVELADZE 2012. 'Ordinanza di custodia cautelare' against DZHANGVELADZE Merab, known as 'Jango' and others (5492/12 RGNR, 10922/12 RG GIP), Bari Tribunal, 2012.

BOLKVADZE 2011. Applicazione della misura della custodia cautelare in carcere' against BOLKVADZE Besik and others (37244/11 RGPM), Rome Tribunal, 2011.

DIA. 2013. Direzione Investigativa Antimafia, 'Eastern European Organised Crime', document prepared for the FP EEOC Operation Meeting, The Hague, 16–18 October 2013, Rome.

I also obtained documents from the Portuguese Supremo Tribunal de Justiça, 3ª Secção.

Relevant newspaper articles appeared in *Il Fatto Quotidiano*, 1 July 2013; *Il Tempo*, 24 October and 27 October 2013; 'La mafia russa nelle case degli italiani', *Corriere della Sera*, 30 June 2013.

For background information on the *vory* in Georgia, see Gavin Slade, *Reorganizing Crime*, and Alexandre Kukhianidze, 'Corruption and

Organised Crime in Georgia before and after the "Rose Revolution"', *Central Asian Survey,* 28(2), 2009, pp. 215–34.

Ellada Larionidou, 'The Emergence of Russian-speaking Mafia in Greece: Culture and Crime', MSc Dissertation, London Metropolitan University, 2015 (supervised by Dr Daniel Silverstone), explores in depth the presence of the *vory* in Greece. I am grateful to the author for allowing me to read her unpublished dissertation.

See also the timely piece by Mark Galeotti, 'The Other Greek Tragedy: Georgian and Russian/Eurasian organized crime', *In Moscow's Shadows,* 24 December 2013 at: https://inmoscowsshadows.wordpress. com/2013/12/24/the-other-greek-tragedy-georgian-and-russianeurasian -organized-crime/. On the Russian Mafia in Italy, see Ombretta Ingrascì, 'La mafia russa in Italia. Lavori in corso', *Rivista di Studi e Ricerche sulla criminalità organizzata,* 1(1), 2015, pp. 37–55.

p. 69. Greece is one of the main transition points of drug trafficking because it connects three continents, as pointed out by Larionidou, *The Emergence,* p. 23.

pp. 70–71. On Pontic Greeks, see 'The Odyssey of the Pontic Greeks', *Journal of Refugee Studies,* Special Issue, 4(4), 1991; and Panagoula Diamanti-Karanou, 'Migration of Ethnic Greeks from the Former Soviet Union to Greece, 1990–2000: Policy Decisions and Implications', *Southeast European and Black Sea Studies,* 3(1), 2003, pp. 25–45.

The estimate of 100 Georgian gangs in Greece is in Larionidou, *The Emergence,* p. 29.

p. 74. A prominent Pontic Greek, Lavrentis Tsolakidi, known as 'Leva Grek', organised a Gathering (*shodka*) in 2010 in Greece, which was attended by more than sixty thieves-in-law. Leva was a valuable and high-ranked member of Grandpa Khasan's clan. A few months after that meeting, Leva died. Police did not rule out that he was murdered (see Larionidou, *The Emergence,* p. 8 and p. 18).

p. 74. The practice of not cutting the beard is observed also in southern Italy. Mourners are expected not to shave between the time of somebody's death and his funeral. Al Capone followed this practice after the death of Chicago organised-crime boss James 'Big Jim' Colosimo. See John Kobler, *Capone: The Life and World of Al Capone* (Cambridge, Mass: Da Capo, 2003), p. 73. I have no evidence that Rezo's son admits to being a member of the *vory-v-zakone.*

p. 76. The Kutaisi-based lawyer is cited in Slade, *Reorganizing Crime,* p. 100.

p. 76. Zykov served time with Grandpa Khasan; see V. P. Podatev, *Kniga Zhizni ili Put' k Svetu* (2015) at: https://www.proza.ru/avtor/podatev.

p. 78. 'A *vor* interviewed in 2014 claimed that it could cost up to $1.5 million in Russia': the interview is in Larionidou, *The Emergence,* p. 31 and p. 43.

p. 80. The four Families that run Reggio Calabria are De Stefano, Condello, Libri and Tegano. This has been established by several police investigations, such as *Crimine (Direzione Distrettuale Antimafia presso il Tribunale di Reggio Calabria),* Operazione Crimine: ordinanza di custodia cautelare, vol. 1, p. 316, 2010 and *Meta* (2011), discussed in Direzione Nazionale Antimafia, Relazione semestrale, 2014. See also Direzione Nazionale Antimafia, *Relazione annuale sulle attività svolte dal Procuratore Nazionale Antimafia,* 2011.

p. 86. On Dubai, see Jim Krane, *Dubai* (London: Atlantic Books, 2010), especially p. 224, and Daniel Brook, *The History of Future Cities* (New York: W. W. Norton & Company, 2014), chapter 11. On privatised spaces, see Anna Minton, 'What is the most private city in the world?' *Guardian*, 26 March 2015. Water consumption across the UAE was 82 per cent above the global average and three times higher than average per capita consumption in the European Union in 2013. Waste levels per capita are almost double that of the UK (Sarah Townsend, 'Greening the desert: How the UAE aims to change its carbon footprint', http://www.arabianbusiness.com/greening-desert-how-uae-aims-to-change-its-carbon-footprint-599849.html, 19 July 2015).

p. 90. On PrimeCrime.ru, see Carl Schreck, 'The Who's Who of Moscow mobsters', *The National*, 5 August 2009, at: http://www.thenational.ae/news/world/europe/the-whos-who-of-moscow-mobsters.

Salvatore Lo Piccolo is arrested with the Constitution of the Sicilian Mafia, Giardinello, Palermo Province, November 2007

p. 95. On the arrest of Lo Piccolo, see 'Palermo, catturati i boss Lo Piccolo', *Corriere della Sera*, 7 November 2007.

pp. 95–6. The document found in the possession of Lo Piccolo is in Gotha (2008). See also Morosini, *Il Gotha di Cosa Nostra*, pp. 26–32.

p. 96. The quote is from Joseph Bonanno, with Sergio Lalli, *A Man of Honor* (New York: Simon & Schuster, 1983), p. 147.

p. 96. A reference to the Bontade election is in Gambetta, *The Sicilian Mafia*, p. 294, note 23. See also Falcone, *Cose di Cosa Nostra*, pp. 100–101.

p. 96. Rules asking permission to enter into business with a member of another Family and the use of violence are mentioned respectively in Bonanno, *A Man of Honor*, p. 157, and in Mass, *Underboss*, p. 140.

p. 98. On the *migawari* in the Yakuza, see Hill, *The Japanese Mafia*, p. 73.

p. 98. The importance of legitimacy in the Italian-American Mafia is highlighted by Annelise Graebner Anderson, *The Business of Organized Crime: A Cosa Nostra Family* (Stanford: Hoover Institution Press, 1979), p. 45, see also pp. 36–7.

p. 98. The Henry Hill quote is in Nicholas Pileggi, *Wiseguy: Life in a Mafia Family* (London: Corgi Books, 1996), p. 128. See also Pistone, *Donnie Brasco*, p. 117.

p. 98. Sammy 'the Bull' Gravano on breaking rules is in Maas, *Underboss*, p. 141. Along similar lines, Antonio Calderone, see Arlacchi, *Men of Dishonor*, p. 67.

p. 98. The quote from the former member of the Sicilian Mafia on how bosses could kill members without informing anybody is in Morosini, *Il Gotha di Cosa Nostra*, p. 58.

pp. 98–9. On Scalise selling membership, see Joe Valachi cited in Hortis, *The Mob and the City*, p. 233 and p. 237. See also John H. Davis, *Mafia Dynasty: The Rise and Fall of the Gambino Crime Family* (New York: Harper Torch, 1993), p. 75; Peter Maas, *The Valachi Papers* (New York: Perennial, 2003); p. 227, Maas, *Underboss*, p. 51. Pistone mentions that occasionally prospects paid their *capo regime* to get made (cited in Hortis, *The Mob and the City*, p. 195).

p. 98. The scholar who recorded the instance of a Yakuza boss failing to keep his promise towards a member arrested in his stead is Hill, *The Japanese Mafia*, pp. 73–4. The scholar who noticed a high degree of animosity within Yakuza gangs is Hiroaki Iwai, 'Organized Crime in Japan', p. 222.

p. 100. On the Commission decision to switch party, see Morosini, *Il Gotha di Cosa Nostra*, p. 58, and Dino, *Spatuzza*, p. 127. As for the effects of the decision, see Attilio Bolzoni, 'Nei feudi della mafia il PSI al primo posto', *La Repubblica*, 18 June 1987.

p. 101. On the Perseus Operation, see: http://www.monrealepress.it/2016/03/16/Mafia-vecchi-e-nuovi-boss-che-si-organizzano-i-dettagli-delloperazione-dei-carabinieri-di-monreale/; http://www.antiMafiaduemila.com/home/primo-piano/34495-operazione-perseo-la-nuova-commissione-provinciale-di-cosa-nostra.html. The investigation also revealed several attempts to restructure the Palermo Families and join some of them together, given their small size. The attempt to restructure the Palermo Families was discovered by the 'Nuovo Mandamento' police investigation. For instance, the territories of Partinico and San Giuseppe Jato were to be merged and the area ruled over by San Lorenzo Families was to be extended. This is an indication of the difficulties in finding enough bosses and of the reduction in activities. See F. Moiraghi, 'Cosa Nostra a Palermo oggi', an inverview with Umberto Santino, in *I Siciliani giovani*, June 2014; Attilio Scaglione, 'Mafia ed Economia. La diffusione del fenomeno estorsivo in Sicilia e i costi dell'illegalità', p. 91, and Punzo, 'Le nuove dinamiche', p. 121, both in *Non è più quella di una volta*.

p. 101. Testimony of Joseph Massino: http://www.nydailynews.com/boss-rat-joseph-massino-admits-court-Mafia-commission-hasn-met-25-years-article-1.114750. Thomas Reppetto's quote is from the same article.

p. 103. 'Georgiano ucciso in piazza Moro: Procura chiede cinque condanne', *BariToday*, 20 December 2016, at: http://www.baritoday.it/cronaca/processo-omicidio-georgiano-rezav-tchuradze-chieste-condanne.html. See also Georgiano ucciso in piazza Moro, 5 condanne: 'Fu vendetta personale, non omicidio di mafia', *Bari Today*, 18 January 2017, http://www.baritoday.it/cronaca/georgiano-ucciso-bari-condanne-esclusa-aggravante-mafiosa.html.

4. Money

Moscow–Italy, 1996

My main source for this section is an extensive investigation into the Russian Mafia conducted by a special branch of the Italian police. The people involved in the investigation were never charged with any crime in Italy. I have published some material related to the story presented in this chapter in Varese, *Mafias on the Move*.

The Service Providers

p. 106. On the Solntsevo district, see Varese, *Mafias on the Move*, p. 65, and Misha Glenny, *McMafia* (London: Bodley Head, 2008), p. 79.

p. 106. The FBI report is cited in *Moscow Times*, 22 February 2000. The 2014 *Fortune* magazine investigation is available at: http://fortune.com/2014/09/14/biggest-organised-crime-groups-in-the-world/.

The Banks

p. 108. A brief summary of anti-money-laundering legislation can be found in Stephen Platt, *Criminal Capital: How the Finance Industry Facilitates Crime* (London: Palgrave Macmillan, 2015), pp. 22–3. The quotation in the text is from p. 74. The list of signatories of the 1988

Convention is found at: https://treaties.un.org/Pages/ViewDetails.
aspx?src=TREATY&mtdsg_no=VI-19&chapter=6&lang=en.

On the BCCI affair, see the 1992 US Congress Investigation, available
at: http://fas.org/irp/congress/1992_rpt/bcci/.

p. 108. The full and precise title of the British government report is 'UK
national risk assessment of money laundering and terrorist financing',
https://www.gov.uk/government/publications/uk-national-risk-assessment-
of-money-laundering-and-terrorist-financing. See especially p. 12 and
p. 32.

p. 109. On the Wachovia scandal, see, for example, http://www.justice.gov/
archive/usao/fls/PressReleases/Attachments/100317-02.Statement.pdf and
Platt, *Criminal Capital*, p. 41.

p. 109. On the HSCB scandal, see: 'U.S. vulnerabilities to money laundering,
drugs, and terrorist financing: HSBC case history', at www.gpo.gov/fdsys/
pkg/CHRG ... /pdf/CHRG-112shrg76646.pdf; 'United Sates *v.* HSBC
Bank USA, Case No. 1:12-cr-00 763-ILG', Document 3-3, 61 (EDNY, 11
December 2012), available at: http://www.justice.gov/opa/documents/hsbc/
dpa-attachment-a.pdf, p. 50.

p. 110. The quotation is from the November 2014 FCA report, 'How
small banks manage money laundering and sanctions risk', available
at: https://www.fca.org.uk/news/tr14-16-how-small-banks-manage-
money-laundering-and-sanctions-risk. See also: Platt, *Criminal Capital*,
p. 47; James Titcomb, 'Is this a new golden age for London's private
banks?', *Telegraph*, 5 May 2015, at: http://www.telegraph.co.uk/finance/
newsbysector/banksandfinance/11582477/Is-this-a-new-golden-age-for-
Londons-private-banks.html; BBA, 'A wealth of opportunities: Private
banking and wealth management attracts investment, creates jobs and
boosts growth', 2 October 2014, at: https://www.bba.org.uk/news/
press-releases/a-wealth-of-opportunities-private-banking-and-wealth-
management-attracts-investment-creates-jobs-and-boosts-growth/#.
V5T_RDXPb54; Martin Arnold, 'UK now main rival to Swiss private
banks', *Financial Times*, 2 October 2014, at: https://www.ft.com/content/
c1b99226-4a55-11e4-b8bc-00144feab7de.

The protected world of private banking is described masterfully in
John le Carré, *A Most Wanted Man* (London: Hodder & Stoughton,
2008).

pp. 110–11. Oliver Bullough, 'Offshore in central London: the curious case
of 29 Harley Street', *Guardian*, 19 April 2016. Michael Findley, Daniel
Nielson and Jason Sharman, *Global Shell Games: Experiments in
Transnational Relations, Crime, and Terrorism* (Cambridge: Cambridge
University Press, 2014).

pp. 110–12. See Platt, *Criminal Capital* (p. 30 and p. 32) on how criminals use corporations.

p. 111. On the Russian Underground, see: https://www.trendmicro.com/cloud-content/us/pdfs/security-intelligence/wp-russian-underground-2.0.pdf.

p. 112. Lansky's investments in Cuba are the subject of many books and films. See, for example, Robert Lacey, *Little Man: Meyer Lansky and the Gangster Life* (Boston, MA: Little Brown & Co., 1991); T. J. English, *Havana Nocturne* (New York: HarperCollins, 2008); Jack Colhoun, *Gangsterismo* (New York: OR Books, 2013); James Cockayne, *Hidden Power: The Strategic Logic of Organised Crime* (London: Hurst & Company, 2016), pp. 203–26.

pp. 112–13. I discussed the notion of trust in Paolo Campana and Federico Varese, 'Cooperation in Criminal Organizations: Kinship and Violence as Credible Commitments', *Rationality and Society*, 25(3), 2013, pp. 263–89; and Federico Varese, 'Underground Banking and Corruption', in Susan Rose-Ackerman and Paul Lagunes (eds), *Greed, Corruption, and the Modern State: Essays in Political Economy* (Cheltenham: Edward Elgar, 2015), pp. 336–58.

See also Klaus Von Lampe and Per Ole Johansen, 'Organized Crime and Trust: On the Conceptualization and Empirical Relevance of Trust in the Context of Criminal Networks', *Global Crime* 6(2), 2004, pp. 159–84.

p. 113. The quote from Calderone is in *Men of Honor*, p. 146.

5. Love

Via Meli, Palermo, 2004

pp. 119–21. The conversations between Nicola Mandalà and *Amalia* are contained in several unpublished court files: see 'Requisitoria, Seconda Parte, De Lucia', in Villabate (2009); and the 'La Famiglia di Villabate' in Grande Mandamento (2005) and Gotha (2008). These documents also offer details on Provenzano's secret trip to France.

p. 121. On men of honour kissing after the ceremony on the lips (but 'without the tongue'), see Leonardo Vitale's description of his ritual initiation in Gambetta, *The Sicilian Mafia*, p. 131, and Rossella Merlino, 'Tales of Trauma, Identity, and God: The Memoirs of Mafia Boss Michele Greco and Leonardo Vitale', *European Review of Organised Crime*, 2(1), 2014, pp. 49–75.

p. 122. Women were not excluded entirely from the labour market in Sicily. For instance, they were employed as manual workers and peasants (I am grateful to Valeria Pizzini-Gambetta for bringing this point to my attention).

p. 122. On the current attitudes of the Russian Orthodox Church towards feminism, see the *Guardian*, 9 April 2013, available at: http://www. theguardian.com/world/2013/apr/09/feminism-destroy-russia-patriarch-kirill.

p. 122, note 1. The Gender Gap Index is produced by the Economic World Forum and is available at: http://reports.weforum.org/global-gender-gap-report-2015/.

p. 123. On the creation of the Mafia Commission in Sicily in the late 1950s, see the testimony of Tommaso Buscetta in Pino Arlacchi, *Addio Cosa nostra: La vita di Tommaso Buscetta* (Milan: Rizzoli, 1994), pp. 60–66, and Enzo Biagi, *Il Boss è solo* (Milan: Mondadori, 1986), pp. 147–54. See also Commissione Parlamentare Antimafia, 'Relazione sul traffico mafioso di tabacchi e stupefacenti nonché sui rapporti tra mafia e gangsterismo italo-americano'. Relatore: senatore Michele Zuccalà, 1976, p. 329; Commissione Parlamentare Antimafia, 'Relazione sul caso Impastato', Doc. XXIII, N.50, XIII Legislatura, 2000, pp. 19–20.

p. 123. On the Italian-American Mafia rules around admission, see Varese, *Mafias on the Move*, p. 123. Buscetta claims that even Jews and Irish had been admitted at the height of the Castellammare War (see *Mafias on the Move*, p. 225, note 65). Ernest Volkman, *Gangbusters* (London: Faber & Faber, 1998) claims that the year in which it was decided that a perspective member needed to be Italian on his father's side only was 1975. The 'zips' were young Sicilians imported into the Bonanno Family by Carmine Galante in the 1970s (Selwyn Raab, *Five Families*, New York: St Martin's Press, 2005, p. 205). Brusca in Lodato, *Ho ucciso Giovanni Falcone*, p. 160, mentions an instance in which a Family is under pressure and does not recruit women or even rely on them.

p. 123. The review of women's roles in terrorist organisations is by Karen Jacques and Paul J. Taylor, 'Female Terrorism: A Review', *Terrorism and Political Violence*, 21(3), 2009, pp. 499–515. See also Kim Cragin and Sara Daly, *Women as Terrorists* (Santa Monica, CA: Praeger Security, 2009), who offer plenty of details on how the PKK, the Tamil Tigers, the FARC, the Zapatista Army and Sendero Luminoso have used women in combat.

pp. 123–4. A proponent of the argument that violence accounts for women's exclusion from the Mafia is Hill, *The Yakuza*, p. 51.

p. 125. The point that the Mafia is not under pressure from the feminist movement to open its ranks is made by Valeria Pizzini-Gambetta, 'Gender

Norms in the Sicilian Mafia' (1999), reprinted in Federico Varese (ed.), *Organized Crime: Critical Concepts in Criminology* (London: Routledge, 2010), vol. 2, p. 218. See also Valeria Pizzini-Gambetta, 'Organized Crime', in Rosemary Gartner and Bill McCarthy (eds), *The Oxford Handbook of Gender, Sex, and Crime* (Oxford: Oxford University Press, 2014), pp. 448–67.

p. 125. The quote 'true love is irresponsible' comes from https://www.adbusters.org/magazine/122/falling-love.html. The point that love engenders other emotions and cannot be artificially induced can be found in Jon Elster, 'Rationality and the Emotions', *Economic Journal*, 106(438), 1996, pp. 1386–97. Nando Dalla Chiesa ('Introduzione', in Marika Demaria, *La Scelta di Lea. Lea Garofalo. La ribellione di una donna alla 'ndrangheta*, Milan: Melampo, p. 15) mentions 'la forza rivoluzionaria dei sentimenti'.

Renate Siebert, *Secrets of Life and Death: Women and the Mafia* (London and New York: Verso, 1996), pp. 175–88, discusses the role of women's emotions as a resource to fight the Mafia.

pp. 125–6. The quote from Felicia Impastato comes from Felicia Bartolotta Impastato, *La Mafia in casa mia*, ed. Anna Puglisi and Umberto Santino (Palermo: La Luna, 1986), p. 11. On Ms Impastato, see also Nando Dalla Chiesa, *Le ribelli* (Milano: Melampo, 2006), pp. 39–82. The point that marriages are designed to build alliances is expanded upon in Renate Siebert, *Le Donne, la Mafia* (Milan: Il Saggiatore, 1994). Jane Schneider and Peter Schneider, *Culture and Political Economy in Western Sicily* (New York: Academic Press, 1976), pp. 73–9, find that families associated with the Mafia are more likely than non-Mafia families to arrange cousin marriages, requiring a special dispensation from the Catholic Church. American Mafia wives are less likely than their Sicilian counterparts to come from Mafia families, but they tend to come from the same neighbourhood, what Pizzini-Gambetta calls 'territorial endogamy' (Valeria Pizzini-Gambetta, 'Mafia Women in Brooklyn', *Global Crime* 8(1), 2007, pp. 80–93, especially pp. 89–91).

p. 126. The Sicilian saying on women is mentioned by Pizzini-Gambetta, 'Gender Norms in the Sicilian Mafia', p. 220.

p. 126. The quotations from Calderone are to be found in Arlacchi, *Men of Dishonor*, p. 163.

pp. 126–7. The story of Serafina Battaglia is mentioned by Calderone in Arlacchi, *Men of Dishonor*, p. 167. See also Anna Puglisi and Umberto Santino, 'La ricerca del Centro Impastato su Donne e Mafia', in Fedele Ruggeri (ed.), *La società e il suo doppio* (Milan: Angeli, 2001), pp. 23–42; Anna Puglisi, *Donne, Mafia e Antimafia* (Trapani: Di Girolamo, 2012);

and Alessandra Dino, *La Mafia devota* (Bari: Laterza, 2010), p. 91. Battaglia's partner, murdered by the Mafia on 9 April 1960, was Stefano Leale. Her son, Salvatore Lupo Leale, was murdered on 30 January 1962.

   Serafina Battaglia started to collaborate with prosecutor Cesare Terranova, himself murdered by the Mafia. The citation referring to her carrying a gun is taken from 'Morta Serafina Battaglia, fu la prima a testimoniare contro i boss della Mafia', *Il Piccolo*, 10 September 2004. The second quote is from Mauro De Mauro, 'La vedova Battaglia accusa', *L'Ora*, 21 January 1964. Mauro De Mauro was also killed by the Mafia in 1970. For a rare interview with Battaglia, see: http://www.raistoria.rai.it/articoli/serafina-battaglia-la-prima-donna-contro-la-Mafia/11936/default.aspx.

p. 127. Giacoma Filippello's words are cited in Puglisi and Santino, 'La ricerca del Centro Impastato su Donne e Mafia', p. 37. In her second life, Giacoma opened a brothel in Rome in the 1990s and was arrested for pimping in 1997. See Enrico Deaglio, *Raccolto rosso* (Milan: Saggiatore, 2010), p. 312.

p. 127. The man eased out of Falcone's murder plot is Mario Santo di Matteo. The man in charge of the murder is Giovanni Brusca, who is quoted in the text (Lodato, *Ho ucciso Giovanni Falcone*, p. 98 and p. 145).

p. 127. The 'sponge' quote is from Piera Aiello (in Puglisi and Santino, 'La ricerca del Centro Impastato su Donne e Mafia', p. 38).

p. 127. The story of Damiano Caruso is in Arlacchi, *Men of Dishonor*, pp. 160–61. Brusca mentions a similar more recent case: Antonella Bonomo, the pregnant partner of Mafioso Vincenzo Milazzo, was killed after him because 'it was thought that she knew all the ins and outs of Milazzo's business' (Lodato, *Ho ucciso Giovanni Falcone*, p. 109).

p. 128. The quotations from Brusca are in Lodato, *Ho ucciso Giovanni Falcone*, pp. 181, 182 and 183. See also p. 35 and p. 41. Jane Schneider and Peter Schneider, *Reversible Destiny: Mafia, Antimafia and the Struggle for Palermo* (Berkeley, CA: University of California Press, 2003), p. 95, also cite from Brusca and discuss this aspect of Mafia life. See also Jane Schneider and Peter Schneider, 'Gender and Violence: Four Themes in the Everyday World of Mafia Wives', in Dana Renga (ed.), *Mafia Movies: A Reader* (Toronto: University of Toronto Press, 2011), p. 39.

pp. 128–9. The new role of women in the Sicilian Mafia is highlighted by Punzo, 'Le nuove dinamiche', pp. 131–3. See also A. Ziniti, 'E la donna del capo tentò di impadronirsi di una taverna', *La Repubblica*, 24 June 2014. On the Brancaccio story, see A. Ziniti, 'Nunzia, la regina dal pugno di ferro da Roma governava su Brancaccio', *La Repubblica*, 30 November 2011, and Dino, *Spatuzza*, pp. 91–92; 'Blitz anti mafia nel Trapanese.

Tra i capi-clan anche due donne', *Corriere della Sera*, 3 November 2009. Anna Greco pleaded guilty and was sentenced to two years and two months (http://liliumjoker-liliumjoker.blogspot.co.uk/2010/10/mafia-otto-rinviiguidizio-alcamo.html). Matteo Messina Denaro's sister was sentenced to fourteen years and six months for mafia association in 2016. Anna Maria Accurso has since been acquitted.

Italian-American Mafia

p. 129. The story of 'Big Jim' Colosimo's love for his second wife, and the negative effect it had on his underworld reputation, is in Kobler, *Capone*, pp. 65–6.

p. 130. The story of Al Capone's test is in Kobler, *Capone*, p. 141.

The vory-v-zakone

p. 131. For the women in the *vory*, I draw upon material I published in Varese, *The Russian Mafia*, p. 153. See also Svetlana Stephenson, *Gangs of Russia* (Ithaca, NY: Cornell UP, 2015), pp. 106–7.

The Yakuza

p. 131. The 'masculine narcissism' ideology of the Yakuza is mentioned by Hill, *The Yakuza*, p. 74. The excellent study by Rie Alkemade, '"Outsiders Amongst Outsiders": A Cultural Criminological Perspective on the Sub-Subcultural World of Women in the Yakuza Underworld', is available at: http://www.japansubculture.com/?s=Rie+Alkemade+. The quote regarding women as objects is taken from Alkemade's paper.

p. 132. Miyazaki Manabu talks about his absentee Yakuza father in *Toppamono* (Tokyo: Kotan Publishing, 2005), p. 19 and p. 29.

p. 133. The quote from the Yakuza boss's son is taken from Alkemade, 'Outsiders Amongst Outsiders': chapter V, section II.

p. 133. The quote from Emiko Hamano is in Ryu Otomo, 'Women in Organized Crime in Japan', in Giovanni Fiandaca (ed.), *Women and the Mafia: Female Roles in Organized Crime Structures* (New York: Springer, 2007), p. 214.

p. 134. Miyazaki recounts how his mother would scold gang members (*Toppamono*, p. 21, p. 23).

p. 134. Miyazaki makes the point that women acted as myth-makers (*Toppamono*, p. 22). The story of Uncle Yamane's wife is also told by Miyazaki, *Toppamono*, p. 72.

p. 134. On the current size of Yamaguchi-gumi, see Alexander Martin, 'Japan's Biggest Mob Group Splits Under Money, Police Pressure', *Wall Street Journal*, 9 September 2015, available at: http://www.wsj.com/ articles/japans-gangsters-find-extortion-no-longer-pays-forcing-yakuza-split-1441773870.

pp. 134–5. The quote from Yuki Taoka is from her autobiography *Otosan no sekkenbako: aisareru koto o wasurete iru hito e (My Father's Soap Box: For Those Who Have Forgotten That They Are Loved)* 2003, p. 27 (cited in Alkemade, 'Outsiders Amongst Outsiders').

pp. 135–6. The conflict over the succession of Kazuo Taoka led to the Yama–Ichi War (1985–9). See David Kaplan and Alec Dubro, *Yakuza: Japan's Criminal Underworld*, pp. 121–3.

p. 136. The quote from Yuki Taoka is on p. 160 of her autobiography (cited in Alkemade, 'Outsiders Amongst Outsiders').

p. 136. The figure on the growth of the Yamaguchi-gumi during Fumiko's tenure is taken from Kaplan and Dubro, *Yakuza: Japan's Criminal Underworld*, p. 120.

6. Self-image

Macau, 1999–2014

pp. 137–40. The film *Casino* is available on DVD and I have a copy. I have taken additional information on the movie from Alison Dakota Gee, 'Capturing Macau's Gangland – on Camera', *New York Times*, 11 June 1998. There are many sources on 'Broken Tooth' Wan. A good general discussion is in João De Pina-Cabal, *Between China and Europe: Person, Culture and Emotion in Macau* (London-New York: Continuum, 2002), especially chapter 10. See also Bertil Lintner, 'Organised Crime: A World Wide Web?', *Global Dialogue*, 1999; 'Tales from the Dragonhead', *Time* magazine, 20 April 1998. Several articles published in *South China Morning Post* are useful, especially 17 April 2011; 26 November 2012; 1 December 2012; 28 February 2013; 2 March 2013; 16 May 2014. Other sources are the *Macau Daily Times* (especially 14 September 2012), *CasinoLeaks* and the *Standard* (especially 28 September 2012).

p. 138. Gambling revenues for 2013 are cited in Kate O'Keeffe, 'Macau's 2013 gambling revenue rose 19 per cent to $45.2 billion', *Wall Street Journal*, 2

January 2014 (http://www.wsj.com/articles/SB1000142405270230364060457929588426 1629874).

Most recent data cited in the text on the profits in VIP rooms are taken from GGRAsia, 'VIP-room revamp hurt Wynn Macau's market share', 10 July 2014, available at: http://www.ggrasia.com/vip-room-revamp-hurting-wynn-macaus-results-analyst/.

p. 138. Descriptions of baccarat's rules abound. The Wikipedia entry is quite clear: http://en.wikipedia.org/wiki/Baccarat_ per cent28card_game per cent29. See also Lawrence Osborne, *The Ballad of a Small Player* (London-New York: Hogarth, 2014), especially pp. 38–40. However, the best way to understand the game is to play it.

p. 139. Chairman A. G. Burnett gave his testimony on 27 June 2013 before the US-China Economic and Security Review Commission. The text is available at: http://www.uscc.gov/sites/default/files/A.G. per cent20Burnett per cent20Testimony.pdf.

p. 140. The interview with the producer of *Casino* is in Alison Dakota Gee, 'Capturing Macau's Gangland – on Camera', *New York Times*, 11 June 1998.

p. 141. Tullio Kezich's story is from *Corriere della Sera*, 1 July 1998. See also J. D. Pistone, *The Way of the Wiseguy* (Philadelphia and London: Running Press, 2004), p. 46. Diego Gambetta, *Codes of the Underworld*, chapter 10, 'Why (Low) Life Imitates Art' (Princeton, NJ: Princeton University Press), pp. 251–74 discusses how Mafiosi imitate films. He also refers to Kezich's article, and to Donnie Brasco.

Yakuza movies

pp. 141–7. This section is derived in part from Federico Varese, 'The Secret History of Japanese Cinema: The Yakuza Movies', *Global Crime*, 7(1), 2006, pp. 107–26 (http://www.tandfonline.com/doi/full/10.1080/17440570600650166), where the reader can find detailed references. Below are the sources of direct quotations. I am grateful to the editors for allowing me to use sections of the paper in this book.

p. 143. Fukasaku's words on the use of hand-held cameras are cited in Patrick Macias, *Tokioscope: The Japanese Cult Film Companion* (San Francisco: Cadence Books, 2001), p. 154.

p. 143. Satō's 1997 interview is from Chris Desjardins, *Outlaw Masters of Japanese Film* (London: I.B. Tauris, 2005), p. 82.

p. 144. Fukasaku's 1997 interview is in Desjardins, *Outlaw Masters,* p. 23.

p. 144. On *Anti-Extortion Woman* (also known as *Minbō: The Gentle Art of Japanese Extortion*), see Biennale di Venezia, *Mostra Internazionale d'Arte Cinematografica*, official catalogue (Edizioni Biennale-Fabbri Editori, Venice, 1992), pp. 152–5.

p. 145. For Schilling on Itami, see Mark Schilling, *Contemporary Japanese Film* (New York and Tokyo: Weatherhill, 1999), p. 258.

p. 145. Itami describing his ordeal is in Schilling, *Contemporary Japanese Film*, p. 83.

p. 146. On *A Band of Daredevils*, see *Asahi News Service,* 30 December 1986. The actor in question is Tsuruta Koji. *A Band of Daredevils* was directed by Yamashita Kōsaku.

p. 147. Paul Schrader, 'Yakuza-Eiga: A Primer', *Film Comment*, 10(1), 1974, pp. 8–17.

p. 147. On Andō, see *Japan Times,* 17 April 2002. The most important in this long series of movies about this gang was released by Tōei in 1973 as *True Account of Andō Gang*. Andō was president of the film production company Andō Kikaku until his death in 2015.

The Godfather (1972)

p. 147. On Mafiosi discussing the casting of *The Godfather*, see *New York Times*, 9 September 1990, and Gambetta, *Codes*, p. 259.

p. 147. Lynda Milito discusses her husband's fascination for *The Godfather* in *Mafia Wife: My Story of Love, Murder and Madness*, with Reg Potterton (New York: HarperCollins, 2004), pp. 126–7. See also Sammy 'the Bull' Gravano on Milito in Maas, *Underboss*, pp. 389–95.

p. 148. Sammy 'the Bull' Gravano's quotations are taken from Maas, *Underboss*, p. 114 and p. 115.

p. 148. The reference to Joe Paruta by Gravano as his 'Luca Brasi' is mentioned in Jerry Capeci and Gene Mustain, *Gotti: Rise and Fall* (New York: Onyx, 1996), p. 118.

p. 148, note 2. The 2011 biopic of Gotti starring Al Pacino was to be directed by Barry Levinson: http://pagesix.com/2016/02/07/travoltas-gotti-film-mobbed-with-trouble/.

p. 148. Pileggi's words are taken from Jack Newfield, 'Little Big Man', *New York Magazine*, 24 June 2002: http://nymag.com/nymetro/news/trends/columns/cityside/6160/. A similar point is made also by the biographer of Meyer Lansky. See Lacey, *Little Man*, p. 319.

p. 149. Gotti's wedding reception is mentioned in Capeci and Mustain, *Gotti: Rise and Fall*, p. 86.

p. 149. The citation from Albert DeMeo comes from Albert DeMeo, *For the Sins of My Father: A Mafia Killer, His Son, and the Legacy of a Mob Life*, with Mary Jane Ross (New York: Broadway Books, 2003), p. 166. On Roy DeMeo, see Gene Mustain and Jerry Capeci, *Murder Machine: A True Story of Murder, Madness and the Mafia* (London: Ebury Press, 2013). On *The Godfather*, see p. 62.

p. 149. The request of the music theme by Donnie Brasco's associates is mentioned in Pistone, *Donnie Brasco*, p. 219. The use of *The Godfather*'s soundtrack in a Mafia wedding in Sicily is mentioned in Gambetta, *The Sicilian Mafia*, p. 135.

p. 149. Calderone's reference to the Di Cristina's murder is in Arlacchi, *Men of Dishonor*, p. 159. The instance of building contractors finding a severed head in their company in Palermo is mentioned by Gambetta, *Codes*, p. 265. The original story was published by *La Repubblica*, 31 May 1991.

Curiously, when John Torrio was critically wounded and lying in a hospital bed in late January 1925, 'three carloads of armed men' were seen circling the building, and four of Torrio's bodyguards joined the police to protect him (Kobler, *Capone*, p. 138). Puzo might have been inspired by this story for the scene in *The Godfather*.

p. 149. On children of bosses not inheriting the title and role of boss, see Calderone, *Men of Dishonor*, p. 21.

p. 150. The definitive debunking of the notion that the Italian-American Mafia did not deal in drugs is in the excellent Hortis, *The Mob and the City*, pp. 127–53. I cite data from his book (p. 131). See also Davis, *Mafia Dynasty*, pp. 112–13; and Philip Jenkins, 'Narcotics Trafficking and the American Mafia: The Myth of Internal Prohibition', *Crime, Law and Social Change*, 18(3), 1992, pp. 303–18. Of course the myth was peddled by real mobsters as well, such as Bonanno, Costello and Lucchese, in their writing and testimonies (see Hortis, *The Mob and the City*, p. 127).

p. 150. For Mario Puzo's prior knowledge of Mafia matters, see his obituary in the *Independent*, 5 July 1999, cited by Gambetta, *Codes*, p. 258. Martin Scorsese and the co-writer of *Mean Streets*, Mardik Martin, 'had contempt for Puzo's *The Godfather*, then a bestseller, which Scorsese knew bore no relation to the truth' (Peter Biskind, *Easy Riders, Raging Bulls*, London: Bloomsbury, p. 229).

p. 150. Information on Radik Galiakbarov and his fascination for *The Godfather* come from a lengthy article by Roman Obolenskii, 'Chertova dyuzhina poluchila po zaslugam', *Respublika Tatarstani*, 14 February 2002: http://rt-online.ru/p-rubr-prav-25774/. See also Aleksandr Shagulin, 'Groza iz "Khadi Taktash" vozvrashaetsya v Kazan', БИЗНЕС Online, 15

May 2012: http://www.business-gazeta.ru/print/59466/; and http://kpk.org.ua/2007/10/03/postsovetskijj_banditizm_banda_chertova_djuzhina.html.

In English, see Svetlana Stephenson, *Gangs of Russia*, p. 95. Stephenson also mentions the leader of the 29th Kompleks gang (also in Kazan), Adygan Saliakhov, who 'made young gang members watch *Once Upon a Time in America* and *The Godfather* as training videos. It was said that his favourite phrase was "Kill him!"' (p. 95).

p. 150, note 1. The words of Simone Pepe are cited in, among other places, Rich Calder, 'Mobster left to be eaten alive by pigs', *New York Post*, 29 November 2013: http://nypost.com/2013/11/29/mobster-left-to-be-eaten-alive-by-pigs/. This article also makes a reference to the film *Hannibal*. Other observers have made reference to a scene in *Snatch* (2000), directed by Guy Ritchie, in which a British gangster called Brick Top recommends disposing of a dead body by feeding it to pigs.

Giuseppe Greco (1953–2015), the worst Mafia film-maker

pp. 151–3. On Michele Greco, see Rossella Merlino, 'Tales of Trauma, Identity, and God'; Lodato, *Ho ucciso Giovanni Falcone*, pp. 53–4; Felice Flaro, 'Greco, il "papa" che predicava la pace e ordinava gli omicidi', *Corriere della Sera*, 14 February 2008; Francesco Viviano, *Michele Greco: Il memoriale* (Rome: Aliberti, 2008).

A six-minute appreciation of Castellani filmed by Daniele Ciprì and Franco Maresco, entitled 'Chi è Giorgio Castellani?' (2006), is available at: https://www.youtube.com/watch?v=CjYk7C_BgJc.

Crema, Cioccolata e Pa...prika (1981) is available at https://www.youtube.com/watch?v=r8QleESu2bA. For the analysis of the film, I draw upon Gordiano Lupi, 'Crema, Cioccolata e Pa...prika (Film, 1981)', 4 June 2014, available at: http://www.futuro-europa.it/7025/cultura/crema-cioccolata-e-paprika-film-1981.html.

The news of Giuseppe Greco's death was reported by, among others, *La Repubblica*, 12 February 2011, at: http://palermo.repubblica.it/cronaca/2011/02/12/news/e_morto_il_regista_giuseppe_greco_il_figlio_del_papa_della_Mafia-12378758/.

p. 152. The interview with Giuseppe Greco is in: 'Un Film su papà, il boss', *La Repubblica*, 21 December 1997.

p. 153. The words of Michele Greco were spoken at the Maxi Trial and reproduced in Gaetano Savatteri and Pietro Calderoni, *Voci del verbo Mafiare* (Naples: Pironti, 1993). An English translation is in Attilio

Bolzoni, *White Shotgun: The Sicilian Mafia in Their Own Words* (London: Pan Books, 2013), p. 369.

p. 153. The actors of *Crema, cioccolata e pa...prika* (1981) included Renzo Montagnani, Barbara Bouchet and Silvia Dionisio.

p. 153. The actor who admitted that the movie is 'quite horrid' is Giorgio Bracardi in an interview with Ciprì and Maresco.

p. 153. On the Maxi Trial, see La Spina, 'The Fight against the Italian Mafia', p. 605.

p. 153. *Vite perdute* (1992) is available at: https://www.youtube.com/watch?v=PVMZxsjGQEA. To discuss the film, I draw upon: Filippo Mammì, '"Vite perdute", un "film contro" impossibile da rivalutare e difficile da guardare. Analisi di una pellicola su cui nessuno osa chiedere', 7 October 2013, available at: http://www.edicoladipinuccio.it/blog/vite-perdute-un-film-contro-impossibile-da-rivalutare-e-difficile-da-guardare-analisi-di-una-pellicola-su-cui-nessuno-osa-chiedere/; and Ciprì and Maresco, *Vite perdute (I migliori nani della nostra vita)* (2007), available at: https://www.youtube.com/watch?v=UPgIpLG85cQ. The film is loosely inspired by a successful prison film released a few years earlier, Marco Risi's *Mery per sempre* (1989). Some of the actors are in both movies.

pp. 154–5. Unfortunately *I Grimaldi* (1997) is not available. For more on this, see Ciprì and Maresco, *I Grimaldi (I migliori nani della nostra vita)*, available at: https://www.youtube.com/watch?v=DOWAGMjXNsQ.

p. 155. Interview with Attilio Bolzoni, 4 April 2016.

p. 155. Interview with Francesco Maresco, 30 April 2016.

Macau, November 2012–2014

p. 156. See Interview with 'Broken Tooth' in: '"Broken Tooth" pledges to return to the gaming industry', *Macau Daily News*, 19 July 2013.

p. 157. 'L'arc theft allegedly involves "Broken Tooth" VIP room', *Macau Daily Times*, 22 February 2016.

7. Politics

The people we interviewed in Hong Kong included: a professor of social sciences and supporter of Umbrella Movement (6 November 2014); a professor of social sciences and trade union activist (2 November 2014); a professor of social sciences present in Mong Kok on 3 October (2 November

2014); a nail salon owner, Mong Kok (17 October 2014); Mary, a volunteer at the Mong Kok First Aid Station (18 March 2015); a minibus driver, Mong Kok (15 October 2014); a senior member of a trade union for minibus drivers (27 July 2015); a news reporter stationed in Mong Kok for the entire period of Umbrella Movement (30 January 2015); a senior news editor, independent news outlet (6 November 2014 and 17 December 2014); a taxi driver on the Kowloon side (8 October 2014); a taxi driver (15 November 2014); a taxi driver (17 October 2014); a taxi driver (10 October 2014); a taxi operator and owner of a taxi company, also the owner of minibuses (27 August 2015); *Shek*, a Triad member (10 November 2014); *Brick Brother*, a senior Triad Member in Wo Shing Wo group (9 March 2015); Ben, a Chinese university graduate present in Mong Kok on the night of the attacks (18 March 2015); Yvonne Leung, leader of Hong Kong University Student Union (2 November 2014 and 10 February 2017).

The two sections on the Occupy Movement and the role of the Triads are based on: Federico Varese and Rebecca Wong, 'Resurgent Triads? Democratic Mobilization and Organised Crime in Hong Kong', *Australian & New Zealand Journal of Criminology*, 17 March 2017, 10.1177/0004865817698191.

The chapter also draws upon: Federico Varese, 'Quei 50 giorni di Hong Kong, tra studenti, Mafia e illusioni', *La Stampa*, 19 November 2014; and Federico Varese, 'Quei ragazzi contro Mafia e potere. A Hong Kong una lezione di libertà', *La Stampa*, 29 March 2015.

Mong Kok district of Hong Kong, 3 October 2014

pp. 158–76. The *South China Morning Post* has published a detailed timeline entitled 'Occupy Central – Day Six: Full coverage of the day's events', available at: http://www.scmp.com/news/hong-kong/article/1608680/live-student-protestors-await-dialogue-date-lung-wo-road-open-traffic?page=all. See also R. Mackey and P. Pan, 'Updates on Hong Kong protests', *International New York Times*, 3 October 2014. Available at: http://news.blogs.nytimes.com/2014/10/03/live-updates-from-hong-kong-protests/?_r=0.

p. 162. The police official spokesman is cited in the *South China Morning Post* timeline.

p. 164. Interview with *Shek* (10 November 2014); Interview with *Brick Brother* (9 March 2015).

p. 165. The names mentioned by *Brick Brother* match those reported in 'National Bureau of Security infiltrates Occupy Central, Shanghai Boy's top personnel disrupts Mong Kok', *Apple Daily*, 7 October 2014, available at: http://hk.apple.nextmedia.com/news/first/20141007/18892050. According to this paper, members of the Wo Shing Wo gang associated with known Triad leaders 'Shanghai Boy' and 'Kiddo' were among those involved in the Mong Kok attacks. It should be noted that *Apple Daily* is a vocal, anti-China tabloid.

p. 165. Chan Wai Man interview: 'Chan Wai Man watches triad involvement in Anti Occupy central movement and claims to recognize some of the faces involved', *Apple Daily*, 9 October 2014, available at: http://hk.apple. nextmedia.com/entertainment/art/20141009/18893709. The notion of a 'patriotic Triad' is discussed in the academic literature as well: T. W. Lo, 'Beyond Social Capital: Triad Organized Crime in Hong Kong and China', *British Journal of Criminology*, 50(5), 2010, pp. 851–72. See p. 864.

p. 166. See D. Tweed, 'Triads see underworld business hurt by Hong Kong protests, *Bloomberg*, 10 October 2014, available at: http://www. bloomberg.com/news/articles/2014-10-09/hong-kong-s-triads-see-underworld-business-squeezed-by-protests.

pp. 166–7. Interview with taxi driver (15 November 2014); taxi operator and owner of taxi company; also the owner of minibuses (27 August 2015).

p. 167. On the red minibuses connection to Triads, see Chu, *Triads as Business*, pp. 56–8. The alterations to the minibus routes were regularly reported and updated. A news reporter added that the local population was not hostile to Umbrella Movement and many supported the protestors (30 January 2015). Indeed, a colleague of his pointed out that 'Mong Kok is famous for its street artists, so residents are used to people being in the streets' (interview with senior news editor, 6 November 2014). The owner of a nail salon also said that she never felt threatened by the protestors, although she did not support the occupation (17 October 2014).

p. 167. Interview with a senior member of a trade union for minibus drivers (27 July 2015); interview with *Shek* (10 November 2014); interview with *Brick Brother* (9 March 2015).

p. 167. Interview with a news reporter stationed in Mong Kok for the entire period of the occupation (30 January 2015).

p. 168. Interview with a senior news editor, independent news outlet (6 November 2014 and 17 December 2014). The land speculations in the New Territories mentioned by the interviewee are narrated in the *Overheard* film trilogy directed by Alan Mak and Felix Chong, and released in 2009, 2011 and 2014.

p. 169. The operation to rescue the leaders of the 1989 students' protests is known as Yellowbird. See Lo, 'Beyond Social Capital', pp. 851–72; Congde Feng, *A Tiananmen Journal: Republic on the Square* (Hong Kong: Sun Chung Books, 2009 [in Chinese]).

pp. 169–70. I discuss Triad investments in mainland China in *Mafias on the Move*, pp. 150–51.

p. 170. It has been alleged that the attack against Kevin Lau had been carried out by the Shui Fong Triad: G. Mullany, 'Hong Kong editor whose ouster stirred protests is slashed', *New York Times*, 25 February 2014; D. Levin, 'Triad links to attack on protestors raise some old questions', *International New York Times*, 4 October 2014.

p. 171. Calderone is cited in Arlacchi, *Men of Dishonor*, p. 201.

p. 171. Marsala is cited in Gambetta, *The Sicilian Mafia*, p. 185.

p. 171. Calderone is cited in Arlacchi, *Men of Dishonor*, pp. 200–201 and p. 202.

p. 172. On the mayor of Reggio Calabria, see Pino Arlacchi, *La mafia imprenditrice* (Bologna: Il Mulino, 1983), pp. 50–51.

p. 172. The point that violence and democracy are intimately linked in Japan is made by Eiko Maruko Siniawer, *Ruffians, Yakuza, Nationalists: The Violent Politics of Modern Japan, 1860–1960* (Ithaca, NY: Cornell University Press, 2008). See especially p. 9, p. 119 and p. 163 for relevant examples.

p. 173. I draw upon material already published in Varese, *The Russian Mafia*, pp. 182–3. The story of the Vorgashurskaya coal mine is mentioned in Varese, *The Russian Mafia*, p. 71.

p. 173. John Landesco, *Organized Crime in Chicago* (Chicago University Press, 1929), p. 169. On Capone's control of Cicero, see Kobler, *Capone*, pp. 109–23.

p. 173. On the deal between the American Mafia and the US Navy during the Second World War, see Alan A. Block, 'A Modern Marriage of Convenience: A Collaboration between Organized Crime and U.S. Intelligence', in Kelly (ed.), *Organized Crime*, pp. 58–77. Other studies include Rodney Campbell, *The Luciano Project* (New York: McGraw-Hill, 1977) and Tim Newark, *Mafia Allies: The True Story of America's Secret Alliance with the Mob in World War II* (St Paul, MN: Zenith Press, 2007). The most recent take on the story is Cockayne, *Hidden Power*, pp. 147–60.

p. 174. On Fascist repression of the Mafia, see Salvatore Lupo, *Storia della Mafia dalle origini ai giorni nostri* (Rome: Donzelli, 1996), pp. 181–91, and Vittorio Coco, *La mafia, il fascismo, la polizia* (Palermo: Fondazione La Torre, 2012).

p. 174. In contemporary Egypt, the authorities employ thugs (*baltagya*) to intimidate students and activists. See Maha Abdelrahman, 'Policing neoliberalism in Egypt: the continuing rise of the "securocratic state"', *Third World Quarterly*, 38(1), 2017, pp. 185–202, especially pp. 189–90. A similar phenomenon is happening in mainland China. Criminals are hired to repress citizens and coerce them into complying with unpopular policies and decisions. They are mostly recruited to enforce illegal housing demolitions and evictions, land expropriations, collection of taxes and illegal fees. See Lynette H. Ong, 'Thugs-for-Hire: State Coercion and Everyday Repression in China', presented at Workshop on Collective Protest and State Governance in China's Xi Jinping Era, Harvard-Yenching Institute, Harvard University, 18 May 2015.

When Mafia and state coincide

p. 175. On the US landing in Sicily and the movement for Sicilian independence, see Salvatore Lupo, 'The Allies and the Mafia', *Journal of Modern Italian Studies* 2(1) 1997, pp. 21–33. Manoela Patti (*La Sicilia e gli alleati. Tra occupazione e Liberazione*, Introduction by Salvatore Lupo, Rome: Donzelli, 2013) debunks the thesis that the US invading authorities had coordinated the landing with the Mafia, or that they entered a pact with them after the invasion. Cockayne, *Hidden Power*, pp. 169–202, writes of 'deliberate neglect' of the Mafia problem on the part of the Allies (p. 200).

p. 175. On the pact between the Mafia and the Christian Democratic Party, see Lupo, *Storia della Mafia dalle origini ai giorni nostri*, and Leoluca Orlando, *Fighting the Mafia and Renewing Sicilian Culture* (New York, London: Encounter Books, 2001). Gaspare Mutolo's words are cited in Roberto Scarpinato, 'Il Dio dei mafiosi e dei dittatori', *Micromega* 1, 1998, online at: http://www.laltrariva.net/?p=136 and in English, in Cockayne, *Hidden Power*, p. 7, although my translation is closer to the original. On the use of military metaphors by Mafiosi, see in particular the conversation of Gaspare Spatuzza with Alessandra Dino. Spatuzza, the man responsible for the terrorist attacks in Florence and Milan, refers to his victims and to the Italian State as 'enemies', and to his time in Cosa Nostra as a 'service' (*militanza*) (Dino, *Spatuzza*, pp. 55, 70, 73, 74 and 138).

p. 176. On Escobar, see Mark Bowden, *Killing Pablo* (New York: Penguin Books, 2002). See also the terrorist campaign of a Brazilian prison gang, Primeiro Comando, in 2012 (Cockayne, *Hidden Power*, p. 286). Misha Glenny, *Nemesis: One man and the battle for Rio* (London: Bodley Head, 2015) is a fascinating study of Antônio Lopes, known as 'Nem', one of the leaders of the gang *Amigos dos Amigos*. Paul Collier ('Rebelling as a Quasi-Criminal Activity,' *Journal of Conflict Resolution*, 44(6), 2000, pp. 839–53) has shown the analytical similarities between insurgencies and organised crime.

Muse–Ruili border, Burma–China, July 2011

I have written several newspaper articles on Burma and the Golden Triangle upon which I draw upon here: Federico Varese, 'L'ipoteca dell'eroina sul futuro della nuova Birmania', *La Stampa,* 27 November 2011; Federico Varese, 'Is Burma the next Mexico?' *Reuters,* 6 December 2011; and Federico Varese, 'Droga, fedi, etnie contro: tutti i demoni della Birmania', *Origami-La Stampa,* 7 April 2016.

On the history of the border areas of Burma and the production and trade of drugs in the Golden Triangle, see Ko-lin Chin's remarkable *The Golden Triangle: Inside Southeast Asia's Drug Trade* (Ithaca, NY: Cornell University Press, 2009), especially pp. 7–9 and p. 21 and Ko-lin Chin and Sheldon X. Zhang, *The Chinese Heroin Trade* (New York: New York University Press, 2015). Estimates of heroin production in the 1990s are in Chin, *The Golden Triangle*, pp. 8–9 and p. 86. More recent estimates are cited in: Chin and Zhang, *The Heroin Trade*, p.4; Liana Sun Wyler, *Burma and Transnational Crime*, Congressional Research Service, 2010; UNODC, *Southeast Asia Opium Survey*, 2013; Transnational Institute, *Bouncing Back: Relapse in the Golden Triangle*, 2014. These works also have data on families working in the opium farms, and the effects of drug addiction on local communities. See also the recent work by Richard Cockett, *Blood, Dreams and Gold: The Changing Face of Burma* (New Haven, CT: Yale University Press, 2015), especially pp. 137–51, and Mary P. Callahan, *Political Authority in Burma's Ethnic Minority States: Devolution, Occupation, and Coexistence* (Singapore: ISEAS Publishing, 2007), p. 25.

p. 177. On the Muse–Ruili drug route, see Chin and Zhang, *The Chinese Heroin Trade*, pp. 44–7.

p. 178. Formally, Mengla banned opium growing in 1997, Kokang in 2003 and Wa in 2005. The local population were driven into destitution by these bans and soon went back to harvesting opium (Callahan, *Political Authority*, p. 25).

p. 179. Useful information on the Wa Army and state structure, and the protection system, is in Chin, *The Golden Triangle*, pp. 39, 45, 78, 80, 93 and 99. For the protection system, see Chin, *The Golden Triangle*, p. 45 and p. 93; Chin and Zhang, *The Chinese Heroin Trade*, p. 56; and Hideyuki Takano, *The Shore Beyond Good and Evil: A Report from Inside*

Burma's Opium Kingdom (Reno, NV.: Kotan Publishing, 2002), pp. 55, 99 and 137.

p. 179. 'Simply because they inadvertently crossed paths with a heroin laboratory hidden in a remote area', Chin and Zhang, *The Chinese Heroin Trade*, p. 56.

p. 181. The drugs enforcement officer has spoken to Chin and Zhang, *The Chinese Heroin Trade*, p. 45.

p. 181. Wei Xuegang is also known as Wei Hsueh-Kang and Prasit Cheewinnitipanya. Basic information on him cited in the text is taken from Chin, *The Golden Triangle*, especially pp. 140–43, 26 and 199, and Anthony Davis and Bruce Hawke, 'Burma: The Country That Won't Kick the Habit', *Jane's Intelligence Review*, 10(3), 1998, pp. 26–31, here p. 28.

p. 182. The words from Milsom are taken from Jeremy Milsom, 'The Long Hard Road out of Drugs: The Case of the Wa', in Martin Jelsma, Tom Kramer and Pietje Vervest (eds), *Trouble in the Triangle: Opium and Conflict in Burma* (Chiang Mai: Silkworm Books, 2005), p. 75.

p. 182. On Indonesian Free Aceh Army, see *Jakarta Post*, 23 January 2003; on the National Liberation Army of Colombia, see *Houston Chronicle*, 28 October 2001.

pp. 182–3. On the FARC, see *New York Times*, 21 April 2000; *San Francisco Chronicle*, 18 December 2000; Zenaida Rueda, *Confesiones de una guerrillera* (Bogotá: Editorial Planeta Colombia, 2009); *Independent*, 21 July 2013; Mario Aguilera Peña, 'Las guerrillas marxistas y la pena de muerte a combatientes. Un examen de los delitos capitales y del "juicio revolucionario", *Anuario Colombiano de Historia Social y de la Cultura*, 41(1), 2014, pp. 201–36; and Francisco Thoumi, 'Organized Crime in Colombia', in Paoli (ed.), *The Oxford Handbook of Organized Crime*, p. 187.

pp. 183–4. For the discussion on Somali piracy, I draw upon: Anja Shortland and Federico Varese, 'State-Building, Informal Governance and Organised Crime: The Case of Somali Piracy', *Political Studies* (2015), doi:10.1111/1467-9248.12227; and Anja Shortland and Federico Varese, 'The Protector's Choice: An Application of Protection Theory to Somali Piracy', *British Journal of Criminology*, 54(5), 2014, pp. 741–64.

p. 184. 'Anyone involved in the provision of a ransom payment must satisfy themselves that there is no reasonable cause to suspect that the money ... will or may be used for the purposes of terrorism.' HM Treasury and the Home Office, *Supplementary Memorandum (3)*, 2009, Annex A: 13–14.

pp. 184–5. Data and information in this paragraph is taken from Ioan Grillo, *El Narco: Inside Mexico's Criminal Insurgency* (New York: Bloomsbury, 2012), p. 271 and p. 270 (interview with major of Ciudad Juarez); Robert

J. Bunker, 'Strategic Threat: Narcos and Narcotics Overview', *Small Wars & Insurgencies*, 21(1), 2010, p. 19; William Finnegan, 'Letter from Mexico. Silver or lead', *New Yorker*, 31 May 2010, pp. 39–51; Benjamin Locks, 'Extortion in Mexico: Why Mexico's Pain Won't End with the War on Drugs', *Yale Journal of International Affairs*, 10, 2014, available at http://yalejournal.org/article_post/extortion-in-mexico-why-mexicos-pain-wont-end-with-the-war-on-drugs; Stephanie Brophy, 'Mexico: Cartels, Corruption and Cocaine: A Profile of the Gulf Cartel', *Global Crime*, 9(3), 2008, pp. 248–61; Eduardo Guerrero-Gutiérrez, 'Security, Drugs, and Violence in Mexico: A Survey', *7th North American Forum* (Washington DC, 2011).

p. 185. 'Cartels are known to offer services of dispute resolution and cheap loans to businesses.' See Tom Wainwright, *Narconomics: How to Run a Drug Cartel* (London: Ebury Press, 2016), p. 91.

p. 185. On the political message of *narcocorridos* and the political nature of Mexican cartels, see Howard Campbell, 'Narco-Propaganda in the Mexican Drug War: An Anthropological Perspective', *Latin American Perspectives*, 41(2), 2014, pp. 60–77.

p. 185. Ioan Grillo, *Gangster Warlords: Drug Dollars, Killing Fields, and the New Politics of Latin America* (London-Oxford-New York: Bloomsbury Circus, 2016), p. 331, argues for a fundamental distinction between mafias and insurgencies.

p. 185. See Thomas Friedman, op-ed column 'Talk Later', *New York Times,* 28 September 2011.

p. 186. On racketeering and informal community policing in Northern Ireland, see *Irish News*, 21 February 2003; Neil Jarman, 'From War to Peace? Changing Patterns of Violence in Northern Ireland, 1990–2003', *Terrorism and Political Violence*, 16(3), 2004, pp. 420–38; Heather Hamill, *The Hoods: Crime and Punishment in Belfast* (Princeton, NJ: Princeton University Press, 2010) and Wainwright, *Narconomics*, p. 95. The UN report cited in the text is available at: http://www.securitycouncilreport.org/atf/cf/%7B65BFCF9B-6D27-4E9C-8CD3-CF6E4FF96FF9%7D/s_2015_79.pdf (see p. 4) and is cited in Cockayne, *Hidden Power*, p. 313.

On people living in Mafia territories labelled as 'subjects' rather than citizens, see Dino, *Spatuzza*, p. 73.

I have discussed some of these themes in 'What is Organized Crime?' in Federico Varese (ed.), *Critical Concepts in Organized Crime* (London: Routledge), vol. 1, pp. 1–33.

Hong Kong, 2015–2016

pp. 187–8. My interview with Yvonne Leung Lai Kwok from November 2014 is in part reported in 'Quei 50 giorni di Hong Kong, tra studenti, Mafia e illusioni', *La Stampa*, 19 November 2014. A subsequent interview with Yvonne took place on 10 February 2017. On the former leader of the Hong Kong Students Union see also: Roula Khalaf, 'Hong Kong's lucky revolutionaries', *Financial Times*, 4 March 2015.

p. 187. The use of injunctions against the Occupy Movement has been stressed by Samson Yuen and Edmund W. Cheng, 'Neither Repression nor Concession? A Regime's Attrition against Mass Protests', *Political Studies*, 30 January 2017, 10.1277/0032321716674024.

8. Death

Via Michelangelo, 24 September 2005, 10.23 a.m.

pp. 189–90. The conversation between Rotolo and Nicchi is in Gotha (2008), p. 476. A partial English translation is in Bolzoni, *White Shotgun*, pp. 61–2.

p. 190. Brusca's words are in Lodato, *Ho ucciso Giovanni Falcone*, p. 180. Giovanni Falcone makes the point that Mafiosi cannot refuse to kill when ordered by the Commission or their Mafia Family head; however, very rarely some have managed to avoid carrying out the order (Falcone, *Cose di Cosa Nostra*, pp. 28–9). It does not follow that in order to enter Cosa Nostra – in Sicily or the US – one has to kill someone. This is a bogus notion found in films such as *The Godfather* (1972) and *Donnie Brasco* (1997). In reality, as noted by Joe Pistone, this 'rule' is often ignored; if enforced, it would, in fact, attract a disproportionate amount of attention to the Mafia. See Joseph Pistone, *Donnie Brasco: Unfinished Business* (Philadelphia: Running Press, 2007), pp. 71–72, cited in Hortis, *The Mob and the City*, p. 195. Antonio Calderone confirms that he was not asked to commit a murder when he joined the Family in 1962 (Arlacchi, *Men of Dishonor*, p. 63).

pp. 191–2. On ambushes, see Gaspare Mutolo and Anna Vinci, *La Mafia non lascia tempo* (Milan: Rizzoli, 2013) and Dino, *Spatuzza*, p. 54. In Cosa Nostra slang, an effective killer is known as 'one who runs fast' (*La Repubblica*, 3 February 1994, cited in Dino, *Spatuzza*, p. 10).

p. 191. The instances when a Mafioso kills in the expectation that he will be killed abound in the history of Italian mafias. Often, members exploit such fear to spread rumours that a murder plot is under way in order to induce others to commit a murder or turn against their bosses. A case in point is the strategy that led to the murder of Paul Castellano. See Capeci and Mustain, *Gotti: Rise and Fall*, pp. 92–3.

p. 191, note 1. The murder of Inzerillo is mentioned by Falcone, *Cose di Cosa Nostra*, p. 36.

p. 191. Roy DeMeo's story is in *For the Sins of My Father*, pp. 155–76. The quotation is from p. 170.

p. 192. The quotation from Brusca on the use of the rope is in Lodato, *Ho ucciso Giovanni Falcone*, p. 162. The Italian rope trick is described in Ovid Demaris, *The Last Mafioso: The Treacherous World of Jimmy Fratianno* (New York: Bantam Books, 1981). *Incaprettare* is described in several places. See, for example, Falcone, *Cose di Cosa Nostra*, p. 27, and Bolzoni and D'Avanzo, *Totò Riina*, p. 187. The first husband of Vito Genovese's wife also died in this way on 16 March 1932 (see Maas, *The Valachi Papers*, p. 130).

pp. 192–3. The discussion on how the Sicilian Mafia uses acid to dispose of bodies is based on Lodato, *Ho ucciso Giovanni Falcone*, pp. 162–4.

p. 193. The local businessman dissolved in acid was Andrea Cottone. See 'Ergastolo per Onofrio Morreale, Michele Rubino e Nicola Mandalà per l'omicidio di Andrea Cottone: decisive le dichiarazioni dei pentiti', *Bagheria News*, 1 December 2015, at: http://www.bagherianews.com/cronaca/16038-ergastolo-per-onofrio-morreale-nicola-rubino-e-michele-mandala-per-l-omicidio-di-andrea-cottone-decisive-le-dichiarazioni-dei-pentiti.html.

p. 193. On the murder of Lea Garofalo, see Marika Demaria, *Lea Garofalo. La ribellione di una donna alla ̓ndrangheta* (Milan: Melanpo Editore), especially p. 139, pp. 145–6. Marcello Ravveduto, 'Lea Garofalo, la scelta di una donna emancipata uccisa dalla ̓ndrangheta', *Fanpage*, 23 November 2016, at: http://www.fanpage.it/lea-garofalo-la-scelta-di-una-donna-emancipata-uccisa-dalla-heta/.

p. 194. By 'early years of Italian organised crime in Chicago', I mean the 1910s. See Kobler, *Capone*, pp. 67, 85 and 35.

p. 194. The key text on the DeMeo crew is Mustain and Capeci, *Murder Machine*. The description of the murder method is on pp. v–vii and pp. 224–5.

p. 194. On the Mafia joke, see N. J. C. Vasantkumar, 'Postmodernism and Jokes', in Arthur Asa Berger (ed.), *The Postmodern Presence: Readings on Postmodernism in American Culture and Society* (Walnut Creek, CA: AltaMira Press, 1997), pp. 212–38; the joke is on p. 226.

pp. 194–5. The murdered man in New Jersey is Pietro Inzerillo. The interpretation of the messages is to be found in Bolzoni and D'Avanzo, *Totò Riina* (p. 188) and Falcone, *Cose di Cosa Nostra* (p. 28). See also Bolzoni and D'Avanzo, *Totò Riina* (pp. 277–8) for a further discussion of the murder of Pietro Inzerillo. A recent instance of a Mafia message is related to the beating of Enzo Fragalà in 2010. A Palermo attorney, Fragalà, had been encouraging some of his clients to turn state evidence. According to evidence heard at the trial, one attacker told his accomplice not to steal anything, so that it would be evidently a punishment rather than a robbery. The attack led to the death of the victim. See 'Omicidio Fragalà: raid punitivo deciso da Cosa Nostra; svola nelle indagini 7 anni dopo uccisione del penalista, sei arresti', *ANSA* 15 March 2017.

p. 195. Kobler, *Capone*, p. 144, reports the practice of pressing a nickel into the hand of a victim.

p. 195. The practice of disfiguring an enemy, 'particularly an informer, by slitting his face from eye to ear' is discussed in Kobler, *Capone*, p. 27.

p. 195. The Sicilian photographer is Natale Gaggioli, who worked for *L'Ora*. Gambetta, *The Sicilian Mafia* (pp. 127–8) calls it a trademark. The original story in Saverio Lodato, *Dieci anni di Mafia*.

pp. 195–6. For a relevant novel by Andrea Camilleri, see *Blade of Light* (London: Mantle, 2015; original edition, *Una lama di luce*, Palermo: Sellerio, 2012).

pp. 196–7. The interview with Yuri Pigolkin, Chair of the Forensic Medicine Department at I.M. Sechenov First Moscow State Medical University, is in 'Kak izmenilis' s 90-x godov banditskie sposoby pytok i sokrytiya tel', *Lenta.ru*, 10 August 2016, at: http://www.ves.lv/kak-izmenilis-s-90-h-godov-banditskie-sposoby-pytok-i-sokrytiya-tel/. See also Aleksandr Sukharenko, 'Transnacional'nye ubiistva rossiiskikh biznesmenov', *EhZh-Yurist*, 31, 2012, at: http://www.justicemaker.ru/view-article.php?art=3654&id=21; and Aleksandr Sukharenko, 'Spiral' "bespredela"', *Nevolya*, 48, 2016, at: http://index.org.ru/nevol/2016-48/10-48-sucharenko.html.

p. 197. The high-ranking member of the Harmoniously United Society – also known as Wo Hop To – is Cheung Chi-tai. The two cases cited are HKSAR v. See Wah Lun, CACC 370/2009 (case of the gambler); and HKSAR v. Wong Fuk Tak, CACC 249/1999.

p. 197. The study of Hong Kong homicides is: K.W. Lee, *Triad Related Homicide in Hong Kong: 1989–1998*, doctoral thesis, University of Hong Kong, 2005. The total number of Triad-related homicides in the 1989–98 period is 95, involving 124 victims, out of 805 recorded homicides. The police report is cited in pp. 419–20. See also p. 451 on the scarce availability of firearms. See summary Table 8.2 on pp. 503–4. A related article is: K. W. Lee, R. G. Broadhurst and P. S. Beh, 'Triad-related Homicides in Hong Kong', *Forensic Science International*, 162(1), 2006, pp. 183–90.

p. 197. Penalties for the illegal possession of firearms are detailed in 'Hong Kong Ordinances, Cap 238 Firearms and Ammunition Ordinances: 13, Possession of arms or ammunition without licence'.

The text of the Firearms Law is available at: http://law.e-gov.go.jp/htmldata/S33/S33HO006.html. See also Mark Alleman, 'The Japanese Firearm and Sword Possession Control Law: Translator's Introduction', *Pacific Rim Law & Policy Journal*, 9, 2000, pp. 165–74.

p. 198. The 41-year-old executive of a crime group is Kosuke Hata. He belongs to a particularly vicious gang called Kudo-kai: see 'The need to protect lay judges', *Japan Times*, 23 July 2016.

p. 198. On the Yakuza wielding swords, see, for example, Mark Schilling, 'Yakuza movie lines without honor or humanity', *Japan Times*, 26 January 2011.

p. 198. Yakuza-related shooting incidents went from over 200 in 2000 to around 50 in 2011. See Andrew Rankin, '21st-Century Yakuza: Recent Trends in Organized Crime in Japan – Part 1', *Asia-Pacific Journal*, 10(7), no. 2, 13 February 2012, p. 14. See also Max Fisher, 'A Land Without Guns: How Japan Has Virtually Eliminated Shooting Deaths', *Atlantic*, 23 July 2012.

p. 198. Rankin, '21st-Century Yakuza: Recent Trends in Organized Crime in Japan – Part 1', p. 14, discusses penalties for carrying guns in Japan.

p. 198. The low-level Yakuza was interviewed by Jake Adelstein, 'Even gangsters live in fear of Japan's gun laws', *Japan Times*, 6 January 2013.

p. 200. I draw here upon reflections published in Varese, *Mafias on the Move*, pp. 12, 193–5, and Varese, 'Protection and Extortion', in Paoli (ed.) *Oxford Handbook of Organized Crime*, pp. 343–58.

p. 202. On 25 May 2001, Gravano pleaded guilty in a New York federal court to drug trafficking charges (http://www.nytimes.com/2001/05/26nyregion/gravano-and-son-plead-guilty-to-running-ecstacy-drug-ring./html). On 29 June 2001, Gravano pleaded guilty in Phoenix to the state charges (http://www.nytimes.com/2001/06/30/nyregion/gravano-pleads-guilty-to-drug-sales-in-arizona.html). See also the case of Maurizio Avola, a member of Cosa Nostra who defected to the authorities. Lorenzo Tondo, 'Meet the Sicilian Mafia Hitman Who Killed 80 People and Will Be Free in 5 Years', *Time* magazine, 21 October 2015 at: http://time.com/4062017/sicilian-mafia-hitman/

p. 204. I draw here upon a piece I have written on Ciprì and Maresco in *Cinico TV, vol. 3, 1998–2007*, DVD and book, Cineteca di Bologna, 2016. See also Emiliano Morreale, *Ciprì e Maresco* (Alessandria: Falsopiano, 2003).

p. 204. On the risk of devolution, see Federico Varese and Paolo Campana, 'Serious and Organised Crime in 2015 and Beyond – Priorities for Business and Government', paper presented at Cityforum, London, 17 March 2015.

p. 205. On the so-called 'new' crime-terror nexus, see Rajan Basra and Peter R. Neumann, 'Criminal Pasts, Terrorist Futures: European Jihadists and the New Crime-Terror Nexus', *Perspectives on Terrorism,* 10(6), 2016.

p. 206. Felicia Bartolotta Impastato, *La Mafia in casa mia*, p. 49.

p. 207. For a description of Massey's funeral, see Helen Pidd, 'Funeral for Salford's "Mr Big" takes place with armed police on standby', *Guardian*, 28 August 2015.

Post-mortem

p. 208. I have expanded on my November 2016 trip to Russia in: Federico Varese, 'La Russia post-mafiosa', *Corriere della Sera-La Lettura*, 4 December 2016. For a damming critique of current Russia, see Luke Harding, *Mafia State: How One Reporter Became an Enemy of the Brutal New Russia* (London: Guardian, 2011). I found Anna Garrels, *Putin Country. A Journey into the Real Russia* (New York: Farrar, Strauss and Giroux, 2016) an insightful and touching portrait of life in the provinces.

Appendix: Mafia Rules

Sources for the rules cited in the table are:
Hill, *The Japanese Mafia*, pp. 72–3; Stark, 'The Yakuza', p. 241; Varese, *The Russian Mafia*, p. 151; Gambetta, *The Sicilian Mafia*, p. 147; Morgan, *Triads*, p. 157.

Appendix: Mafia Structure

Sources for the Appendix are the document found in the possession of Lo Piccolo cited above; Anderson, *The Business of Organized Crime,* pp. 34–36; Stark, 'The Yakuza', pp. 64–5, and p. 238; Hill, *The Japanese Mafia*, pp. 65–6; Chu, *Triads as Business*, pp. 27–8; Morgan, *Triads*.

On the Triads 'headquarter system', and 'Central Committee', see Chu, *Triads as Business*; and Morgan, *Triads*, p. 95. On the *Kanto* in the Yakuza, see Hill, *The Japanese Mafia*, pp. 70–71, and Stark, 'The Yakuza', pp. 235–7.

INDEX

Page numbers for illustrations are given in italics; those for notes are followed by n

Personal names written in *italics* are pseudonyms